The Mexican Masked Wrestler
and Monster Filmography

The Mexican Masked Wrestler and Monster Filmography

Robert Michael "Bobb" Cotter

McFarland & Company, Inc., Publishers
Jefferson, North Carolina, and London

This, my first book, is dedicated to:
Dad and Brownie, who couldn't be here to see it;
Mom, who threw away my comic books and
thus kept my interest in such things alive;
Rogelio Agrasanchez, Jr., and David Wilt,
who taught me most everything I know about Mexican movies;
all of my family and friends who love me or put up with me.
I can never love or thank you all enough.

The present work is a reprint of the illustrated case bound edition of The Mexican Masked Wrestler and Monster Filmography, *first published in 2005 by McFarland.*

LIBRARY OF CONGRESS CATALOGUING-IN-PUBLICATION DATA

Cotter, Robert Michael "Bobb."
The Mexican masked wrestler and monster filmography / Robert Michael "Bobb" Cotter.
p.   cm.
Includes bibliographical references and index.

ISBN 978-0-7864-4104-4
softcover : 50# alkaline paper ∞

1. Wrestlers in motion pictures.   2. Masks in motion pictures.
3. Motion pictures — Mexico — Catalogs.   4. Horror films —
Mexico — History and criticism.   I. Title.
PN1995.9.W74C68   2008   791.43'6528796812 — dc22   2005000889

British Library cataloguing data are available

On the cover: Top: Lina Marín in *Chanoc contra el Tigre y el Vampiro,* 1970.
Center: The flame pistol of El Santo in *Santo en la Venganza de la Momia,* 1970.
Bottom: Azteca lobby card detail from *El Barón del Terror,* 1961

Manufactured in the United States of America

McFarland & Company, Inc., Publishers
Box 611, Jefferson, North Carolina 28640
www.mcfarlandpub.com

Table of Contents

Preface

"Thank You, Masked Wrestler"

The author feels it would be a little unkind to present this book without just a word of friendly warning. We are about to unfold the story of the Mexican masked wrestler/monster movies. It is one of the strangest stories ever told. It deals with the two great mysteries of creation: monsters and wrestling. And while it does strive to be a comprehensive look at that subgenre, it's not meant to be an exhaustive study of Mexican fantasy films as a whole; rather, it examines how they relate to the evolution of the masked wrestler subgenre, and the creatures and creators that influenced both.

If imitation is the sincerest form of flattery, then the creators of the classic Universal monster movies and serials must have been flattered indeed by their imitators south of the border. Or maybe not. Bemused might be a better word... Or perhaps just puzzled. For in the annals of cinema, no country's "take" on the monsters of legend and action heroes is as unique as Mexico's. Maybe bizarre would be a better word, or simply surreal.

There are many genres of cinema: comedies, dramas, musicals, horror films, action films, science fiction movies, sports, sex. In most countries, filmmakers are content to sink or swim within the confines of their chosen subject matter. Not so with Mexican horrors, in which all of the above, and more, can usually be found commingled in the same movie — practically every movie — practically every time. Why? Well, monster movies anywhere are generally aimed at an audience that expects certain conventions of the genre to be observed. In Mexico, by contrast, the "target audience" is the whole family, and therefore their monster movies are more likely to contain something for everybody. That's one reason the Mexican monsters seem to flout the rules. Also, like the Japanese, Mexicans seem more willing to accept obviously manufactured elements and to suspend disbelief when things go beyond the boundaries of a particular genre.

Take action heroes, for instance. The cinema has certainly had its share: Indiana Jones, Flash Gordon, James Bond, Batman... But in Mexico's case, well... Try to imagine for a moment that Batman were real. A powerfully built man in cape, tights and mask walks among us in broad daylight, recognized everywhere by his adoring fans. Anywhere else, this is a situation out of a comic book. In Mexico, however, they ask for his autograph, then pay money at the local arena or movie theater to watch him do his thing, be it real or imaginary.

For, in Mexico, the action heroes are

Somos Uno magazine, June 1995 — If a picture is worth a thousand words, then this *Somos Uno* cover pretty much sums up what this book is all about.

professional wrestlers. A few non–Mexican wrestlers have made the transition to the big screen, like "Rowdy" Roddy Piper and "the Rock," but none have been consistent in terms of roles or drawing power on the screen (and besides, they always play fictional characters). Mexico's greatest action heroes parlayed success in the ring into profitable and decades-long screen careers *as themselves*. You could go to the Saturday afternoon matinee and see El Santo or Blue Demon fight monsters; then you could go to the arena that night and watch him wrestle. You could go to the supermarket the next day and still see him — in all his masked glory! None of this dual-persona Clark Kent/Superman nonsense for these Mexican heroes. The only Bruce Wayne bits were for home or family or close friends. In public, they were El Santo or Blue Demon to the core, and everybody knew it.

Could they act? Well, that depends on your definition of acting — if you're talking in the Laurence Olivier vein, of course not. But, in a way, they were already actors before they even hit the screen, because professional wrestling is nothing if not knowing how to play to a crowd. And, after a couple of movies, like anyone else, the masked wrestlers certainly became competent professionals. They knew their roles and played them with all their hearts.

So, just how do their movies rate as movies? Well, I remember a time, not so long ago (about 30 years), when the B-movies of the world were looked upon sneeringly (and worse), when looked upon at all. Fans and critics alike considered them trash. Even a classic like *Abbott and Costello Meet Frankenstein*, which today securely rests in its rightful position as the greatest horror-comedy of all time, was scorned as a sad end to the careers of comedians and monster characters alike. Bela Lugosi's films produced by Monogram or PRC were viewed in a similar manner, yet today have entire expensive, hardbound books devoted to them. Edward D. Wood, Jr., has become the subject of a big-budget Hollywood "biopic." But those pundits who now extol the virtues of those and many similar gems now harbor a snobbish and uninformed attitude towards Mexican monster/wrestler movies. And while perhaps the combination of those two seemingly incompatible genres in itself will forever consign these films to the pit of cult movies, the best of the Mexican breed can indeed go toe-to-toe with many an American "B." They aren't cheap rip-offs. Sure, the budgets weren't the biggest, and many times they stole (sometimes outrageously), both cinematically and graphically, from their inspirations. But the settings, design, and atmosphere are all generally solid, and certainly comparable to the sources. They just used those sources as a base from which they took off on unbridled flights.

Unlike American "B" films, the Santo and Blue Demon and other assorted monster/wrestler movies were not considered lower-half-of-the-double-bill fodder, but were rather the main event. Of course, they are onscreen comic books, but even in that realm, there is a world of difference between quality graphic work and that ground out by cynical hacks just to meet a deadline. It is sometimes that very cynicism which gives a film that special quality of "badness," but this is based on the prevailing opinion that the monster/wrestler movies are bad — and that, of course, is a very relative term. Considering them to be bad just because they may be bizarre is a very patronizing view.

I'm certainly not arguing that these films are anything more than what they are. They are, however, fun with a capital F; and rather than laughing at us, they encourage us to join in the fun. And I'm not trying to say they're somehow better than American B-movies, just that there's a whole big wonderful world of psychotronica out there, and if some sort of cinematic or cultural bias is preventing you from enjoying these movies, then you're missing out on a fiesta.

The first time I encountered images from a Santo movie was in issue number four of *Monsters of the Movies*, a magazine published by Marvel in the mid-seventies. It featured an article titled "Superheroes vs. Monsters in Distant Lands," accompanied by a double-page shot from *Santo y Blue Demon vs. los Monstruos*, with Santo taking on the five titular monsters. Who was that masked man, and what were these bizarre variations on the classic monsters I knew and loved? Also included was a photograph of another guy in a mask (with a different design) fighting a moustached and goateed Frankenstein Monster! What was up with that? Mysteries—for which the fine article by Don Glut provided only partial answers—mysteries that needed to be solved. Undoubtedly that spark led to what you're reading right now.

So come, join me now, and we'll celebrate a world where men are masked, women are wrestlers, and sometimes monsters are both!

A quick note about some of the Mexican titles of movies that appear throughout this book. We have followed the practice of the Mexican film industry of using the words "*contra*" and "*vs.*" interchangeably. Movies are discussed herein as "*vs.*" when a lobby card illustration might show "*contra*"—and vice versa. Also, in Mexican movies "Frankenstein" is frequently but not always spelled "Frankestein"—and at least once even "Franquestein"—but throughout this book for the sake of consistency we use the spelling with the *n*. The reader should note, for example, the film on page 113 and its lobby card, showing both variances, *contra* and *Frakestein*.

Gracias, y vayan con dios, mis amigos.

Alphabetical List of Films

El Águila Real
Anónimo Mortal
Arañas Infernales
El As Negro
Asesinato en los Studios
El Asesino Invisible
Asesinos de Otros Mundos
Atacan las Brujas
El Ataúd del Vampiro
Autopsia de un Phantasma
Aventura al Centro de la Tierra
El Barón Brákola
El Barón del Terror
Las Bestias del Terror
Blue Demon contra Cerebros Infernales
Blue Demon, Destructor de Espías
Blue Demon, el Campeón
Blue Demon, el Demonio Azul
Blue Demon vs. el Poder Satánico
Blue Demon vs. las Diabólicas
Blue Demon y las Invasoras
La Bruja
La Cabeza Viviente
La Cámara del Terror
Campeones del Ring
Los Campeones Justicieros
Los Canallas
Capulina contra los Monstruos
Capulina vs. las Momias
Capulina vs. los Vampiros
La Casa del Terror
La Casa Embrujada
El Castillo de las Momias de Guanajuato
El Castillo de los Monstruos
Cerebro del Mal

Chabelo y Pepito vs. los Monstruos
Chanoc vs. el Tigre y el Vampiro
Chanoc y el Hijo del Santo contra los
    Vampiros Asesinos
Con Licencia para Matar
De Sangre Chicana
Dr. Satán
Dr. Satán y la Magia Negra
Drácula
Los Endemonadios del Ring
Enigma de Muerte
El Enmascarado de Plata
El Espectro de la Novia
El Espectro del Estrangulador
Frankenstein, el Vampiro y Compañía
La Furia de las Karatecas
Gigantes Planetarios
El Hacha Diabólica
El Hijo de Alma Grande
El Hijo de Huracán Ramírez
El Hijo del Santo en Frontera sin Ley
El Hombre Que Logró Ser Invisible
El Hombre y el Bestia
El Hombre y el Monstruo
La Horripilante Bestia Humana
Huracán Ramírez
Huracán Ramírez y la Monjita Negra
El Imperio de Drácula
La Invasión de los Muertos
La Invasión de los Vampiros
Invasión Siniestra
El Investigador Capulina
La Isla de los Dinosaurios
Los Jaguares contra el Invasores Miste-
    riosos

Karla vs. los Jaguares
Ladrón de Cadáveres
Los Leones del Ring
Los Leones del Ring contra la Cosa Nostra
Leyendas Macabras de la Colonia
La Llorona
La Loba
Las Lobas del Ring
Las Luchadoras contra el Robot Asesino
Las Luchadoras vs. el Médico Asesino
Las Luchadoras vs. la Momia
La Mafia Amarilla
La Maldición de la Llorona
La Maldición de la Momia Azteca
La Maldición de Nostradamus
La Mano Que Aprieta
La Mansión de las Siete Momias
Mantequilla en la Venganza de la Llorona
Mil Máscaras
Misión Suicida
El Misterio de Huracán Ramírez
Misterio en las Bermudas
La Momia Azteca
La Momia Azteca contra El Robot Humano
Las Momias de Guanajuato
Las Momias de San Ángel
El Monstruo de la Montaña Hueca
El Monstruo de los Volcanes
El Monstruo Resucitado
La Muerte Viviente
La Mujer Murciélago
La Mujer sin Cabeza
Las Mujeres Panteras
El Mundo de los Muertos
El Mundo de los Vampiros
El Museo del Crimen
Museo del Horror
La Nave de los Monstruos
Neutrón contra el Criminal Sádico
Neutrón contra los Asesinos del Karate
Neutrón contra los Automatas de la Muerte
Neutrón, el Enmascarado Negro
Neutrón vs. el Dr. Caronte
Noche de Muerte
Nostradamus
Nostradamus, el Genio de las Tinieblas
Nostradamus y el Destructor de Monstruos
Operación 67
Orlak, el Infierno de Frankenstein
El Pantano de las Ánimas
Pasaporte a la Muerte
El Planeta de las Mujeres Invasoras
Platillos Voladores
El Poder Negro de Sangre Chicana
Profanadores de Tumbas
El Puño de la Muerte
El Regreso del Monstruo
El Robo de las Momias de Guanajuato
Una Rosa Sobre el Ring
Santo contra Blue Demon en el Atlántida
Santo contra Capulina
Santo contra el Asesino de la T.V.
Santo contra el Cerebro Diabólico
Santo contra el Dr. Muerte
Santo contra el Rey del Crimen
Santo contra Hombres Infernales
Santo contra la Mafia del Vicio
Santo contra la Magia Negra
Santo contra los Cazadores de Cabezas
Santo contra las Mujeres Vampiro
Santo contra los Jinetes del Terror
Santo contra los Sequestadores
Santo contra los Zombies
Santo, el Enmascarado de Plata: El Infraterrestre
Santo en el Hotel de la Muerte
Santo en el Misterio de la Perla Negra
Santo en el Museo de Cera
Santo en el Tesoro de Drácula
Santo en la Frontera del Terror
Santo en la Venganza de la Momia
Santo en Oro Negro
Santo frente a la Muerte
Santo: La Leyenda del Enmascarado de Plata
Santo vs. el Estrangulador
Santo vs. la Hija de Frankenstein
Santo vs. la Invasión de los Marcianos
Santo vs. las Lobas
Santo vs. los Villanos del Ring
Santo y Blue Demon contra el Dr. Frankenstein

Santo y Blue Demon contra los Monstruos
Santo y Blue Demon vs. Drácula y el
 Hombre Lobo
El Secreto de Pancho Villa
Serenata Macabra
La Sombra Blanca
La Sombra del Murciélago
La Sombra Vengadora
La Sombra Vengadora contra La Mano
 Negra
El Superloco
Superzán el Invencible

Superzán y el Niño de Espacio
El Terrible Gigante de las Nieves
El Tesoro de Moctezuma
El Tesoro de Pancho Villa
El Triunfo de los Campeones Justicieros
Las Vampiras
El Vampiro
El Vampiro Sangriento
Los Vampiros de Coyoacán
La Venganza de Huracán Ramírez
La Venganza de las Mujeres Vampiro
Vuelven los Campeones Justicieros

Chronological List of Films

1931
Drácula

1933
La Llorona

1936
El Superloco

1937
Nostradamus

1943
El Espectro de la Novia
La Mujer sin Cabeza

1944
El As Negro
La Casa Embrujada

1945
El Museo del Crimen

1946
Asesinato en los Studios

1952
Huracán Ramírez
El Enmascarado de Plata

1953
El Monstruo Resucitado

1954
La Bruja
El Monstruo de la Montaña Hueca
El Secreto de Pancho Villa
La Sombra Vengadora
La Sombra Vengadora contra La Mano
    Negra
El Tesoro de Pancho Villa

1955
Platillos Voladores

1956
Ladrón de Cadáveres
El Pantano de las Ánimas

1957
El Ataúd del Vampiro
El Castillo de los Monstruos
El Hombre Que Logró Ser Invisible
La Maldición de la Momia Azteca
La Momia Azteca
La Momia Azteca contra El Robot Hu-
    mano
El Vampiro

1958
Cerebro del Mal
El Hombre y el Monstruo
Santo contra Hombres Infernales

1959
La Casa del Terror

La Maldición de Nostradamus
La Nave de los Monstruos
Nostradamus, el Genio de las Tinieblas
Nostradamus y el Destructor de Monstruos
El Regreso del Monstruo
La Sangre de Nostradamus

1960

El Mundo de los Vampiros
Neutrón, el Enmascarado Negro
Neutrón contra los Automatas de la Muerte
Neutrón vs. el Dr. Caronte
Orlak, el Infierno de Frankenstein

1961

El Barón del Terror
La Cabeza Viviente
Frankenstein, el Vampiro y Compañía
La Invasión de los Vampiros
La Maldición de la Llorona
Santo contra los Zombies
Santo contra el Rey del Crimen
Santo en el Hotel de la Muerte
Santo contra el Cerebro Diabólico

1962

El Misterio de Huracán Ramírez
El Monstruo de los Volcanes
Santo contra las Mujeres Vampiro
El Terrible Gigante de las Nieves
El Vampiro Sangriento

1963

El Espectro del Estrangulador
Las Luchadoras vs. el Médico Asesino
Museo del Horror
Santo en el Museo de Cera
Santo vs. el Estrangulador
La Sombra Blanca

1964

El Asesino Invisible
Atacan las Brujas
Aventura al Centro de la Tierra

Los Endemonadios del Ring
El Hacha Diabólica
La Loba
Las Luchadoras vs. la Momia
La Mano Que Aprieta
Neutrón contra el Criminal Sádico
Neutrón contra los Asesinos del Karate

1965

El Barón Brákola
Blue Demon, el Demonio Azul
Blue Demon vs. el Poder Satánico
Gigantes Planetarios
El Hijo de Huracán Ramírez
Las Lobas del Ring
El Planeta de las Mujeres Invasoras
Profanadores de Tumbas

1966

Arañas Infernales
Blue Demon contra Cerebros Infernales
Blue Demon vs. las Diabólicas
Los Canallas
Dr. Satán
Dr. Satán y la Magia Negra
El Imperio de Drácula
La Isla de los Dinosaurios
Mil Máscaras
Las Mujeres Panteras
Santo vs. la Invasión de los Marcianos
Santo vs. los Villanos del Ring
La Sombra del Murciélago

1967

Autopsia de un Phantasma
Blue Demon, Destructor de Espías
Con Licencia para Matar
La Mujer Murciélago
Operación 67
Pasaporte a la Muerte
El Tesoro de Moctezuma
Las Vampiras
La Venganza de Huracán Ramírez

1968

Blue Demon y las Invasoras

La Cámara del Terror
Enigma de Muerte
La Horripilante Bestia Humana
Invasión Siniestra
Las Luchadoras contra el Robot Asesino
La Muerte Viviente
Santo contra Capulina
Santo contra Blue Demon en el Atlántida
Santo en el Tesoro de Drácula
Sereneta Macabra

1969

El Mundo de los Muertos
Santo y Blue Demon contra los Monstruos
Santo contra los Cazadores de Cabezas
Santo frente a la Muerte

1970

Los Campeones Justicieros
Capulina vs. los Vampiros
Las Momias de Guanajuato
Santo contra los Jinetes del Terror
Santo contra la Mafia del Vicio
Santo en la Venganza de la Momia
La Venganza de las Mujeres Vampiro

1971

El Águila Real
Asesinos de Otros Mundos
Chanoc vs. el Tigre y el Vampiro
La Invasión de los Muertos
Misión Suicida
Santo vs. la Hija de Frankenstein
Superzán el Invencible
Superzán y el Niño de Espacio

1972

Anónimo Mortal
Las Bestias del Terror
Campeones del Ring
Capulina vs. las Momias
El Castillo de las Momias de Guanajuato
El Hombre y el Bestia
Huracán Ramírez y la Monjita Negra
La Mafia Amarilla

Noche de Muerte
El Robo de las Momias de Guanajuato
Una Rosa Sobre el Ring
Santo contra la Magia Negra
Santo contra los Secuestadores
Santo vs. las Lobas
Santo y Blue Demon vs. Drácula y el Hombre Lobo
Vuelven los Campeones Justicieros

1973

Chabelo y Pepito vs. los Monstruos
El Investigador Capulina
Los Jaguares contra el Invasores Misteriosos
Karla vs. los Jaguares
Leyendas Macabras de la Colonia
Las Momias de San Ángel
El Poder Negro de Sangre Chicana
Santo contra el Dr. Muerte
Santo y Blue Demon contra el Dr. Frankenstein
El Triunfo de los Campeones Justicieros
Los Vampiros de Coyoacán

1974

El Hijo de Alma Grande
Los Leones del Ring
Los Leones del Ring contra la Cosa Nostra
Santo en el Misterio de la Perla Negra
Santo en Oro Negro
Santo y Mantequilla en la Venganza de la Llorona

1975

La Mansión de las Siete Momias

1977

Misterio en las Bermudas

1979

Santo en la Frontera del Terror

1981

Chanoc y el Hijo del Santo contra los Vampiros Asesinos

1982

La Furia de las Karatecas
El Puño de la Muerte

1983

El Hijo del Santo en Frontera sin Ley

1989

Blue Demon, el Campeón

1992

Santo: La Leyenda del Enmascarado de Plata

2000

Santo, el Enmascarado de Plata: El Infraterrestre

ONE

The Bat Flies South

Early Mexican Fantasy and Horror

It was a dark and stormy night. The wind howled outside the walls of the ancient castle, scraping the branches of gnarled trees against the weather-beaten stone battlements. It was not the storm, however, which caused the chill to race down the spine of the man standing at the foot of a great staircase — it was the man standing at the head of those stairs. Tall, aristocratic, possessed of a hawk-like visage, he held a lit candle aloft as his cloak wrapped around him like the spiderwebs that adorned the walls and he introduced himself: "Yo soy ... Drácula!"

Two very important things happened in Mexico in the 1930s: In 1931, the Spanish-language *Drácula* was released. In 1933, Salvadore Lutteroth introduced masked wrestlers to Mexican arenas. Mexican wrestling, or "Lucha Libre" ("Free Wrestling"), takes on a whole new personality and dimension.

And so the seed was planted for the weird, wonderful world of Mexican horror films as we know and love them. No, the Spanish-language version of *Drácula* (Universal, 1931) was not a Mexican production. An alternate version of the Bela Lugosi classic, it was shot simultaneously by George Melford, who filmed on the same sets after the regular production had gone home for the night. It did, however, utilize

well-known Mexican actors in the lead roles, and it was a great success in Mexico. Unlike the more famous Lugosi version, however, it did not inspire an industry. To be sure, there was a Mexican film industry; but whereas America's 1931 *Dracula* immediately begat *Frankenstein*, *The Mummy*, *The Wolf Man*, et al., there would be no such onslaught in Mexican films — at least, not for another twenty years.

This is not to say that there was a dearth of fantasy in Mexican films of the '30s and '40s; on the contrary, numerous fantastic elements featured in many "straight" movies. But there just weren't many monsters. There was, however, more of a fantastic element to everyday life in Mexico (i.e. the Day of the Dead, the Mummies of Guanajuato display), so it was more readily accepted in everyday films.

The part that the wrestling mask played in this process cannot be overestimated. The part that wrestling played, period, cannot be underestimated. As opposed to its status in the United States, where wrestling has always been more of a "fringe" sport (and viewed by some as not a sport at all), wrestling ranks as one of Mexico's top attractions. Aspiring to be a Mexican pro wrestler (males are "luchadores," females are "luchadoras") is much the same as aspiring to be a football or baseball star in América.

In América, however, the mask did not quite mean the same thing. In the U.S., a mask denoted villainy, or a recognized star who was "on the run." In any event, masks were either meant to be defeated or discarded. Not so in Mexico. A tradition of masks, which dates back to the Aztecs, re-invented itself in a modern fashion. In Mexico, the wrestling mask became the symbol of the wrestler who wore it; it became his identity. The masked wrestlers never appeared in public without those masks; and, in time, the mask became a legacy to be passed from generation to generation, much like the fictional Phantom. To be unmasked was the ultimate disgrace and defeat, and once unmasked, a wrestler could never wrestle with a mask again.

Monsters. Masked wrestlers. Both made their way into Mexico in the 1930s, and when they finally cross-pollinated, the world would never be the same.

Drácula (1931)

(Universal) *Prod:* Carl Laemmle, Jr.; *Dir:* George Melford/Enrique Tovar Avalos; *Scr:* B. Fernández Cué, Garrett Fort, Dudley Murphy (based on the novel by Bram Stoker); *Asst. Prod:* Paul Kohner; *Cinematography:* George Robinson; *Film Ed:* Arturo Tavares; *Art Dir:* Charles D. Hall; *Asst. Dir:* Charles S. Gould, Jay Marchant; *Rec. Suprvsr:* C. Roy Hunter.

Cast: Carlos Villarias (Drácula), Lupita Tovar (Eva), Barry Norton (Juan Harker), Pablo Álvarez Rubio (Renfield), Eduardo Arozamena (Van Helsing), José Soriano Viosca (Doctor Seward), Carmen Guerrero (Lucia), Amelia Senisterra (Marta), Manuel Arbó (Martín).

Although not a Mexican production, Universal's 1931 Spanish-language version of its classic *Drácula* was designed for Latino audiences. It is included in this volume because it's the very first south-of-the-border appearance of a "classic" monster, and features Mexican principals in the cast who would become identified with the

genre. Director George Melford filmed on the *Drácula* sets at night, with a different cast and crew, and it has been opined by many (including this author) that in most every way except one (which also happens to be the most important), it is superior to the Tod Browning version. Pictorially and atmospherically, it remains much more cohesive than the famous English-language version. But it lacks one very important element — Bela Lugosi. Carlos Villarias, a respected actor in the young Mexican cinema, certainly looked the part, but he could not duplicate Lugosi's skill, unique charm, and powerful presence. This does not make the Spanish-language effort less enjoyable as cinema, however, and the power achieved in parts by this version only make one wish Tod Browning had taken as much care with the same basic tools. Apart from Villarias, the ensemble work is stronger in this version, and since it isn't dominated by a single presence, the other players have more of a chance to shine. Particularly impressive is the raven-haired Lupita Tovar, Helen Chandler's replacement as Mina, who is much more passionate than the frigid Miss Chandler, and much more openly sensual in her low-cut black silk negligees. Her performance (and appearance) highlights one of those elements that the Spanish-language version captures far more successfully than its more stage-bound model — the inherent sexuality so crucial to the vampire mythos.

Born in 1892, Carlos Villarias not only looked like Lugosi, his career followed a similar path — a major star in the thirties, he was consigned to "B" productions in the forties. He passed away April 27, 1976, and even though his genre credits were relatively slight compared to Lugosi, it seems that if there was a major fantasy production, Villarias was in it. His genre credits include: *El Misterio del Rostro Palido* (The Mystery of the Pallid Face, 1935), *El Super-loco* (see subsequent entry), and *Nostra-*

damus (1937). Among his "B" roles were two turns in the "Fu Manchu" series, *El Museo del Crimen* and *Asesinato en los Estudios.*

Lupita Tovar, besides appearing in the Spanish-language versions of Universal chillers like *Dracula* and *The Cat and the Canary,* also crossed the border to find work in American productions like *The Cat Creeps, Green Hell,* and *The Crime Doctor's Courage.*

La Llorona (*The Crying Woman,* 1933)

Dir: Ramón Peón; *Story:* A. Guzmán Aguilera, Fernando de Fuentes, Carlos Noriega Hope.

Cast: Ramón Pereda (Dr. Ricardo de Acuna/ Capitan Diego de Acuna), Virginia Zurí (Ana María de Acuna), Carlos Orellana (Mario), Adriana Lamar (Ana Xicontencatl), Esperanza del Real (Nana Goya), Alberto Martí (Rodrigo de Cortes, Marques del Valle), Paco Martínez (Don Fernando de Moncada), María Luisa Zea (Dona Marina, La Malinche), Alfredo del Diestro (Inspector de policia), Conchita Gentil Arcos (Sirvienta), Antonio R. Frausto (Francisco), Victoria Blanco, Manuel Dondé.

La Llorona was the first Mexican horror film based on an actual Mexican legend, that of "the Crying Woman." A woman of the lower classes bears the children of a rich man, only to have him marry another. Driven mad, she kills the children and then commits suicide. She becomes the spectre known as "the Crying Woman," because her wailing for her lost children ("Ayyy, mis hijos!") can be heard on the wind.

In this first filmic version of the legend, the peasant Ana is the lover of wealthy Don Rodrigo Cortes, who abandons her and their children to marry another. Crashing the wedding, Ana kills the children and herself. Because of this, every first-born male Cortes is cursed to die on his fourth birthday. Ricardo Cortes' son Juanito turns four, and, sure enough, he is abducted by a hooded figure. Ricardo rescues him, and in the process learns the story of the curse. But then Juanito is kidnapped again. The police get the boy back this time, killing the hooded figure, who is really the child's nanny — she had been possessed by "the Crying Woman," whose spirit leaves the nanny as she expires (in a well-filmed scene which is genuinely creepy).

Besides several other films (offering quite different takes on the legend) devoted to the character herself, the old girl makes a couple of cameos in later movies. *Grito de la Muerte* ("The Living Coffin" 1958), is another Gaston Santos Western with horror overtones, and it turns out pretty much like *Swamp of the Lost Monster,* in that, instead of using a fake lagoon creature to scare away pesky intruders, they use "La Llorona" masks. Another very, very, very brief appearance of the Crying Woman comes in the 1973 Mil Máscaras film *Leyendas Macabras de Colonia;* and her tie with the monster/wrestler genre (which I'm sure the legends never envisioned!) was cemented the year after that with *Santo y Mantequilla vs. la Venganza de la Llorona.*

El Superloco (*The Super Madman,* 1936)

Dir: Juan José Segura; *Scr:* Jorge Cardeña Álvarez, Juan José Segura; *Music:* Chucho Monge, Daniel Pérez Castañeda; *Cinematography:* Jack Draper; *Film Ed:* José Marino; *Prod. Design:* José Rodríguez Granada.

Cast: Carlos Villarias (Dr. Dienys), Emilio Fernández ("Indian" Fernández), Ramón Armengod, Aurora Campuzano, Jorge Cardeña Álvarez, Consuelo Frank, Manuel Noriega, Polo Ortín, Armando Rosendal, Galdino R. Samperio, Raúl Urquijo (Monster).

This pioneering effort of Mexican genre cinema is significant for being the first Hollywood-style Mad Scientist epic, with a dash of *Forbidden Planet* (20 years beforehand!) and *The Picture of Dorian Gray* thrown in for good measure. The story concerns Dr. Dienys ("Drácula" himself, Carlos Villarias), who theorizes that controlling emotions can lead to eternal life. Though ridiculed (naturally) by his scientific brethren, Dr. Dienys takes on a young assistant, who aids him in his experiments. What the new fellow doesn't know is that the doc keeps a brutish monster locked up in the basement. In a Dorian Gray-esque twist, all of the good doctor's lusts and forbidden passions have taken shape in hideous real form! When the assistant inadvertantly releases the monster, the doc's passions overload, and the nutty professor ages right before our eyes. To add insult to injury, the monster then tosses Dienys out a window, before getting his. All the classic mad science elements are here, well-filmed and well-played.

Again, one wishes there had been more of a demand for genre pictures at the time, as well as wondering why fine efforts like this one didn't inspire further films along these lines. Carlos Villarias, with his Lugosi-style looks, had the presence to become a dominant force in horror character roles. Like Lugosi, Villarias' acting in such parts is certainly "baked ham," and he was an all-around fine actor; but, unlike "Poor Bela" (and, to a certain extent, Germán Robles), he wasn't typecast by playing Drácula, and received much more of a chance to showcase his skills in many other types of big-budget mainstream Mexican films.

Nostradamus (1937)

Prod: Francisco Beltrán, Salvador Bueno; *Dir:* Juan Bustillo Oro, Antonio Helú; *Scr:* Juan Bustillo Oro, Antonio Helú; *Novel:* Michel Zevaco; *Music:* Max Urban; *Cinematography:* Víctor Herrera; *Film Ed:* Juan Bustillo Oro; *Prod. Design:* Jorge Fernández, Salvador Tarazona; *Asst. Dir:* Miguel M. Delgado.

Cast: Carlos Villarias (Nostradamus), Valentín Asperó, Luis G. Barreiro, Rodolfo Calvo, Aurora Campuzano, René Cardona, Joaquín Coss, Consuelo Frank, Alfonso Landa, Carlos López, Juan José Martínez Casado, José Elías Moreno, Manuel Noriega, Polo Ortín, Miguel Ruiz, Miguel Wimer.

Somewhat like Universal's *Tower of London* two years in the future, *Nostradamus* is a more or less historical account of the famed medieval prophet, with the spooky elements emphasized. Twenty-two years later, the name would be utilized for a four-picture series featuring a relative who has become a vampire and perpetrates a reign of terror not unlike some of those envisioned by his famous ancestor. *Nostradamus* features one of the first film appearances of René Cardona, Sr., who would shortly turn to directing, although he never completely give up acting (he continued to essay genre roles right up through the end of the El Santo series, 45 years later). Cardona's influence on the genre is inestimable.

"Fu Manchu" Series

El Espectro de la Novia (*The Spectre of the Bride*, Films Mundiales, 1943)

Prod: Felipe Subervielle; *Dir/Adapt:* René Cardona; *Collab:* Xavier Villaurrutia; *Story:* David T. Bamberg, Agustín J. Fink; *Photo:* Gabriel Figueroa; *Music/Music Rec:* Manuel Esperón; *Prod. Chf:* Armando Espinosa; *Asst. Dir:* Felipe Palomino; *Film Ed:* Jorge Bustos; *Art Dir:* Jorge Fernández; *Cam Op:* Domingo Carrillo; *Sound Dir:* Howard E. Randall; *Dialog Rec:* José de Pérez; *Makeup:* Ana Guererro.

Cast: David T. Bamberg (Fu Manchu), Manuel Medel (Satanas), Josefina Escobedo (Madame Dupont), Miguel Ángel Ferriz (Gout), Narciso Busqueta (Juanito), Mimi Derba (Snra. Guzmán), José Pidal (Dr. Sumo), Ángel T. Sala (Lt. Palomino), Agustín Sen, Julio Ahuet, "Cucuita."

La Mujer sin Cabeza (*The Headless Woman*, Films Mundiales, 1944)

Prod: Felipe Subervielle; *Dir:* René Cardona; *Scr/Story:* David T. Bamberg, René Cardona, Xavier Villaurrutia; *Music:* Manuel Esperón; *Cinematography:* Gabriel Figueroa; *Film Ed:* Gloria Schoemann; *Cam. Op:* Domingo Carrillo.

Cast: David T. Bamberg (Fu Manchu), Manuel Medel (Satanas), Alfonso (Bedoya) Bedolla, Roberto Cañedo, Paco Fuentes, Ramón G. Larrea, Manuel Noriega, Fransisco Pando, Carlos Riquelme, Humberto Rodríguez, Fernando Romero, Ángel T. Sala, Milisa Sierra, Arturo Soto Rangel, Jeusus Valero, "Cucuita."

El As Negro (*The Black Ace*, Films Mundiales, 1944)

Prod: Felipe Subervielle; *Dir:* René Cardona; *Scr/Story:* David T. Bamberg, René Cardona, Xavier Villaurrutia; *Music:* Manuel Esperón; *Cinematography:* Gabriel Figueroa; *Film Ed:* Gloria Schoemann; *Cam. Op:* Domingo Carrillo; *Prod. Design:* Jorge Fernández; *Costume Design:* Royer, Henri de Chatillon.

Cast: David T. Bamberg (Fu Manchu), Manuel Medel (Satanas), Janice Logan, Tony Díaz, Chel López, Tito Novaro, Salvador Quiroz, Milisa Sierra, Charles Stevens, Mario Tenorio, Victor Velázquez.

La Casa Embrujada (*The Bewitched House*, Producciones Eduardo Quevedo, 1944)

Prod: Quevedo; *Dir/Adapt:* Fernando A. Rivero; *Story:* Norman Foster, David T. Bamberg; *Photo:* Ignacio Torres; *Music:* Jorge H. Pérez; *Prod. Chf:* Luis Bustos; *Asst. Dir:* Valerio Olivo; *Film Ed:* Rafael Portillo; *Art Dir:* Luis Moya; *Decor:* Francisco Zarraga; *Camera Op:* Andrés Torres; *Makeup:* Felisa L. de Guevara; *Sound:* Rodolfo Solis; *Sound Ed:* Lupe Marino.

Cast: David T. Bamberg (Fu Manchu), Pituka de Foronda (Margarita Palacios), Ricardo Mondragón (Dr. Busquet), Emma Roldan (nurse), Ramón Vallarino (Manuel Ramos), Ángel T. Sala (Lt. Palomino), Katy Jurado (Sara Cardoso), Cuca Escobar (Cuca), Rafael Icardo, Octavio Martínez (Dr. Andrade), Concha Gentil Arcos (Clementina Cardoso de Ramos), José Morcillo (salesman), Fernando Curiel (Dr. Osorio), Carlos Villarias (detective), Ernesto Monato (Dr. Villanueva), José Escanero (hotel mgr), Humberto Rodríguez (medical examiner).

El Museo del Crimen (*The Museum of Crime*, Astro Films, 1945)

Prod: José D. Sotomayor; *Co-Prod/Dir/Scr:* René Cardona, Sr.; *Dialog:* Ramón Pérez; *Adapt/Story:* David T. Bamberg; *Photo:* José Ortiz Ramos; *Prod. Chf:* Luis Sánchez Tello; *Asst. Dir:* Luis Abadie; *Film Ed:* José Marino, Sr.; *Art Dir:* Ramón Rodríguez; *Cam Op:* José Gutierrez Zamora; *Makeup:* Felicia (Ladrón de Guevara); *Sound:* B.G. (*sic*) Kroger; *Sound Engineer:* Rodolfo Solis.

Cast: David T. Bamberg (Fu Manchu), Pituka de Foronda (Margarita Palacios), Ricardo Mondragón (Dr. Busquet), Emma Roldán (nurse), Ramón Vallarino (Manuel Ramos), Ángel T. Sala (Lt. Palomino), Katy Jurado (Sara Cardoso), Cuca Escobar (Cuca), Rafael Icardo, Octavio Martínez (Dr. Andrade), Concha Gentil Arcos (Clementina Cardoso de Ramos), José Morcillo (salesman), Fernando Curiel (Dr. Osorio), Carlos Villarias (detective), Ernesto Monato (Dr. Villanueva), José Escanero (hotel mgr), Humberto Rodríguez (medical examiner).

Asesinato en los Studios (*Murder in the Studios*, Astro Films, 1946)

Prod: José D. Sotomayor; *Dir/Scr:* Rafael J. Sevilla; *Dialogue:* "Fu Manchu"*, Ramón Pérez; *Add'l Dialogue:* Rafael J. Sevilla, Adelaida Noriega; *Adapt/Story:* David T. Bamberg; *Photog:* José Ortiz Ramos; *Music:* Jorge Pérez; *Prod. Chf:* Luis Sánchez Tello; *Asst. Dir:* Luis Abadie; *Film Ed:* José Marino; *Art Dir:* Ramón Rodríguez; *Cam Op:* José

**Yes, he's listed in the credits as both himself and his alter-ego. Did he get two paychecks?*

Gutierrez Zamora; *Sound Rec:* B.J. Kroger; *Sound Op:* Rodolfo Solis; *Sound Ed:* Lupita Marino.

Cast: David T. Bamberg (Fu Manchu), María de los Ángeles (Santa) (Pola Blanqui), Ricardo Mondragón (González), José Morcillo (Bernal), Ángel T. Sala (Lt. Palomino), Fredy Romero (Lucifer), José Pidal (Santos), Víctor Velázquez (Pepe), Alma Lorena (Elena Palmer), Salvador Lozano (David Martin), Ángel di Stefani (Raúl Roldan), Carlos Villarias (doctor), Roberto Cañedo (cameraman), René Cardona (himself), Rafael J. Sevilla (himself), María Enriqueta Reza, Natalia Ortiz, Rusty Russell.

David T. Bamberg (1904–1974) was one of the most famous stage magicians of his generation. After serving his apprenticeship with various magicians, Bamberg received the backing to put on his own show, and adopted the persona of "Fu Manchu," obviously based on Sax Rohmer's evil Asian mastermind. After emigrating to Mexico, Bamberg transferred the name recognition of his extremely popular character to a series of motion pictures, although the complete "Fu" persona, makeup and all, was used only when recreating portions of Bamberg's real-life show.

For most of the films—detective thrillers with supernatural overtones—Bamberg appears in the standard '40s suit and fedora. Even in civvies, however, he was referred to as "Fu Manchu"; as with Hollywood sleuths, you didn't have to have a secret identity, just a cool nickname.

The films themselves are handsomely mounted B products, and match up quite well in comparison with their foreign counterparts of the same mettle. They play like a cross between RKO's *Falcon* and Universal's *Inner Sanctum* series, with Bamberg's suave sleuth echoing *Falcon*'s Tom Conway and George Sanders, and the mood and supernatural elements were pure Laemmle.

The series is significant not only because it featured the first supernaturally themed series character, but also because many of the names which pop up here for the first time would later become heavily associated with the Monster-Wrestler genre, including Roberto Cañedo, Aztec Mummy Ángel Di Stefani, Tito Novaro, Jorge Pérez, Rafael Portillo, José Sotomayor, and many others. René Cardona cut his directorial teeth on the series; twenty years later, he paid tribute to Bamberg in *Las Luchadoras vs. la Momia*, in which the villainous Prince Fujiyata bore a strong resemblance to Bamberg's Fu.

All in all, the *Fu Manchu* films are a pretty satisfying little group. Bamberg's no Charles Laughton, but he sure performed his duties adequately, and perhaps better than the comparable World War II–era leading men north of the border. All the films have their moments, with perhaps *Museo del Crimen* and *Asesinato en los Studios* emerging as the popular favorites.

Museo del Crimen has a genuinely creepy and effective sequence where, in flashback, Fu is in a suitably noirish motel room, at the mirror, preparing to shave. The face of a bearded man with a straight razor appears in the mirror, making slashing gestures with the razor, and Fu is nearly moved to cut his own throat! *Asesinato* takes place at the actual Azteca Studios, and features not only scenes of real directors like Cardona directing real movies, but a film-within-a-film that is like a mini–Universal.

La Casa Embrujada has a great over-the-top villain (Baena) and his brutish, moronic henchman. That film's decidely different tone and bizarre scenarios are something of a foreshadowing of the next decade's monster madness, especially as the monsterish henchman is played by future Aztec Mummy Ángel Di Stefani.

Other notable faces include Drácula himself, Carlos Villarias; Katy Jurado, the beautiful, gutsy "other woman" from *High Noon*; the striking Janice Logan (*Dr. Cyclops*), and the unforgettable Alfonso Bedolla: "Badges?! We don't need no stinking badges!"

Two

Who Was That Masked Man?

The Spirit of the Serials

Like horror films, the serial (i.e. cliffhanger or chapter play) was a thriving genre in the Golden Age of Hollywood. Fans flocked to the theaters week after week to see the latest installment of their favorite heroes (like Captain Marvel, Flash Gordon or Batman) doing battle with their favorite villains (like the Crimson Ghost or Ming the Merciless). Heroes were stalwart, villains nefarious, the plots diabolical, the gadgetry outrageous, and the action non-stop. But, unlike Mexican horror movies, which at least made a late start, south-of-the-border serials never even got off the ground. In fact, only *one* real cliffhanger was ever made *and* shown in Mexico, *Las Calaveras del Terror*. No, it was more the spirit of the serials which manifested itself so deeply in the wrestler/monster genre—upstanding heroes versus wacky villains with even wackier machines. The Mexicans actually pushed this concept much farther over the top than their American counterparts, and the best part was that you didn't have to wait a week to see what happened next!

But wait a minute—wasn't *El Enmascarado de Plata* a serial? And don't a lot of the early monster-wrestler films have numbered episodes and chapter titles in them? Well, yes it is, and yes they do, little amigos, and here's how they both work: *El Enmascarado de Plata* was made as a serial, but it was only shown that way in the United States! The print that survives is the feature version, which was the way it was seen in Mexico. As for the features, like El Santo's *Profanadore de Tumbas*, the different "episodes" contained within the films were never shown separately. This shot-as-a-serial-but-shown-as-a-feature method was infended to circumvent regulations pertaining to the making of feature films. Of the movies discussed that display the spirit of the serials, only *El Enmascarado de Plata* was a true cliffhanger (but, again, only for its U.S. release); but it, along with *La Sombra Vengadora*, *Huracán Ramírez*, and *Ladrón de Cadáveres*, pretty much laid out all the ground rules for a genre that was soon to explode higher than Captain Marvel could fly! (And even though it came first, for continuity's sake, *Huracán Ramírez* is listed and discussed with the other films featuring the character, in Chapter Eight.)

El Enmascarado de Plata (*The Silver-Masked Man*, 1952)

(Filmex) *Prod*: Antonio de Castillo; *Dir*: René Cardona, Sr.; *Adapt*: Ramón Obón; *Story*: José G. Cruz, René Cardona, Sr.; *Photo*: Raúl Martínez Solares; *Music*: Rafael Carrión; *Prod. Chief*: Luis Busto; *Asst. Dir*: Julio Cahero; *Film*

El Enmascarado de Plata, 1952 — The one-sheet for the seminal "Masked Wrestler as Action Hero" movie.

Ed: Rafael Ceballos; *Art Dir*: Jorge Fernández; *Camera Op*: Cirilo Rodríguez; *Lights*: Carlos Najera; *Makeup*: Concepción Zamora; *Music/Dialogue Rec*: Enrique Rodríguez; *Sound Ed*: Abraham Cruz.

Cast: El Médico Asesino (El Médico), Victor Junco (Alfredo), Crox Alvarado (Julio), Luis Aldas (Kroger), Aurora Segura (Elena), René Cardona, Jr. (Pecas), Carlos Muzquez (Risueno), Jack O'Brien (Jack, henchman), Guillermo Hernández "Lobo Negro" (Lobo, henchman), Sergio Llanes, José Pulido, Mario Llanes, Julio Ahuet, Pedro Ortega, Roberto G. Rivera (Henchmen), Hermanitas Julián (Singing group), Elena Julián (Miraya), Fransisco Llopis (Uncle), Felipe Montoya (Inspector), José Luis Moreno (Pepe), Cuco Sánchez (Radio perator), Ignacio Peon (Old man in bed).

The mexican wrestler/horror film did not spring full-blown from the screen when some producer simply decided to pit El Santo against some vampire women. No, that early apex of the genre came about only after some ten years of refining elements which had already been in place, but had (almost) never before been brought together with such audacity. Four films in particular from the early 1950s contributed these elements: *El Enmascarado de Plata*, *La Sombra Vengadora*, *Huracán Ramírez*, and *Ladrón de Cadáveres*. None of the four alone contains all the requisite attributes (although *Ladrón* comes close), but certain facets from each of them were later combined to create what we know as the classic Mexican wrestler/horror movie.

Two of the four were made in 1952. *Huracán Ramírez* came first, but it was a rather ordinary sports drama, its distinguishing feature being, of course, that it featured a masked wrestler rather than a ball player or fighter. He wasn't really a crime-fighter, although he battled corruption in the wrestling business itself. Actually, he wasn't even played by a real wrestler either; but it was the fact that the character *was* a wrestler and not another sports figure that proved important (that,

and his distinctive mask). The character proved so popular that the name and mask were adopted for the ring by Daniel García, who carried the mantle ably and proudly for many years.

El Enmascarado de Plata released a short time later, comes much closer to what we think of as a classic Santo or Blue Demon movies. In fact, this historic serial could have become even more historic had it been Santo's first film. Though it bears his familiar nickname, Santo did not appear in *El Enmascarado de Plata*. Why? Well, therein hangs the tale.

When we think of El Santo nowadays, we think of the crime-busting superhero idol of millions and all-around good guy. In his pre-movie championship days, however, it was quite the opposite. El Santo was a rudo, a villain in the ring, an image completely belying his ironic monicker, "the Saint." But as he was quickly on his way to becoming the most popular wrestler in Mexico, it was decided that he undergo a gradual change of image — gradual in that in the ring he was still mostly a bad guy, but in the comic books he was all hero! The comic books (and the Santo heroic persona contained therein) were the work of José G. Cruz. So was the major part of the story for *El Enmascarado de Plata*. The role, obviously, was created with Santo in mind. However, El Santo passed on the picture, doubting either his own screen appeal or the commercial potential of the venture itself. As a slap at Santo, Cruz kept the name intact, and instead of referring to the film's hero, the titular character was now one of the film's two major villains. Here was one of the earliest examples of the Mexican wrestler/ horror films' tendency to pile it on. In American serials, the audience was often asked to play a guessing game as to the identity of a masked hero (the Lone Ranger, the Masked Marvel) or masked fiend (the Scorpion, the Lightning), but generally not both in the same serial! So not only are we supposed to guess the identities of the hero *and* villain in *El Enmascarado de Plata*, but we get another masked mastermind thrown in for good measure!(The plot device of making the viewer wonder who was under a wrestling mask was pretty much dispensed with when the real-life wrestlers, such as Santo and Blue Demon, started making movies as themselves, although filmmakers gave it another go-round with the Neutrón character.)

Despite the secret identity tomfoolery it shares with *Huracán Ramírez*, there's one important difference in the hero of *El Enmascarado de Plata*. Whereas Huracán was a character created for the screen whose persona was later transferred to the ring, El Médico Asesino was a real-life grappler who played himself in the movie, and thereby set the stage for the others. Like the filmic El Santo, he had a secret lab, but unlike in Santo's movies, the wrestling aspect of his career was not emphasized very much. *El Enmascarado de Plata* offers only one wrestling scene, and that is staged for the film; and in another eerie foreshadowing of (too many) later lucha films, he fights an evil double of himself! (Thank God it was just for one scene, and not a recurring subplot.) The other main difference between El Médico and the famous wrestlers of filmland who followed in his wake was, unfortunately, beyond his control: screen presence. Whereas El Santo, Blue Demon and Mil Máscaras had charisma to spare, El Médico came up, shall we say, a little short in that department. He cuts a dashing enough figure when totin' a tommy gun or while astride his 'cycle (a vintage Indian), but there's not much else to give him much of a personality (he's too busy disappearing so that the audience can wonder which one of the intrepid male leads he "really" is).

Overall, though, the film satisfies. The pacing and tone strive to emulate the product of Republic, and the filmmakers do a reasonable job. The director was a well-respected man on both sides of the camera, René Cardona, Sr., who would be responsible for many of the best wrestler/horror movies, including the classic Wrestling Women series (see Chapter Seven). Hooded villains were nothing new to serials, but not only did Cardona up the ante by featuring two (El Tigre and the titular mastermind), he added the uniquely Mexican twist of making the hoods wrestling masks, a theme he would repeat in *Las Luchadores vs. El Médico Asesino*. And these are some stylish baddies—El Tigre sports a black-and-white tiger-striped mask and gloves, along with a dark fedora and overcoat, while El Enmascarado favors (obviously) a silver mask (the only difference from El Santo's being the little black lightning bolts that adorn it, giving him sort of a reverse–Neutrón look). In another twist, the title villain actually dies midway through the proceedings, revealing with his dying gasp that he is not the true mastermind of the group! (Perhaps another shot at Santo?) It is actually El Tigre, who has been more or less absent since the beginning. Actually, it should have been obvious it was him all along, because he sported a much more impressive mask (and don't forget his matching accessories)! Also, it was El Tigre's striped-gloved hands seen operating the death ray at the beginning, even though El Enmascarado seemed to be giving the orders. Okay, maybe it wasn't a death ray, it was merely a weapon of unspecified power (seemingly able to both divert storms and level buildings), but it sure looked superscientific, and that was all that mattered.

El Enmascarado de Plata not a bad serial in and of itself, and remains historically important for the introduction of the masked-wrestler-as-action-hero genre (no small feat). All it would take was a couple

Above: An "Azteca" lobby card for *El Enmascarado de Plata,* named for the U.S. Distributor of Mexican films. *Below:* Biker Boyz El Médico Asesino and Rene Cardona, Jr., cruisin' on El Médico's vintage Indian cycle.

more pictures and a few monsters, and then they had it down for the count!

THE *LA SOMBRA VENGADORA* SERIES

La Sombra Vengadora (*The Avenging Shadow*, 1954)

Prod: Luis Manrique; *Dir*: Rafael Baledón; *Screenplay*: Ramón Obón.

　Cast: Fernando Osés (La Sombra Vengadora), Armando Silvestre (Rogelio), Alicia Caro (Margarita), Perdo D'Aguillon (Eduardo), Rodlfo Landa, Yerye Bierute.

La Sombra Vengadora contra la Mano Negra (*The Avenging Shadow versus the Black Hand*, 1954)

(Technical credits and castare the same as above.)

El Tesoro de Pancho Villa (*The Treasure of Pancho Villa*, 1954)

Prod: Luis Manrique; *Dir*: Rafael Baledón; *Screenplay*: Ramón Obón.

　Cast: Fernando Osés (La Sombra Vengadora), Alicia Caro, Rodlfo Landa, Pascual García Pena, Rafael Banquells.

An Azteca lobby card for *La Sombra Vengadora,* 1954.

El Secreto de Pancho Villa (*The Secret of Pancho Villa*, 1954)

(Technical Credits and Cast: Same as above.)

Two years later, another piece of the puzzle fell into place with the apperance of the La Sombra Vengadora series. The first entry was the biggest part of that piece, for reasons explored in a moment, but the sequels that soon followed proved significant for one important reason: they showed that a popular wrestling/superhero character could sustain more than just one film, and so set the tone for all future series featuring real-life wrestling heroes.

La Sombra, like Huracán Ramírez, was a character created for the screen who later transferred to the ring. However, while Huracán Ramírez was a masked wrestler in his film, La Sombra was "just" a masked superhero who wrestled (complete with fancy cape and buccaneer boots). Yet his attire suggested that, given a more colorful costume and dynamic personality (with action to match), a real-life wrestler could easily play that role, and shortly one would.

The character of La Sombra was created and owned by Ramón Obón. The character, like Huracán Ramírez, made the transition to the ring; but, unlike Huracan, he was not a great success. Interest-

More serial-type thrills and a solidification of the wrestling-masked hero concept, brought to life by luchador-of-all-trades Fernando Osés (publicity photograph for *La Sombra Vengadora*, 1954).

ingly, another wrestler soon appeared, Rayo de Jalisco, whose costume was identical to La Sombra's, except that the lightning bolt adorning the front of the mask zig-zagged in a different direction. And real life imitated reel life when Rayo de Jalisco replaced La Sombra in the "Champeons of Justice" series. Apparently, Obón wanted too many pesos for the use of his character.

The La Sombra series turned to the serials for their inspiration, and, although not actual cliffhangers, the movies came out so quickly in succession that they must have seemed like chapterplays. The pacing and plot devices were very serial-like, and the action proved quite spectacular, damn near up to the standards of the Republic Studio classics. This was due to the brisk direction by Baledón, and, more importantly, the spectacular athletics of Fernado Osés. Osés is one of the key figures in Mexican wrestler/horror movies, on both sides of the camera. A former pro himself, Osés virtually created the genre. Using lessons learned from the preceding films, this one, and at least one more key entry to follow, he gave birth to the real-life-masked-wrestler-as-superhero, combining serial-type thrills with fantastical menaces. Osés not only wrote many of the classics of the genre, he appeared in many, both as heavy (Barón Brákola, numerous henchmen) and hero (he played La Sombra Vengadora in every screen appearance of the character). And like the stuntman Tom Steele in the Republic serial *The Masked Marvel* (1943), in the first two Sombra movies Osés always appears as the title character in costume, but never appears on-screen as one of the men suspected to be him. After the first two, there was never much palaver about secret identities; La Sombra was La Sombra all the time — another precedent for the real-life wrestlers who needn't be bothered with such plot devices.

Ladrón De Cadáveres (*Body Snatchers,* 1956)

Prod: Sergio Kogan; *Dir*: Fernando Méndez; *Scr/Story*: Fernando Méndez, Alejandro Verbitzky; *Music*: Federico Ruiz; *Cinematography*: Víctor Herrera; *Film Ed*: Jorge Bustos; *Prod. Design*: Gunther Gerszo; *Makeup*: Margarita Ortega; *Prod. Sprvsr*: Armando Espinosa; *Asst. Dir*: Américo Fernández; *Sound*: James L. Fields; *SPFX*: Juan Muñoz Ravelo; *Still Photo*: Rafael García.

Cast: Wolf Ruvinskis (Guillermo Santana), Carlos Riquelme (Mad Doctor), Crox Alvarado (Capt. Rodríguez), Columba Domínguez (Secretary), Yerye Beirute, Eduardo Alcaraz, Alberto Catalá, Alejandro Cruz, Guillermo Hernández, Arturo Martínez, Lee Morgan, Ignacio Navarro.

The more-or-less final piece of the puzzle, *Ladrón de Cadaveres* is the first full-fledged example of what we now know as Mexican Film Insanity. Taking from one rising genre (the masked wrestler action movie), it melded with another (which didn't just rise, it *exploded* the very next year) … the monster movie. But the film was not the wrestler-*meets*-monster epic which would become so prevalent in a very short time; no, *Ladrón de Cadáveres* takes it "one step beyond," and the wrestler actually turns into the monster!

Ladrón de Cadáveres features the first appearance of a plot device which would be utilized over and over again (particularly by screenwriter Alfredo Salazar) — a mad scientist wants to create a monster via brain transplants, and decides that a pro wrestler would be the perfect specimen! The initial recipient of this treatment is Wolf Ruvinskis, a former wrestler turned actor, as "Guillermo Santana," a po' boy who wants to become a wrasslin' star. Of course, this makes him perfect fodder for the nutty Doc Ogden. On the night of his first important match, Ogden kills the likeable Santana and steals his corpse, whereupon he performs the expected surgery. Amusingly, Guillermo's wrestling character is named "El Vampiro," a name adopted by another wrestler in the '80s who became infamous via his association with legendary punk rock band the Misfits.

The brain takes, and Ogden has his monster — and what's the first thing a Mexican mad scientist who has created a monster does with his crowning achievement? Why, he sends him out to wrestle, of course! In another blueprint scene, the now-monsterized Santana (wrestling as "El Vampiro 2," another great joke) makes short work of his opponent — and since his opponent isn't El Santo or Blue Demon, he actually gets killed! El Vampiro 2 then rips off his own mask to reveal a snarling ape-man! He then goes on the expected rampage. A nice touch has Ruvinskis' makeup becoming more and more monstrous as the picture races to its climax; he starts out ape-like, but by the time he's gunned down on the rooftops, he's become a slobbering, fanged, scaly, bug-eyed, vaguely reptilian fiend (readers of *Famous Monsters* magazine will recall a startling full-page shot of this horrifying visage from an early issue).

Although it's not generally seen today, *Ladrón de Cadávares* is a piece of Mexican film history that cries out for the dubbing or subtitling that would make it accessible to gringos, because it's one of the most important films in establishing the ground rules for pretty much everything that followed. *Huracán Ramírez, El Enmascarado de Plata*, and the *La Sombra Vengadora* series each performed an important function in that they introduced and sold to the public the idea of wrestlers (and wrestler-like heroes) as action stars; but *Ladrón* introduced the crucial element of monsters, and the floodgates opened.

THREE

Universal con Carne

New Lives for the Old Undead

In 1931, the Spanish-language version of Universal's classic Drácula was a popular picture in Mexico, but unlike its northern cousin, it failed to spawn a rash of similarly-themed films. Twenty-six years later, another vampire movie *El Vampiro* (described by its own producer, Abel Salazar, as "Drácula set on a hacienda") did the trick — in a major way and at a very important time. Coinciding with the renewed interest in the classic Universal horrors via television's "Shock Theater" package, and the beginning of vivid new treatments of the same subjects by Hammer films in England, Mexico began its own "Golden Age" of Horror, initiating their own uniquely Mexican take on the classic monsters (and more). There had been a slight increase in actual monster pictures in the mid–1950s (including the seminal *Ladrón de Cadáveres*), but in '57 the dam broke. And then Mexican filmmakers added one magical ingredient that Universal or Hammer never dreamed of: masked wrestlers. This uniquely Mexican addition to monster movie lore really kicked into gear with the start of El Santo's long reign as King of Mexican Cinema, so we'll reserve discussion of that aspect for the next chapter. But the table was being set, and what a feast it turned out to be!

El Monstruo Resucitado (*The Resuscitated Monster*, 1953)

Prod: Sergio Kogan; *Dir*: Chano Urueta; *Scr/Story*: Dino Maiuri, Chano Urueta; *Music*: Raúl Lavista; *Cinematography*: Víctor Herrera; *Film Ed*: Jorge Bustos; *Prod. Design*: Gunther Gerszo, Mario Padilla; *Makeup*: Armando Meyer; *Sound*: José de Pérez; *SPFX*: Jorge Benavides.

Cast: Miroslava Stern (Nora), Carlos Navarro (Ariel/Serguei Rostov), José María Linares-Rivas (Hermann Ling), Fernando Wagner (Gherásimos), Alberto Mariscal (Mischa), Stefan Berne (Crommer).

For all their uses of the monster bearing the name (and, for that matter, the name itself), Mexican horror cinema really never did a "straight" version of *Frankenstein* (although it can also be argued that they never really did a straight version of anything!). Oddly, the Universal/Karloff-inspired monster showed up in plenty of productions, as well as the good doctor or his offspring, but never together in the same picture, and never in a "re-telling" of the classic story. One of the first variations on the theme was *El Monstruo Resucitado*, and like 1936s *El Superloco*, the variation proved surprisingly novel, another instance where the normally-viewed-as-derivative Mexican horror genre trumped its rivals. The film does in-

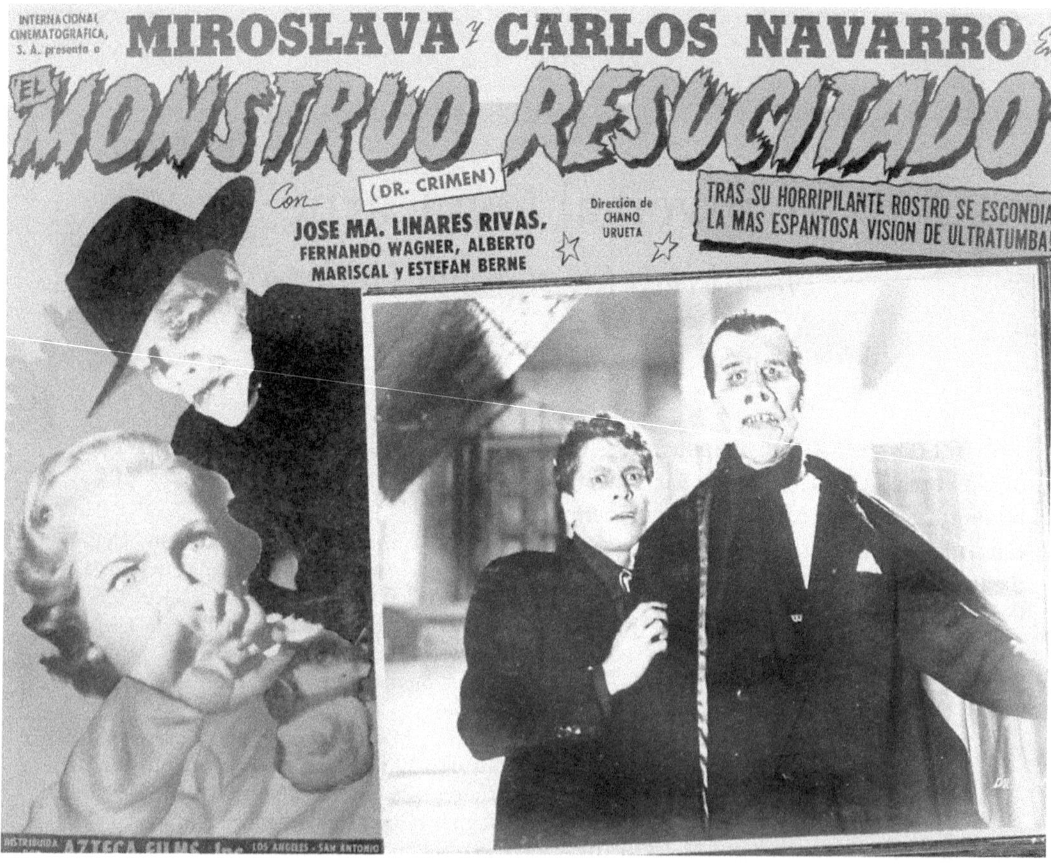

Azteca lobby card for *El Monstruo Rescusitado*.

deed feature a mad doctor, Ling, who reanimates a corpse (although not a pieced-together one); the twist in the tale is that the "monster" is handsome, and it is the doctor, the cunning Ling, who is horribly scarred (a memorable makeup job). The "beautiful monster" theme would be put to use in such later efforts as Hammer's *Frankenstein Created Woman* (1967) and NBC's *Frankenstein: The True Story* (1974).

La Bruja (*The Witch*, 1954)

Prod: Sergio Kogan; *Dir*: Chano Urueta; *Scr*: Chano Urueta; *Story*: Alfredo Salazar; *Music*: Raúl Lavista; *Cinematography*: Víctor Herrera; *Film Ed*: Jorge Bustos; *Prod. Design*: Gunther Gerszo; *Sound*: Javier Mateos; *SPFX*: Jorge Benavides, Antonio Bustos.
    Cast: Lilia del Valle (La Bruja), Luis Aceves

Castañeda, Victorio Blanco, Ángel Di Stefani, Emilio Garibay, Ramón Gay, Guillermo Hernández, Vicente Lara, Diana Ochoa, José Pardavé, Charles Rooner, José René Ruiz, Guillermina Téllez Girón, Julio Villarreal, Fernando Wagner.

Another of the early scattered efforts which preceded the boom caused by *El Vampiro*, *The Witch* is not about a witch in the classical sense, but more like a precursor to *Frankenstein Created Woman* (1967). A woman, called "the witch" because she is so ugly, is transformed into a beauty by a mad scientist, who then uses her as his instrument of revenge against a large company that stole another of his experimental formulas and murdered his daughter. His formula-created female assassin does his nefarious bidding—until he bids her to kill a man that she's fallen for, and then the bidding ends early.

El Monstruo de la Montaña Hueca (*The Beast of Hollow Mountain*, 1954)

Prods: Edward/William Nassour; *Dirs*: Edward Nassour, Ismael Rodríguez; *Story* ("El Toro Estrella"): Willis H. O'Brien; *Scr*: Robert Hill, Jack DeWitt; *Music*: Raúl Lavista; *Cinematography*: Jorge Stahl Jr.; *Film Eds*: Fernando Martínez, Holbrook N. Todd, Maury Wright; *Art Dir*: Jack DeWitt; *Prod. Mgr*: Henry Spitz; *Asst. Dir*: Gene Anderson Jr.; *Sound*: James L. Fields; *Dialogue Rec*: Nick Rosa; *SPFX*: Willis H. O'Brien (suprvsr), Louis DeWitt, Jack Rabin, Henry Sharp; *Script Suprvsr*: Bobbie Sierks.

Cast: Guy Madison (Jimmy Ryan), Patricia Medina (Sarita), Carlos Rivas (Felipe Sánchez), Mario Navarro (Panchito), Pascual García Peña (Pancho), Eduardo Noriega (Enrique Rios), Julio Villarreal (Don Pedro), Lupe Carriles (Margarita), Manuel Arvide, José Chávez, Roberto Contreras, Armando Gutiérrez, Margarito Luna, Jorge Treviño, Guillermo Hernández.

In 1942, Willis O'Brien, animator of the 1925 silent dinosaur classic *The Lost World*, and the legendary *King Kong*, wrote a treatment called "Valley of the Mist," which pitted cowboys against dinosaurs; but O'Brien could never find funding for the project. Subsequently elements of this concept showed up in both *The Beast of Hollow Mountain* and *Mighty Joe Young* (1949), although it took O'Brien's assistant on "Joe," Ray Harryhausen, to fully realize the idea with *The Valley of Gwangi* (1969).

O'Brien used one of the dinosaur models created for his died-aborning "Valley of the Mist" project for the title star of *The Beast of Hollow Mountain*, a U.S.-funded Mexican production, and one of the few Mexican genre films to feature the outsized thunderlizards. The Allosaurus is animated by O'Brien's crew with skill, and, for some reason, sports a waggling tongue

that makes it look like Gene Simmons of Kiss! The movie's main problem basically boils down to too much cowboy, not enough dinosaur; the first hour or so of the film is more or less a standard oater, with some mysterious disappearances thrown in. No significant dino action occurs until the last third of the movie (a problem that Harryhausen subsequently corrected with his *Valley of Gurangi*).

Though no award-winner, *Beast of Hollow Mountain* proved a landmark of sorts, in that it was the first stop-motion monster film to be shot in color. O'Brien and crew terrorized Mexico again two years later with *The Black Scorpion*, a U.S. production shot in black-and-white, and starring *Hollow Mountain* alumnus Carlos Rivas and another gringo, Richard (*Creature from the Black Lagoon*) Denning.

Platillos Voladores (*Flying Saucers*, 1955)

Prod: Óscar J. Brooks, Felipe Mier; *Dir*: Julián Soler; *Scr/Story*: Carlos León, Carlos Orellana, Pedro de Urdimalas; *Cinematography*: Augustín Martínez Solares.

Cast: Adalberto "Resortes" Martínez (Marciano), Evangelina Elizondo (Saturnina), Amalia Aguilar, Famie "Vitola" Kaufman, Bertha Lehar, Andrés Soler (Prof. Saldana), José "El Bronco" Venegas.

Platillos Voladores is an early sci-fi effort from an industry that never had much truck with such efforts, although the attempts they did make generally proved satisfactory in a "space-opera" kind of way. In fact, most of the Mexican treatments of such subjects have either been in this "pulpy" form or been comedies (serious science-fiction, *à la 2001*, is pretty much non-existent). *Platillos Voladores* is the latter variety, a comedy that features Resortes as a nerdy inventor who is mistaken for a man from outer space. The focus is on Resortes and musical comedy, but actual Matians do appear, and the film overall possesses engaging and costume elements, particularly the space-babes' skimpy outfits and the Robots, which seem to have taken a cue from Gene Autry's *Phantom Empire* (1935). The attractive visual design extends to the poster art, which features a *Planet Stories* pulp swipe of flying saucers and a floating space-maiden.

El Pantano de las Ánimas (*The Swamp of the Spirits,* a.k.a. *The Swamp of the Lost Monster,* 1956)

(Alameda Films) *Prod*: Alfredo Ripstein Jr.; *Dir*: Rafael Baledón; *Scr*: Ramón Obón; *Photo*: Raúl Martínez Solares; *Mus. Dir*: Gustavo César Carrión; *Asst. Dir*: Jesús Marin; *Makeup*: Concepción Zamora; Eastmancolor.

Cast: Gaston Santos (Gaston), Manola Savedra (Julieta), Manuel Donde (Nacho), Sara Cabrera, Salvador Godinez, Pedro de Aguillon, Rayo de Plata.

Gaston Santos was a noted bullfighter, horseman and playboy when he was signed in 1956 to do a series of Hollywood-style westerns (as opposed to the homegrown ranchera films), some of which contained fantastic elements. The best of these is *Swamp of the Lost Monster*, in which Gaston and his trusty steed Rayo de Plata battle a "swamp monster" apparently inspired by *The Creature from the Black Lagoon* and *Gorgo*, as it resembles both! (Just picture Gorgo's head on the Gill Man's body, and you've got it.) That there is room in the costume for a scuba-tank is pretty obvious, but, as it turns out, this bit of cheesiness is excusable, because it's a fake monster anyway. It seems a crooked old ratbastard faked his own death to get his mitts on a pile of loot—and he would've gotten away with it, too, if it hadn't been for that meddling cowboy and his wonder horse. In fact, fans of equestrian antics will love this movie, as Rayo de Plata does a boatload of showy tricks, and

ultimately proves himself more talented than the human masked wrestler of the same name ("Los Campeones del Ring")!

El Vampiro (*The Vampire,* 1957)

(ABSA) *Prod*: Abel Salazar; *Dir*: Fernando Mendez; *Music*: Gustavo César Carrión; *Cinematography*: Rosalío Solano; *Film Ed*: Jorge Bustos; *Art Dir*: Gunther Gerszo; *Prod.* (English-language version): K. Gordon Murray; *Dir.* (English-language version): Paul Nagle.

Cast: Germán Robles (Count Karol de Lavud/Duval), Abel Salazar (Dr. Enrique), Ariadna Welter (Marta González), Carmen Montejo (Eloisa), José Luis Jiménez (Emilio), Mercedes Soler (María), Alicia Montoya (María Teresa), José Chávez (Anselmo), Julio Daneri, Amado Zumaya, Guillermo Álvarez Bianchi, Margarito Luna.

As stated previously, *El Vampiro* was the opening salvo of the Mexican horror boom, and remains one of its most recognizable examples, outside of the Santo movies and possibly *The Brainiac*. It's the only Mexican horror to ever grace the cover of *Famous Monsters* (#124), a fine Ken Kelly portrait of star Germán Robles. And although he only essayed the role of "Count Lavud" twice, Robles, like Lugosi and Lee before him, became forever identified with fangs. And, speaking of fangs, score one for the Mexican horrors— up until *El Vampiro*, cinema vampires left plenty of puncture holes in necks, but became curiously tight-lipped when it came to actually showing the instruments of incision. Oversized choppers are now standard screen issue for vamps, and most people think that *Horror of Dracula* was the first, but *El Vampiro* beat that Hammer classic to the big screen by well over a year. Heck, the Mexicans were putting huge fangs and bloody cleavage on posters even earlier, and the film didn't even feature a vampire! The movie in question was the Ed Wood "classic" *Bride of the Monster*; though lacking a vampire, it did have Bela

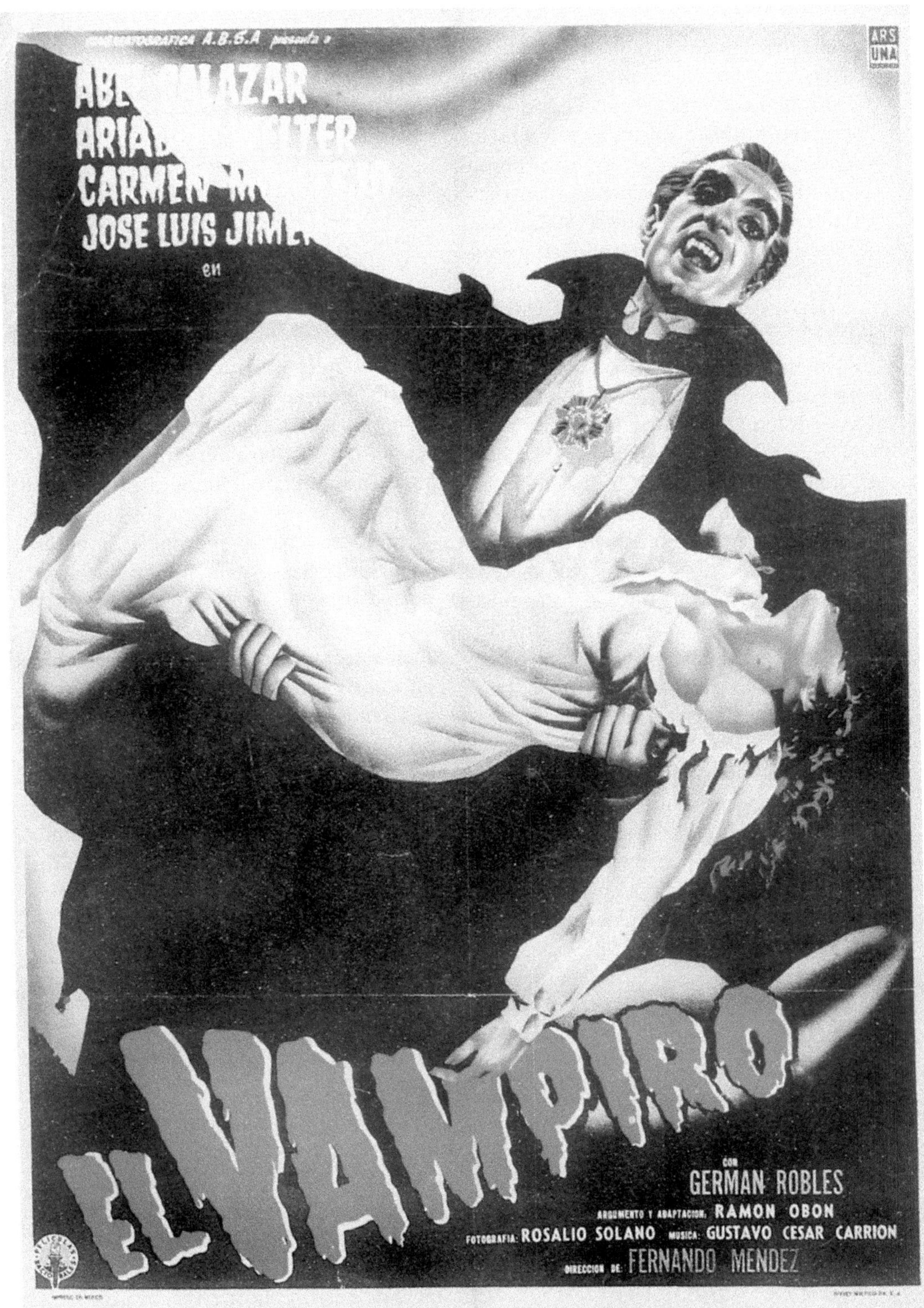

The one-sheet for the one that started the Mexican horror boom, *El Vampiro*.

"Drácula" Lugosi, and that was enough for the art department! They took the basic design and poses from the American poster, and then tricked up Lugosi with the aforementioned outsize fangs, and sent blood running down his chin, dripping onto the also-more-exposed-than-the-original breasts of the damsel in his arms. The result: Artwork that out–Hammered Hammer.

Having no real Mexican cinematic or literary vampire tradition to draw upon, *El Vampiro* borrows heavily from the Universal canon. In one instance, however, the viewer is tempted to wonder exactly why. In Universal's *Son of Dracula* (1943), Lon Chaney, Jr., travels under the guise of "Count Alucard." The yokels are in a tizzy until one of 'em hits on spelling it backwards, revealing the Count's true colors. So in *El Vampiro*, our undead antagonist goes by the name "Count Lavud," and, of course, the yokeleros are aghast to discover it's really ... Count Duval! Yee! Yeah, that Duval the Impaler was one nasty hombre...

Naming nonsense aside, *El Vampiro* is a moody horror classic, one fully deserving of its rep, and a worthy start to the trend. Robles is ultra-suave, and not as given to outbursts of boorish behavior as Christopher Lee. Robles made an indelible impression in the role in Mexico, and, while not encountering the dearth of work which haunted Lugosi because of his association with a vampire (Robles was part of the ABSA "stock company"), Robles was nonetheless typecast in the minds of the public. Then again, typecasting is just another way of saying you own a role, and that's really not such a bad thing.

El Ataúd del Vampiro (*The Vampire's Coffin*, 1957)

(ABSA) *Prod*: Abel Salazar; *Dir*: Fernando Méndez; *Scr*: Alfredo Salazar; *Story*: Raúl Zen-teno; *Music*: Gustavo César Carrión; *Cinematography*: Víctor Herrera; *Film Ed*: Alfredo Rosas Priego; *Prod. Design*: Gunther Gerszo; *Sound*: Javier Mateos; *Prod*: K. Gordon Murray (English-language version); *Dir*: Paul Nagle (English-language version).

Cast: Germán Robles (Count Karol de Lavud/Duval), Abel Salazar (Dr. Enrique), Ariadna Welter (Martha), Yerye Beirute (Graverobber), Alicia Montoya (Mary), Carlos Ancira (Dr. Marion), Guillermo Orea, Antonio Raxel, Alicia Rodríguez.

El Vampiro was such an enormous hit that a sequel was unavoidable. Like the hastily conceived and executed *Son of Kong*, the hastily conceived and executed *El Ataúd del Vampiro* contains some good moments, but fails to duplicate the impact of its predecessor. Of course, in some cases a sequel can outstrip the original, but those superior efforts usually have a lot longer period in which to gestate. Abel Salazar and Ariadna Welter are back to reprise their respective roles, and Germán Robles once again hitches up his super-sized fangs as Lavud/Duval. Despite their combined presences, the only really memorable scene comes in the climactic fight, where milksop hero Salazar decides to engage in fisticuffs with the Count. After Abel lands a couple of weakly-placed haymakers, the Count changes into a bat, which gives him a distinct advantage ... but only momentarily, as Salazar grabs a nearby javelin(!) and skewers the bat like so much shish-kabob, pinning him to the wall. It's a most satisfying ending; too bad we had to wade through seventy minutes of uninspired footage to reach it.

Priceless tag line from the American trailer: "From the depths of evil comes the diabolic killer of beautiful women — The Vampire's Coffin!" Funny, I thought it was the vampire.

Regarding the three principals in these pioneering efforts, Abel Salazar went on to produce and star in more genre classics; his career was long and varied, but came to a halt in 1985 when he began to suffer from Alzheimer's Disease. He passed away ten days before Halloween in 1995. Ariadna Welter lent her beauteous looks and solid acting skills to many more genre pieces as well, even replacing Lorena Velázquez for one film in the Wrestling Women series. Germán Robles vowed to play Lavud/Duval no more, and turned up later in the year to spoof the role in *El Castillo de los Monstruos*.

THE *AZTEC MUMMY* SERIES

La Momia Azteca (*The Aztec Mummy*, 1957)

La Maldición de la Momia Azteca (*The Curse of the Aztec Mummy*, 1957)

La Momia Azteca contra el Robot Humano (*The Robot vs. the Aztec Mummy*, 1957)

(The technical and cast credits are identical for all three films.)

(Cinematográfica Calderón) *Prod:* Guillermo Calderón; *Dir:* Rafael Portillo; *Scr/Story:* Guillermo Calderón, Alfredo Salazar; *Music:* Antonio Díaz Conde; *Cinematography:* Enrique Wallace; *Film Eds:* Jorge Bustos, José Li-Ho, Jack Remy; *Prod. Design/Art Dir:* Javier Torres Torija; *Prod. Mgr:* Luis García de León; *Sound:* Luis Fernández; *Aztec Choreography:* Stella Inda.

Cast: Ángel Di Stefani (the Aztec Mummy), Ramón Gay (Dr. Almada), Rosita Arenas (Flora), Luis Aceves Castañeda (Dr. Krupp), Crox Alvarado (Pincate/the Angel), Arturo Martínez (Bruno), Jorge Mondragón, Alejandro Cruz, Julián de Meriche, Guillermo Hernández, Emma Roldán, Francisco Segura, Jesús Vázquez, Alberto Yáñez, Enrique Yáñez.

Hot on the fangs of *El Vampiro* came the second great Mexican monster, one which, like *El Vampiro*, exerted a great influence on the genre and became an icon of Mexican monsterdom, the Aztec Mummy. Also significant was the fact that, while the Vampire was basically a Transylvanian transplant, the Aztec Mummy, though certainly looking to Universal for inspiration, infused many more of its own cultural elements, thereby making him the greatest homegrown Mexi-movie-monster. Of course, he wasn't the first—La Llorona claims that distinction, but the solo features based on her legend weren't nearly as compelling as those featuring the beat of the cloth-wrapped feet (not to mention the fact that she never squared off against the Wrestling Women).

The Aztec Mummy movies resemble the Universal Kharis films to some extent, but only in that the mummy is a warrior who dared the forbidden love of the virgin princess, yadda, yadda, yadda. But Popoca (the warrior/mummy) has not been cursed with eternal un-life to protect the princess (Xochitl), but rather to guard a breastplate that holds the secret of a long-lost treasure. And rather than some High Priest of Karnak exacting vengeance on tomb desecrators, we have two warring factions of scientists—one good (Dr. Almada and co.), who wants to prove his theories of reincarnation, and one bad (Dr. Krupp, who just wants the treasure). Both film series offer extended flashback sequences to show us whence the Mummy came, but the Aztec Mummy scenes ring truer, seeing as how they take place in the time of the Aztecs, a subject the filmmakers knew something about, rather than a Hollywood version of ancient Egypt.

The Aztec Mummy series also eschews the conventional Hollywood Mummy look; the head-to-toe bandages, the lame arm, and the dragging leg are replaced by a, if not terribly more mobile

An Azteca lobby card for one of the most famous Mexican monsters, the Aztec Mummy; Angel Di Stefani hovers over Rosita Arenas.

mummy, at least a fully-operational one, wrapped not in bandages but in ceremonial garb. The face was the most striking difference — instead of a wrinkled mug with a droopy eye and hair plastered down by the ages, the Mexican Mummy possessed a more skull-like visage, topped off by a wildly frizzy "shock" of hair; this look found its ultimate expression in *Wrestling Women vs. the Aztec Mummy*. It certainly resembled real-life examples, such as the famous Mummies of Guanajuato attraction, an aspect which must've made the films even more unsettling for locals.

The second entry in the trilogy, *The Curse of the Aztec Mummy*, finds all of the principals back for another round. Dr. Krupp is still after the treasure, and Dr. Al-

mada, having painfully proved his theories of reincarnation, is content to merely try and thwart Krupp. In another foreshadowing of things to come, Almada is aided by a masked character, "El Angel" (Crox Alvaredo), although not a wrestler either in the film or real life.

In a sense, the third installment, *The Robot vs. the Aztec Mummy*, is most like a Universal offering. Like *The Mummy's Curse* or *The Mummy's Ghost*, a goodly portion of the first half of the film is comprised of clips from the previous pictures, almost making it a "Best of the Aztec Mummy" entry. As the action really gets rolling after the flashbacks, we find that ol' Dr. Krupp, a persistent cuss, still has treasure on his mind, and to combat the Aztec

A considerably less-imposing Aztec Mummy takes five behind Ramon Gay and Crox Alvaredo as "the Angel."

Mummy he has constructed a robot with a human brain! The robot is a wonderful retro-design, and the vacant look on the actor's face inside Krupp's tin can is not only (unintentionally, one presumes) chuckle-inducing, but probably just what somebody's face would look like if they'd just come back to life as a robot! The climax can only be described as the *Frankenstein Meets the Wolfman* of Mexican cinema. As a monster tussle, it's actually a little more satisfying, simply because the two monsters are allowed to fight for more than five seconds without the angry villagers bringing down the castle on them. Our hero (the Aztec Mummy, of course!) pulls out his can of whup-ass on both "El Robot Humano" and Dr. Krupp, and, breastplate in hand, shambles off into the sunset.

Angel de Stefani makes an imposing Aztec Mummy, and Ramón Gay (b. 1917), who would be murdered in a crime of passion the following year (shot and killed by the estranged husband of actress Evangelina Elizondo), is solid as Dr. Almada; but the acting honors for the trilogy must go to Luis Aceves Castaneda as the treasure-grubbing Dr. Krupp. Combining the over-the-top fruitiness of an Ernest Thesiger with the look and bombast of a Lionel Atwill, Castaneda cuts a memorable, entertaining figure, one of the few mad scientists in Mexi-cinema who can make that claim.

Just as *El Vampiro* sired a whole brood of south-of-the-border bloodsuckers, the Aztec Mummy sired a prodigious progeny of petrified princes and other mummified unfortunates, both of the Guanajuato and Hollywood style. The Aztec Mummy as a name character would only feature in one other film, the classic *Wrestling Women vs. the Aztec Mummy*, and even though it was technically a different Aztec Mummy (Tutomec, not Popoca), the modified monster design and outré action make it the Aztec Mummy that most readily comes to mind. (More on this film in the Wrestling Women chapter.) The Aztec Mummy was last seen on the set of the *Incredibly Strange Films Show*, menacing his former co-star, Lorena Velázquez, and in a limited number of public appearances in the company of cult figure Johnny Legend (making his ring debut and introducing rock concerts).

El Castillo de los Monstruos (*The Castle of the Monsters,* 1957)

(Producciones Sotomayor) *Exec. Prod*: Herbert Dávila; *Dir/Scr*: Julián Soler; *Adapt*: Carlos Orellana; *Story*: Fernando Galiana; *Photo*: Victor Herrera; *Asst. Dir*: Jaime L. Contreras; *Music*: Gustavo César Carrión; *Makeup*: Rosa Guerrero.

Cast: Antonio "Clavillazo" Espino, Germán Robles (vampire), Evangelina Elizondo (Beatriz), Carlos Orellana, Guillermo Orea, José Moreno Camacho, José Muñoz Wilhelmy, Alejandro Reyna García, Leopoldo Pineda Magana, Vincente "Indio Cacama" Lara.

In the year following the release of *The Wolf Man* (1941), somebody at Universal had a great idea: if one monster was good, then two monsters would be twice as good, and so on and so forth. The trend began with *Frankenstein Meets the Wolf Man* (1942), and continued through *House of Frankenstein* (1944) and *House of Dracula* (1945). With the end of World War II, the monsters had just about done it all, and the public's tastes were beginning to change anyway. Abbott and Costello's popularity had taken a hit as well, and somebody had another great idea: if three or four monsters were good, then Abbott and Costello made it better. The result was the all-time great horror-comedy and "monster rally" *Abbott and Costello Meet Frankenstein* (1948).

In the months following the release of *El Vampiro* (1957), somebody in Mexico had a great idea: if Universal made money with "monster rallies," then we can too. Unlike in America, however, the monsters hadn't played themselves out yet — they'd only been around for a few months. The Universal idea for teaming up monsters had come near the end of a cycle; Mexico's had barely begun! The Mexi-trend began with *The Robot vs. the Aztec Mummy* (1957), and continued only a few months later with *El Castillo de los Monstruos* (1957). Like the Universal monster rallies, *Castillo* featured Frankenstein's monster, Drácula, a Wolf Man, and a hunchback, but added a mummy, the Creature from the Black Lagoon and a gorilla. Unlike Universal's efforts, which had all-star casts playing the monsters, *Castle* only had the monsters, the only "name" being Germán Robles, who naturally portrays the vampire (but his part amounts to little more than a cameo). Clavillazo is the comedian on the spot, and a lot more of the film is dedicated to his shopworn (but nonetheless amusing) antics than to his tangling with the monsters. But *El Castillo de los Monstruos* cleared the decks for such future epics as *Santo and Blue Demon vs. the Monsters* and the real Mexican remake of *A & C meet Frank*, *Frankenstein, El Vampiro, y Compañía*.

El Hombre Que Logró Ser Invisible (*The New Invisible Man,* 1957)

(Cinematográfica Calderón) *Prod*: Guillermo Calderón; *Dir*: Alfredo B. Crevenna; *Scr/Story*: Alfredo Salazar, Julio Alejandro de Castro; *Music*: Antonio Díaz Conde; *Cinematography*:

Raúl Martínez Solares; *Film Ed*: Jorge Bustos; *Prod. Design*: Javier Torres Torija; *Sound*: Javier Mateos.

Cast: Arturo de Córdova (Carlos), Ana Luisa Peluffo (Beatriz Cifuentes), Augusto Benedico (Luis), Raúl Meraz (Comandante Flores), Jorge Mondragón (Don Ramón Cifuentes), Néstor de Barbosa (José Suárez), Roberto G. Rivera (Mendez), José Chávez, Enrique Díaz "Indiano," Emilio Garibay, José Muñoz, Héctor Gómez, Manuel Dondé, Carlos Robles Gil, Raúl Guerrero, Inés Murillo, Salvador Lozano.

El Hombre Que Logró Ser Invisible continues the "classic monster" remake trend, (before they started meeting the wrestlers more or less full time). Directed by Alfredo B. Crevenna, it was one of the director's personal favorites, and it featured one of his favorite actors to work with, Arturo de Cordova. Crevenna has stated that the producer wanted to bring in help from the U.S. for the numerous trick shots, but Crevenna insisted that his crew accomplish the task, and they prove to be more than up to it. This becomes particularly impressive when you consider that SPFX were never a Mexican genre strong suit. The movie is basically a remake of Universal's Vincent Price–starrer *The Invisible Man Returns* (1940), with de Cordova in the Price role as a scientist who uses his brother's formula to turn himself invisible and clear himself of murder. Ana Luisa Peluffo played the heroine. Also featured was Jorge Mondragón, who not only had a great name for the genre, but made quite a name for himself as a founder of the Mexican actors' union, ANDA. Born in 1903, Mondragón appeared in countless films, plays and television shows. He featured in many genre classics, including *La Momia Azteca*, *Las Luchadoras vs. el Médico Asesino*, *La Mujer Murciélago*, and *Santo y Blue Demon vs. Drácula y el Hombre Lobo*, before his death in 1997.

The strong direction by Crevenna was an early effort in a genre he would come to have an enormous influence on, from this film to the very last of the Santos. In between, he directed a score of classics, including *Adventures in the Center of the Earth*, two Neutróns, four other Santos, and a Blue Demon. Born in Germany in 1914, Crevenna left when the Nazis came to power, and eventually made his way to Mexico, where he directed his first film in 1944. After the monster/wrestler craze faded, he made numerous action and comedy pics, and was actively directing until he passed away in 1996.

El Hombre y el Monstruo (*The Man and the Monster*, 1958)

(ABSA) *Prod*: Abel Salazar; *Dir*: Rafael Baledón; *Scr/Story*: Alfredo Salazar, Raúl Zenteno; *Music*: Gustavo César Carrión; *Cinematography*: Raúl Martínez Solares; *Film Ed*: Carlos Savage; *Production Design*: Javier Torres Torija; *Sound*: Manuel Topete; *Musician, Piano*: María Teresa Rodríguez.

Cast: Abel Salazar (Ricardo), Enrique Rambal (Man/Monster), Martha Roth (Laura/Alejandra/Blonde motorist), Ofelia Guilmáin (Mother), José Chávez, María Roth, Carlos Suárez, Maricarmen Vela.

Rafael Baledón directed this 1958 effort, which blends elements of the werewolf legend, Jekyll and Hyde, and *The Devil and Daniel Webster*. An unsuccessful pianist makes a deal with Ol' Scratch — his soul for talent, fame, and everything that goes with it. But, as is typical of Beelzebub's transactions, the composer gets a lot more than he bargained for — every time he plays his big hit, he turns into a werewolf! But not just any werewolf, mind you. The makeup is actually quite good — if you can get past the huge, bulbous nose! It's as if W.C. Fields came down with lycanthropy, and this image alone is enough to secure *El Hombre y el Monstruo* an immortal place in Psychotronic Heaven. But even W.C. Fields wasn't nasty enough to keep a dead female rival in the closet. And taking a cue from Monogram's *Return of the Ape Man* (Lugosi, Carradine, 1944), even after he's gone animal he can still tickle the ivories with the best of 'em! Rafael Baledón (1919–1995) was an innovator as well as a stylist, having helmed the pioneering *La Sombra Vengadora* series and *Swamp of the Lost Monster*, one of the first Mexican horrors in color, as well as the unforgettable *La Loba*.

La Casa del Terror (*The House of Terror*, a.k.a. *Face of the Screaming Werewolf*, 1959)

(Diana Films) *Prod*: Fernando de Fuentes, hijo; *Dir*: Gilberto Martínez Solares; *Scr*: Fernando de Fuentes, Juan García, Gilberto Martínez So-lares; *Story*: Gilberto Martínez Solares; *Music*: Luis Hernández Bretón; *Song*: Luis Demetrio; *Cinematography*: Raúl Martínez Solares; *Film Ed*: Carlos Savage; *Production Design*: Jorge Fernández; *Set Decoration*: Raúl Serrano; *Makeup*: Román Juárez; *Sound*: Enrique Rodríguez; *SPFX*: Jorge Benavides (as Benavides); *Asst. Ed*: Sigfrido García.

Cast: Lon Chaney, Jr. (the Mummy/the Werewolf), Yerye Beirute (El Professor), Germán "Tin Tan" Valdés (Casimiro), Yolanda Varela (Paquita), José Luis Aguirre, Alfredo Wally Barrón, Rafael Estrada, Agustín Fernández, Jesús Gómez, Dacia González, Consuelo Guerrero de Luna, Óscar Ortiz de Pinedo, Mario Sevilla, José Silva.

La Casa del Terror is almost two completely different films, depending on which version you see. Mexico had been remaking

Lon Chaney, Jr., migrated south to re-play two of his most famous roles, the mummy and werewolf, in *La Casa del Terror*. Azteca lobby cards are unique in that they feature a still from the movie pasted right onto the card, and are especially attractive examples of genre ad art.

the classic Universal horrors for a couple of years, and with this production they took it to the next level and actually got one of the Universal icons, Lon Chaney, Jr., to re-create not one, but two of his most famous roles, appearing as both a werewolf and a mummy in the same movie! (Boris Karloff and John Carradine followed Chaney across the border in later years.) Chaney's makeup as both monsters is very well done, the werewolf here a close approximation of his Universal wolfman (complete with standard-issue Larry Talbot dark shirt and grey pants), and it's a real joy for horror kids to see him return to the roles.

Now, the original Mexican version is first and foremost a "Tin Tan" vehicle — the popular comedian plays a nerd who works in a wax museum for a doctor who just happens to be mad and is conducting life-restoring experiments. His latest subject is a mummy who, after several treatments in the doc's atomic jacuzzi, turns into a werewolf(!) and goes on a killing rampage. The mad médico is played by Yerye Beirute (b. 1928), a veteran heavy who usually played such characters' assistants. The horror scenes (done straightly, and very well at that — Chaney was actually allowed to act a little more savagely in his attacks and draw more blood) and Tin Tan's routines rarely run afoul of each other until the climax. OK, hold that thought.

As noted elsewhere in this tome, Jerry Warren did not so much import films as he did butcher them. Whereas K. Gordon Murray dubbed the originals, Warren took scenes from various pictures (where no or little dubbing was needed) and wrapped them around newly-filmed (and inevitably boring) scenes of dialogue featuring American actors that attempted to connect the other footage, a tactic which failed quite miserably. Warren turned off-center movies into hopeless jumbles. Warren

took all of the mummy and werewolf scenes from *La Casa del Terror*, added sequences from *La Momia Azteca* (and keep in mind here that Chaney's mummy looks like Kharis, which, of course, is completely different than the Aztec Mummy), threw in a few talking-gringo-head scenes and ... voila, fit for American consumption! Now, remember I said that Chaney and Tin Tan have very little recourse until the climax? Well, since both are involved in the event, and since even Jerry Warren wouldn't have been stupid enough to cut out the grand finale, here comes Tin Tan out of nowhere to save the heroine!

When Lon Chaney, Jr., played Larry Talbot, one of his favorite catchphrases was, "But you don't understand!" Chaney doesn't appear in human form in either version of *La Casa del Terror*, but Jerry Warren should have included at least that clip for his version, which would've summed up the audience's feelings perfectly.

La Llorona (*The Crying Woman*, 1959)

Prod: José Luis Bueno; *Dir*: René Cardona; *Story/Scr*: Carmen Toscano de Moreno Sánchez, Adolfo Torres Portillo (as Adolpho Portillo), based on the play by Carmen Toscano de Moreno Sánchez; *Music*: Luis Mendoza López; *Cinematography*: Jack Draper; *Film Ed*: Jorge Bustos; *Prod. Design*: Ramón Rodríguez Granada; *Costume Design*: Bertha Mendoza López; *Assistant Ed*: Joaquín Ceballos; *Assistant Cam*: Carlos Montaño; *Cam. Op*: Urbano Vázquez.

Cast: Luz María Aguilar, Erna Martha Bauman, Manuel Casanueva, Eduardo Fajardo, Mauricio Garcés, Carlos López Moctezuma, María Elena Marqués, Juan José Martínez Casado, Francisco Pando, David Reynoso, Emma Roldán.

In selected instances throughout this book, I have the opportunity to present a movie synopsis provided by the original pressbook for that film. Translated by the producers to encourage distribution in a given foreign country, they are not only of immense historical value, but are almost as deliriously entertaining as the movies themselves— sometimes more!

(Punctuated "as is"): "Man departs … then comes then unknown and goes to the unknown and in that rambling about between two incognitos of life and death sometimes some memento is left that rescues from forgetfulness. The remembrance of a smile or an anxious sorrow or a strange love. A love which has lived beyond the limits of nature which becomes a legend … the steps of a woman can be heard in these places … they go down between the walls … they turn at the corner … we feel a human presence with its torments and grudges, with its passionate love … then the steps are lost and we hear a wail … a deep wail, the lamenting of a crime, condemned forever … the wind carries the voice … now it stops and muffles it … now however it lets it lose itself in the country or drift through the cracks and locks invading everywhere … always trying to escape and always returning to the same place to the same stones that know the story … how to be free and undo what is done … how to knit and unravel the acts that have taken place … the voice is heard in the corners and it is locked in the shadows and it starts again in the twentieth century with the same sorrow of other days and tells a new story … The Weeper."

La Llorona was the genre debut of David Reynoso, one of Mexico's most active character actors. In a career that spanned five decades, before his passing in 1994, Reynoso played numerous types of roles, including real-life ones such as actors' union president and director. His best

genre roles were a pair of Blue Demons from 1966, *Blue Demon vs. las Diabolicas* and *Blue Demon vs. the Infernal Brains.*

Too bad Rondo Hatton never lived long enough to make movies in Mexico— then we could've had "The Creeper Meets the Weeper!"

La Nave de los Monstruos (*The Ship of Monsters,* 1959)

Prod: Jesús Sotomayor Martínez; *Dir*: Rogelio A. González; *Scr/Story*: José María Fernández Unsáin, Alfredo Varela (as Alfredo Varela, Hijo); *Assoc. Prod*: Alberto Hernández Curiel; *Cinematography*: Raúl Martínez Solares; *Film Ed*: Carlos Savage; *Prod. Design*: Javier Torres Torija; *Makeup*: Rosa Guerrero; *Asst. Dir*: Jaime Contreras; *Sound*: James L. Fields (Supervisor),

Francisco Alcayde (Rec); *SPFX*: Juan Muñoz Revenna; *Costumes*: Julio Chávez; *Still Photog*: Ángel Corona; *Musical Dir*: Sergio Guerrero.

Cast: Eulalio (José) "Piporro" González (Lauriano), Ana Bertha Lepe (Gamma), Lorena Velázquez (Beta), Consuelo Frank (Leader of the Space Women), Manuel Alvarado (as Manuel Alvarado Lodoza), Heberto Dávila, Jr., Mário García Hernández, José Pardavé, Jesús Rodríguez Cárdenas.

Amigos, this one has it all. Following in the footsteps of Gene Autry's *The Phantom Empire* (1935), Mexico presents its first sci-fi musical horror comedy western! It's a modern western (with cars and such), but the hero is a singing cowboy (top-billed "Piporro") who comes up against the two sexiest space vamps ever to seduce an earthman, Ana Bertha Lepe (Miss

Opposite and above: Mexican lobby cards for two of the country's most famous horrors. Mexican lobby cards differ from Azteca lobby cards in that they were larger, the inset photograph was printed on the card, and they were printed in Mexico.

Mexico '53) as "Gamma," and Lorena Velázquez (funny how she keeps turning up in all these genre classics) as "Beta." It seems that the Space Sisters, along with their robot (the same one seen in *The Robot vs. the Aztec Mummy*, but without the human face), are prowling the galaxy kidnapping men to help them re-populate Venus. The men they've collected are as follows: a giant spider, a cyclops (who would turn up ten years later in *Santo and Blue Demon vs. the Monsters*), a talking horse skeleton (Paw, they done got Mr. Ed!), and a big-brained baddie who resembles a miniature Metaluna Mutant with oversized rubbery lips. Their names, along with the robot's, are Uk, Utirr, Tagual, Tor and Zok. They make a pit stop on Earth, where the closest thing the bikini'd lady Venusians can find to a man is Piporro ... and, given their other choices in tow, they both fall for him. Gamma insists on taking Piporro back to Venus despite her love, but Beta won't have any of that and shows her true colors by becoming a space vampire, and unleashes their captive creatures to vent their frustrations. Piporro teams up with his son and the robot to defeat Beta and the other creatures; Gamma decides to stay with him on Earth; and the robot, who has found true romance with a jukebox, flies the rocket back to Venus singing a duet with his newfound love!

Now I know you think I must be making some of this stuff up, but it's all there in glorious black and white. Justifiably one of the most famous nondubbed or subtitled Mexican genre pieces, it's right up there with *Santo vs. the Vampire Women* and *Wrestling Women vs. the Aztec Mummy*. It's literally a jaw-dropping experience, and your brain refuses to believe what your eyes are showing it. Any makeup deficiencies in the hypnotically cheesy monsters are completely wiped away by the sheer audaciousness of it all.

To wit: Lorena Velázquez in a one-piece space swimsuit, singing a duet with Piporro and doing some mighty invitin' gyrations; Piporro's son shooting the minimutant, resulting in its oversized brain deflating like a basketball; a huge bat swooping down on a man, only to turn into Lorena; the talking horse-skull (which actually appears to be a Space Vampire Unicorn); the robot singing along with the jukebox. If this film had been dubbed into English, Tim Burton would have made a biopic of Rogelio González instead of Ed Wood!

Señora Lepe was at the center of a scandal the very next year, when her father killed her boyfriend, Augustín de Anda, after discovering they had engaged in premarital sex. De Anda was the son of the chief of the Mexican producers' union, and this tragic situation led to her blacklisting. She returned in 1974, but her roles remained sporadic.

El Regreso del Monstruo (*The Return of the Monster*, 1959)

(Fimadora Mexicana S.A.) *Prod*: Luis Manrique; *Dir*: Joselito Rodríguez; *Scr/Story*: Luis Manrique, Antonio Orellana, Fernando Osés; *Cinematography*: Carlos Najera; *Prod. Mgr*: Fernando Osés; *Music Ed*: Enrique Rodríguez; *Sound*: Consuelo Rodríguez; *Photo*: J. Moreno, Fernando Colin, Eduardo Barrera; Estudios "América" laboratorios "Mexico."

Cast: Luis Aguilar (El Zorro Escarlata), Pascual García Pena (Pascual), Jaime Fernández (Sergio/the Monster), Yolanda del Valle (the Haciendada), Roger López, Arturo Martínez, Sergio Murrieta, Fanny Schiller, Teresita (Tere) Velázquez, "Trio Los Mexicanos."

This, another seriously nutty entry in the Mexi-monster sweepstakes, is the second film featuring El Zorro Escarlata (the Scarlet Zorro), who can be distinguished from the original model by the addition of a large skull to his shirt, making him look like Marvel Comics' the Punisher with a sombrero. It's another monster/western like *Swamp of the Lost Monster*, but here the monster's not only real, he's a real doozy! A local mad médico, Dr. Kraken (great name), has been experimenting on women in hopes of restoring the body of a talking skeleton with glowing eyes! The skeleton's son (who's not a skeleton, but Jaime Fernández) turns into a monster that can be called, well, Frankenstein-esque (but compared to this vision from goofy-hell, Karloff and Lee were matinee idols). Sporting an enlarged bald head spotted with wisps of hair, big bushy eyebrows, and teeth that a mouth could never possibly close around, this creature completes its ensemble by donning a plaid poncho! He gets in some great bits, both intentional (*à la* Chris Lee's spear-in-the-chest in Hammer's *The Mummy*, he takes a pitchfork in the same spot and keeps on ticking) and unintentional (after coming down a ladder hard, he noticeably limps—apparently they couldn't be bothered to shoot it again; and during the climactic battle with El Zorro, he has to adjust his monster mask). He's sort of a were-Frankenstein, because he changes into the monster via a series of haltingly-done dissolves. Dr. Kraken kidnaps another doctor, who begrudgingly aids him in his fiendish work, until his own daughter is kidnapped as well and brought in as the next subject. But El Zorro Escarlata has taken the fight with the Monster to the lab, and not only frees the kidnapees, but destroys the lab and all its malevolent occupants. It's all gloriously cheap and aggressively cheesy.

Star Jaime Fernández had won a Best Supporting Actor "Ariel" award in 1952 for Luis Bunuel's *Robinson Crusoe*, and went on to become one of the most dependable leading men in the genre—think David Manners, but more manly. Among his many credits are the first three Blue demon films, and two with El Santo, including the all-important *Santo vs. las Mujeres Vam-*

piro. He became an influential figure in union circles, and remains active to the present day.

THE *NOSTRADAMUS* SERIES

La Maldición de Nostradamus (*The Curse of Nostradamus,* 1959)

Prod: Victor Parra; *Dir*: Federico Curiel; *Scr/Story*: Alfredo Ruanova, Carlos Enrique Taboada, Federico Curiel; *Music*: Jorge Pérez; *Cinematography*: Fernando Colín; *Film Eds*: Juan José Munguía, Federico Landeros; *Co-Dir*: Alberto Mariscal; *Production Design*: Arcadi Artis Gener; *Sound Editor*: Felipe Marino; *Camera Operator*: Raúl Domínguez; *Prod*. (English-language version): K. Gordon Murray; *Dir*. (English language version): Stim Segar.

(Technical credits are the same for all four films).

Cast: Germán Robles (Nostradamus), Domingo Soler (Professor), Julio Alemán (Antonio), Aurora Alvarado (Anna), Manuel Vergara "Manver" (Leo), Jack Taylor [as Grek Martín] (Igor), Carlos Ancira, Luis Aragón, Roberto Aroya, Carlos Becerril, Guillermo Bravo Sosa, Ramón Bugarini, Manuel Casanueva, Mario Cid [as Mário Chávez], Enrique Couto, Fernando Curiel, Gayo Dante, Eric del Castillo, Cora Del Rey, Manuel Dondé, Rosario Dúrcal, Rafael Estrada, Carlos Hennings, Rogelio "Frijolitos" Jiménez Pons, José Loza, Alejandra Meyer, Celia Monzano, Magda Monzón, Patricia de Morelos, Carlos Nieto, Antonio Raxel, Harapos Guillermo Rivas, Reynaldo Rivera, Fanny Schiller, Amado Sumaya, Rina Valdarno.

Nostradamus y el Destructor de Monstruos (*The Monsters Demolisher,* 1959)

Cast: Germán Robles (Nostradamus), Domingo Soler (Professor), Julio Alemán (Antonio), Aurora Alvarado (Anna), Manuel

Vergara "Manver" (Leo), Jack Taylor [as Grek Martin] (Igor), Luis Aragón, Mario Cid [as Mário Chávez], Fernando Curiel, Rafael Estrada, Rogelio "Frijolitos" Jiménez Pons, José Loza, Alma Margarita, Magda Monzón, Antonio Raxel.

Nostradamus, el Genio de las Tinieblas (*Genie of Darkness*, 1959)

Cast: Germán Robles (Nostradamus), Domingo Soler (Professor), Julio Alemán (Antonio), Aurora Alvarado (Anna), Manuel Vergara "Manver" (Leo), Jack Taylor [as Grek Martín] (Igor), Fanny Schiller (Rebecca, el bruja "the witch"), Rina Valdarno (Nora), Luis Aragón, Guillermo Bravo Sosa, Enrique Couto, Fernando Curiel, Manuel Dondé, Carlos Hennings, Carlos Nieto.

La Sangre de Nostradamus (*The Blood of Nostradamus*, 1959)

Cast: Germán Robles (Nostradamus), Domingo Soler (Professor), Julio Alemán (Antonio), Aurora Alvarado (Anna), Manuel Vergara "Manver" (Leo), Carlos Ancira (Police Chief), Luis Aragón, Carlos Becerra, Fernando Curiel, Gayo Dante, Eric del Castillo, Cora Del Rey, Rosario Dúrcal, Alejandra Meyer, Celia Monzano, Harapos Guillermo Rivas.

Okay, can somebody explain why Germán Robles thought he could escape being typecast as a vampire by refusing to do any more films as Count Lavud/Duval, and then turn around and make these movies? Regardless of his reasoning, the role is strong, and Robles looks a little more comfortable here than he did as Lavud/Duval. Nostradamus, by the way, is not the medieval mystic, but a vampirized descendant. He's quite dapper, and adds a goatee to emphasize his satanic bent.

The Monsters Demolisher is a good example of the series— and genre as a whole. It opens with a genuinely spooky scene of two children skipping school; cutting through the woods, they stumble upon a crypt, the crypt of Nostradamus! They are chased away by a bearded hunchback who wears a hat like Gilligan (and who then proves he is about as good a caretaker as Gilligan, because he doesn't know where his master is until he literally trips over him in the dirt).

The series' Van Helsing figure is visited by a friend, who tells him that "the committee" does not necessarily believe his findings, and demands his evidence. Before he leaves, the friend gives the Professor a note that apparently someone just walked up and handed him (because they know he goes there all the time…), and it turns out to be from the very vampire whose existence the committee doubts! Later, in his study, the Prof is visited by a rubber bat that turns into Nostradamus, top hat in hand.

The film continues like this, veering from creepy atmospherics to head-scratching oddness, very often in the same scene. A man Nostradamus wants to kill turns out to be dead already, so Nosmo goes after his son; and since he's going there anyway, Gilligan the hunchback may as well pick up his luscious teenage daughter! When the Prof and his right-hand man (Julio Aleman) invade the crypt, they are confronted by Nostradamus, whom they attempt to shoot. He keeps disappearing as soon as they fire, taunting them, but they keep on shooting anyway. This is Mexicinema as we've come to know and love it, and the public did, too. Germán Robles, however, tired of the fangs, and after this series played no more vampires.

Co-star Julio Alemán (b. 1933) was almost as in-demand as Jaime Fernández and Armando Silvestre as a lead or supporting character in the halcyon early days of the genre — he appears in all four Nostradamus films, as well as the original Neutrón trilogy. In that series, he was merely suspected of being the hero, but he graduated to full super-status when he played the comic book hero Rocambole. While later turning to politics, he never lost his enthusiasm for his earlier avenue of make believe, and continued to tread the boards.

Santo and Son

The Legend of the Silver-Masked Man

To call El Santo the greatest Mexican wrestler ever would be an understatement. To compare him to John Wayne may be a little more apt — not politically, but certainly in terms of cultural influence and box-office clout. Both were number-one box office attractions for decades, and both transcended the nature of their professions to become legends. But the Duke was legend in a land that manufactures them daily, and even though his star shines brighter than many, he's still got a whole skyful of them surrounding him. El Santo was the supernova in the Mexican heavens.

El Santo was born Rodolfo Guzmán Huerta in 1917. He began wrestling in the 1940s, and by the mid–50s was Mexico's most popular wrestler. His legend grew via not only his numerous ring appearances, but constant exposure in the news and sports publications, plus an overlooked, but maybe even more significant, medium: comic books. The comics helped shape the El Santo mythos in two very important ways. For one, as stated elsewhere, the comics portrayed him as a (super)hero, and until then, El Santo was a rudo, a bad guy in the ring. It also cemented his image as *El Santo*. Of course, he never appeared in public without his mask anyway, but very shortly, Rodolfo Guzmán Huerta vir-

tually disappeared, except to family and close friends. It was as if Batman were really alive (and never bothered switching to Bruce Wayne). So when his persona transferred to the screen, the sense of wonder increased even further, because you knew it wasn't just somebody playing a superhero, it really was El Santo.

El Santo didn't invent the monster/wrestler genre, but he defined it; he was its standard-bearer, a presence against which all others were measured. He made genre pictures before they were fashionable, and continued to make them long after the fashion had passed. In so doing, he helped create a world which, even if he's not in the film, is known as "a Santo Movie." His silver mask became such an icon that the image which adorns the plaque on his crypt is not the face of Rodolfo Guzmán Huerta, but the mask of El Santo.

Cerebro del Mal (*Brain of Evil*, 1958)

Santo contra Hombres Infernales (*Santo versus Infernal Men*, 1958)

(Technical credits and cast are the same for both films)

(Agrupación de Técnicos de la Industria Cinematográfica Cubana y Auxiliares) *Exec. Prod*: Enrique J. Zambrano; *Co-Prod*: Jorge García Besné, Dr. Carlos Garduño, Jesús Alvareno; *Dir*: Joselito Rodríguez; *Co-Dir*: Zambrano; *Script*: Zambrano, Fernando Osés; *Phot*: Carlos Najera; *Music*: Salvador Espinosa; *Prod. Mgr*: Oscar G. Dulzaidez; *Co-Dir*: Enrique J. Zambrano; *Film Ed*: Jesús Echeverria; *Makeup*: Israel Fernández; *Cam. Op*: Minervino Rojas; *Sound*: Modesto Corvision.

Cast: El Santo, Joaquín Cordero (Dr. Campos), Norma Suárez (Elisa), Fernando Osés ("El Incognito"/ Police Sgt.), Enrique J. Zambrono (Lt. Zambrono), Alberto Insua, Los Romero y Estelita, Trio Servando Díaz, Juanito Tremble, Mario Texas.

As has already been noted in Chapter Two, in 1952, Santo passed on the opportunity to star in *El Enmascarado de Plata*. In retrospect, it's difficult to understand why. *El Enmascarado de Plata* was certainly decent in concept and execution, and provided a potential star-making vehicle for

"If you had written a fan letter to El Santo in the '60s, this is one of the autographed photos you might have received (vintage still given to the author by the Son of Santo, from his personal collection)

El Médico Asesino (who, unfortunately, lacked the screen presence to exploit the opportunity). Instead, the Saint waited another six years, then traveled to Cuba for his first two roles. To call them "starring" would be somewhat misleading — although Santo is top-billed and featured prominently in the advertising art, they are more "Joaquín Cordero Pictures Featuring Occasional Cameo Appearances by El Santo." Santo may have felt that *El Enmascarado de Plata* had little chance of success, but at least he would've had the lead role and plenty of screen time. As is, he becomes almost incidental to the plot. He is a famous pro wrestler, but (unlike pretty much every Santo film that followed) does not wrestle in the film. He fights crime, but is not the recognized Defender of Mexico that he would shortly become (but, then again, everybody has to start somewhere). And in a final irony, "El Enmascarado de Plata," Santo's nickname, was applied to a film in which he never appeared; and in his first two movies he's never even called El Santo, just "the Masked Man." All of this would soon be corrected, along with upping the "fantastic" ante, which is nearly nil in these first two installments, consisting of a couple of photo enlargers or something which are supposed to pass for superscientific (*El Enmascarado de Plata* offered for more impressive hardware), and a steel beanie used to brainwash Santo.

Joaquín Cordero is competently malicious as the "mad" scientist, although he's not the classic eye-rolling type that term denotes (he's more just an inventor with a grudge). And although he did not deign to give Santo a name in the affair, producer, co-director and scripter Enrique Zambrano plays a prominent part in the investigative proceedings as "Lt. Zambrano!" It is fitting that Fernando Osés, La Sombra himself, plays significant roles on both sides of the camera — on one side as

The one-sheet for El Santo's very first film.

scripter, and on the other as another masked hero, El Incognito. Although given even less to do than Santo, he plays an important function, freeing Santo from the effects of the evil beanie. Unlike Santo, he is unmasked at the end, revealed to be Lt. Zambrano's assistant; they both wave as the plane bearing the hero and heroine on their honeymoon flies off into the sunset.

The best thing about *Cerebro del Mal* is the poster art, which features a huge central image of a snarling Santo (or as much as you can snarl under a mask) blasting away with a machine gun! If only he'd been featured that prominently in the film, and shown that kind of chutzpah, it would've been a much more memorable debut.

Santo contra los Zombies
(*Santo vs. the Zombies*, a.k.a. *Invasion of the Zombies*, 1961)

(Filmadora Panamericana) *Prod*: Alberto López; *Dir*: Benito Alazraki, Antonio Orellana; *Story*: Orellana, Fernando Osés; *Photo*: José Ortiz Ramos; *Music*: Raúl Lavista; *Prod. Mgr*: Manuel R. Ojeda; *Prod. Chf*: Jorge Cardeña; *Asst. Dir*: Carlos Villatoro; *Film Ed*: José Bustos; *Art Dir*: José Silva; *Cam. Op*: Ignacio Romero; *Makeup*: Carmen Palomino.

Cast: (Character names: Mex/US) El Santo (El Santo/the Saint), Armando Silvestre (Sanmartin/Savage), Lorena Velázquez (Gloria Sandoval/Rutherford), Jaime Fernández (Rodríguez), Irma Serrano (Isabel), Black Shadow (Black Shadow), Dagoberto Rodríguez (Almada), Carlos Agosti (Genaro/Herbert), Ramón Bugarini (Rogelio/Roger), Julián de Meriche (Dino Pavetti), Fernando Osés, Eduardo Bonada, Juan Garza, "Picoro."

Now this was more like it. Having taken a couple of years off to tweak the formula, they finally hit on the filmic Santo we all know and love. Although still not at the peak of his big-screen prowess (that in itself would only take a few more years), Santo receives a much better turn in *Invasion of the Zombies*. Again, he doesn't have a large amount of screen time, but it was a huge slice indeed compared to his initial two outings. Also, his identity(s) are firmly established; not in the secret identity sense — he was Santo all the time (apparently, he even slept with the mask on!) — but in the sense that not only do we know him as a real-life wrestler, he is one in "reel" life too. From this picture on, producers would feature anywhere from one to four wrestling matches, either real bouts or ones filmed for the particular movie. Santo also doesn't just pop out of nowhere anymore, but arrives in full "Batman" mode — in that he has a secret HQ, and the police call on him for assistance (no, they don't shine a mask-symbol in the sky).

For some reason, this is one of only four (out of 50!) Santo movies dubbed into English. It's not part of the K. Gordon Murray package, but apparently the dubbing was done at his studio. The actors are not the recognizable "Murray Stock Voice Company," though, and Santo is referred to by the actual translation of his name (not "Samson," as was heard in the Murray trio). One of the things that always made the Murray dubs so incongruous was that, although his hero was re-dubbed "Samson," the audiences at the wrestling matches (which were not dubbed) always chanted "Santo, Santo, Santo!" Another unfortunate side-effect of this re-christening is that the casual viewer perusing the *TV Guide* to see what the local late-night horror host had to offer might well pass it up, thinking it another Hercules/Goliath–type "sword-and-sandal" epic! Admittedly, the two genres share some similarities; both feature half-naked men and big-chested women in outlandish situations, speaking in a language and voices that are not their own, but only a few of the "sweat sagas" approached the outré level attained by most of the Mexican genre pieces.

In *Santo contra los Zombies* the spirit

of the serials is again in evidence, via the "mystery" hooded villain who kidnaps wrestlers and turns them into zombies (finally, actual monsters!) to carry out his nefarious schemes. Fernando Osés performs double duty again, assisting on the script (which, by coincidence, gives him one of the best scenes—when zombified luchador Osés faces off with Santo in a match, he can't beat the Saint, so he goes into overload and starts to go up in smoke!). The other zombies appear more burly than scary (they are wrestlers, after all), and are saddled with some silly outfits, but there's one great moment in which the bunch attack a group of policemen, and a zombie takes a bullet to the forehead but keeps advancing.

The cast is quite adequate and features many soon-to-be familiar faces, including Armando Silvestre (fresh off the Neutrón series), Jaime Fernández, Irma Serrano, and future Vampire Queen Lorena Velázquez. Santo himself is more relaxed and assured, and has begun to adopt a truly larger-than-life quality.

The poster art for *Zombies* is interesting in that the central motif (used for both this and *Vampire Women*) is that of a three-quarter view of El Santo surrounded by a huge question mark. Of course, the characters usually engaged in at least one mandatory "I wonder who he really is?" scene per film in the early going, but it was never a plot device (like in *El Enmascarado de Plata* or the Neutrón films).

Santo contra el Rey del Crimen (*Santo vs. the King of Crime*, 1961)

(Películas Rodríguez) *Dir*: Fredrico Curiel; *Adapt*: Curiel, Antonio Orellana; *Story*: Orellana, Fernando Osés; *Photo*: Fernando Colin; *Music*: Enrique Cabiati; *Prod. Mgr*: Luis Quintanilla Rico; *Asst. Dir*: Alberto Mariscal; *Film Ed*: J. Juan Munguia; *Art Dir*: Arcado Artis Gener; *Camera Op*: Raúl Rod-

ríguez; *Makeup*: Graciela Muñoz; *SPFX*: Javier Sierra.

Cast: El Santo, Fernando Casanova (Fernando Lavalle), Ana Bertha Lepe (Virginia), Beto "El Bocario" (Conrado), Begonia Palacios (Dancer), René Cardona, Sr. (Señor de la Llata), Yolanda Ciani (Mercedes), Augusto Benedico (Matias), Guillermo A. Bianchi (Don Cosme), Victor Velázquez (Morales), Fernando Osés (Wrestler), "Picoro," Fredy Guzmán Jazz Combo.

Santo en el Hotel de la Muerte (*Santo in the Hotel of Death*, 1961)

(Technical credits same as above.)
Cast: El Santo, Fernando Casanova, Ana Betha Lepe, Beto "El Bocario," Wally Barron (Prof. Corbera), Luis Aragón (Armando Correa), Augusto Benedeico, Fernando Osés (Cook), Black Shadow (Himself), Yolanda Ciani (Daughter).

Santo contra el Cerebro Diabólico (*Santo vs. the Diabolical Brain*, 1961)

(Technical credits same as above.)
Cast: El Santo, Fernando Casanova, Ana Bertha Lepe, Beto "El Bocario," Luis Aceves Castaneda (Refugio Canales), Celia Viveros (La Jarocha), José Chávez Trowe, Fernando Osés (Asian gangster; Canales' assassin), Augusto Benedico, Victor Velázquez, Nothanael "Frankenstein" León, René Cardona, Sr., and Los Trios Gallos.

This 1961 trilogy of Santo films not only shares the same technical credits, but practically the same cast—all the principals are the same, and they play the same characters in all three films; only some of the supporting players differ, and even some of them remain constant, as they just play different characters! All three movies were thought lost for many years, until copies surfaced in 1998. Historically, they provide the all-important link between *Zombies* and *Vampire Women*. While all three certainly offer moments of interest, they ultimately prove somewhat disappointing in terms of content, both Santo-wise and fantasy-wise, despite the lurid titles.

The titles and ad art promised much, and emphasized the sex appeal. *Hotel of Death* presented a particularly striking poster design — a bevy of nightgown-clad beauties undulating beneath a grinning skull; and *Diabolical Brain* features a prominent image of Ana Bertha Lepe being spanked! And while they delivered on these promises (in fact, *Hotel of Death*, like the "Beach Party" movies, seems like nothing more than an excuse for a ninety-minute parade of pulchritude), they delivered very little Santo. Almost reverting to bit-player status, á la his first two movies, Santo appears every once in a while to wrestle or scrap with the baddies, but the bulk of the action and screen time are devoted to Casanova (a popular leading man at the time), Lepe, and comedy-relief "El Bocario." Ana Bertha Lepe was one of the most vivacious of the Mexican beauties, and has a particularly memorable "sexy scene" in *Diaboilical Brain*: in order to infiltrate a crooked bar, she has to "audition" for the sleazy owner (Luis Aceves Castaneda, "Dr. Krupp" from *Robot vs. the Aztec Mummy*). He somehow manages to sequester her in a corner of the crowded saloon, where he sits at a table with his drink and urges her to lift her skirt "higher, higher," which she does quite provocatively, revealing a wonderful pair of legs. Santo, in one of his too-few action scenes, also provides a memorable moment when, like Kirk Alyn in the 1952 *Blackhawk* serial, he manages to take on a moving (on the ground) airplane!

Santo contra las Mujeres Vampiros (*Santo vs. the Vampire Women*, a.k.a. *Samson vs. the Vampire Women*, 1962)

(Filmadora Panamericana) *Prod:* Alberto López; *Dir:* Alfonso Corona Blake; *Scr:* Rafael García Travesi, Blake; *Story:* Antonio Orellana, Fernando Osés, Travesi; *Photo:* José Ortiz Ramos; *Music:* Raúl Lavista; *Prod. Mgr:* Luis García De León; *Prod. Chief:* Jorge Cardeña; *Asst. Dir:* Ignacio Villareal; *Film Ed:* José W. Bustos; *Art Dir:* Roberto Silva; *Makeup:* Ramón Juárez; *Decor:* Ernesto Carrasco; *Sound:* Javier Mateos, Galdino Samperio; *Camera Op:* Manuel González; *Lighting:* Daniel López; *Sound Ed:* Raúl Portillo.

Cast: (Character Names: Mex/U.S.): El Santo (El Santo/Samson), Lorena Velázquez (Zorina), María Duval (Diana), Jaime Fernández (Carlos/Charles Andrews), Augusto Benedico (Prof. Orlof/Rolof), Ofelia Montesco (Tundra), Fernando Osés (Igor), Nothanael "Frankenstein" León (Taras), Guillermo "Lobo Negro" Hernández (Marcus), Cavernario Gallindo, Ray Mendoza, Black Shadow, Bobby Bonales, Eduardo Bonada, Wally Barron, Victor Velázquez, Fabian Grey, "Picoro."

Simply put, this is the all-time greatest Mexican wrestler/monster movie. Ever. Period. Case closed. Well, okay, in my mind, at least, that title would be shared with *Las Luchadoras vs. la Momia*, but mention Mexican monster or wrestler movies to anyone, and this is probably the one they'll think of. *Las Luchadoras* may actually have a slight edge in overall weirdness (in this respect, *El Barón del Terror* is also in the running), but they both lack one very important ingredient: El Santo. Blue Demon may indeed have been the better technical wrestler, and Mil Máscaras may have had more elaborate masks and international fame, but when it came to presence on the screen, nobody, but nobody, could hold a candle to El Santo. Blue Demon came across as likeable but businesslike, a no-nonsense attitude which sometimes sacrificed warmth; Mil Máscaras was a relative latecomer, and though he had charisma to spare, he only made about a third as many pictures as El Santo. And even though his voice was almost always dubbed (both in Spanish and English), the combination of man-of-action,

Above and opposite: The Mexican and Azteca lobby card designs for El Santo's best-loved film. The Mexican card incorporates elements of the one-sheet in its design; the Azteca card features Lorena Velázquez and Ofelia Montesco prominently in both the photograph and the border artwork.

international playboy and father figure helped propel El Santo to the very forefront of the genre, a position he never relinquished.

And this was his finest hour. Many more films followed, some of them very, very good, but this one was magic — one of those instances in which everything comes together just right. It wasn't the first time he had fought monsters. It wasn't even the first time he co-starred with Lorena Velázquez. But let's put it this way: fighting half-naked, burly wrestlers is okay, but fighting buxom beauties with fangs in sheer nightgowns is great! And *Vampire Women* has *the* classic scene from all of wrestler/monsterdom. It's the one that re-

ally says it all — everything there is to say about these movies and their otherworldly spirit and just why we love them — the scene you see in the middle of an all-night, zonked-out movie marathon, the one where everything around you slows down and the sequence imprints itself onto your brain:

El Santo is readying himself for the big match. Unbeknownst to him, his masked opponent has been murdered, and his place taken by one of vampire queen Lorena Velázquez's thuggish fanged henchman (Fernando Osés, naturally). The bell sounds, and after a few minutes, Santo realizes this isn't his scheduled foe: "He's using Karate," says Santo, "and could kill

me with one blow!" But after some furious ring action (Fernando Osés was far and away Santo's best onscreen opponent, and engaged in some exhilarating battles over their long association), in which Santo is almost (gasp, choke) unmasked, Santo turns the tables on the impostor and does a little unmasking of his own … revealing not the expected mustached, fanged features of Osés, but the snarling visage of an enraged werewolf! The werewolf then squares off against Santo and half the police force of Mexico City, who all dogpile on top of the beast. This bothers the monster not at all, as he simply turns into a bat and flies away!

This, my friends, is cinema. Cinema, as this writer understands it, is a vehicle which can transport us out of our wretched daily existence, and the very best examples of this are those films that most completely create another world and make us believe in it. The original *King Kong* and *The Wizard of Oz* are two prime examples. While *Vampire Women* may not be on the same level as those two classics, a weird, wonderful world all its own — one in which anything (like the above-described scene) can and will happen. From the opening scenes of the lady vampires resurrecting their queen, complete with a visit from Ol' Scratch himself (portrayed as a shadow on the wall, complete with horns and pointy tail), to the climax in which Santo races from coffin to coffin, igniting the vampires where they lay, we are completely absorbed.

And it is no coincidence that both *Vampire Women* and *Las Luchadoras vs. la Momia* feature Lorena Velázquez. Equally

Above and opposite: More Azteca lobbies. (***Above***) Look closely at the photograph, and you'll see some smoking vampire women (and I don't mean their looks). Apparently, this shot was taken during a smoke break, and they used it for the lobby card! (***Opposite***) Gina Romand goes wild in the non-sequel.

at home as either the beautiful, heroic Gloria Venus, or the beautiful, evil Zorinna, Señora Velázquez proved to be an actress and siren of the first rank; her appearances in the two finest examples of their genre make her the undisputed queen of this cinematic subset. And, on top of all this, she's one of the few people outside of his family ever to see El Santo unmasked. When asked, on the *Incredibly Strange Films Show*, how she responded to this rare opportunity, she recounted that she quickly advised Santo to "Put it back on!"

As beautiful in her own right was Lorena's right-hand vampire woman, Ofelia Montesco. Born in Peru in 1936, Ms.

Montesco made a large number of films, but only one other in the monster/wrestler camp, *Santo vs. el Estrangulador*. She passed away at only 47 years of age, but her place in Psychotronic Heaven is assured by *Vampire Women* alone.

Santo vs. the Vampire Women is one of the quartet of Santo films dubbed into English and shown north of the border, and one of two included in the infamous K. Gordon Murray package. As such, it features the Murray "stock voice company." Santo's dubber, in particular, remains memorable for a basso profundo rendering that makes Rex Reason (of *This Island Earth* fame) sound like Fay Wray; this, no

doubt, is one of the reasons the movie has attained its exalted "cult" status. Additional foreign dubbings have helped cement that status, making *Santo vs. the Vampire Women*, by far the most recognizable example of the genre to the world at large.

Santo en el Museo de Cera (*Santo in the Wax Museum,* a.k.a. *Samson in the Wax Museum,* 1963)

(Filmadora Panamericana) *Prod*: Alberto López; *Dir*: Alfonso Corona Blake; *Scr*: Fernando Galiana, Julio Porter; *Photo*: José Ortiz Ramos; *Music Dir*: Raúl Lavista; *Music*: Sergio Guerrero; *Asst. Dir*: Mario Cisneros; *Film Ed*: José W. Bustos; *Art Dir*: José Rodríguez Granada; *Sound*: Luis Fernández; *Makeup*: Román Juárez.

 Cast: (Mex/U.S.): El Santo (El Santo/Samson), Claudio Brook (Dr. Karol), Ruben Rojo (Ricardo/Charles), Norma Mora (Gloria), Roxana Bellini (Susana/Susan), José Luis Jimenez (Prof. Galvan), Fernando Osés, Nothanael "Frankenstein" León (Henchmen), "Picoro" (Ring announcer).

This was the eighth Santo movie, and the third title dubbed into English (too bad they only dubbed one more out of forty-two remaining films!). The poster art, although exceedingly well-rendered, is somewhat misleading, and (as usual) inherently bizarre: accompanying a large, beautiful portrait of El Santo are equally large images of a werewolf (wearing a muscle shirt!) and the Frankenstein monster (in a pin-striped jacket!)—suggesting it will be El Santo's first encounter with classic-style, Universal-type creatures. Alas, the two monsters are only exhibits in the titular museum. Ironically, the makeup for

Santo en el Museo de Cera boasts one of the best El Santo one-sheets — beautiful composition and exceedingly well-rendered. Dig those crazy fashions on the werewolf and Frankenstein Monster!

these immobile figures proved far superior to that of any of the ambulatory versions that followed!

The plot takes its inspiration from both *House of Wax* and *Island of Lost Souls*. Dr. Karol (well-played by Claudio Brook) is a scarred madman who performs fiendish experiments while maintaining a benign public face. But unlike Vincent Price in *House of Wax*, Dr. Karol's victims do not end up as exhibits—his wax museum is also a "House of Pain" where unfortunates wind up as "manimals." Emulating Charles Laughton in *Island of Lost Souls*, Karol's supreme creation will likewise be a panther woman! And, like the fate that befell Laughton and so many other mad scientists, Karol's creations turn on him in the end. At the harrowing climax, Santo not only faces off against these creations, but engages in a vicious battle with Dr. Karol's pug-uglies (familiar faces Fernando Osés and Nothanael León), emerging victorious by dumping a vat-ful of hot wax cover them. When it comes to destroying monsters, Santo did not mess around!

Claudio Brook was born in 1927 and died in 1995. A respected performer not only in Mexico but internationally, he appeared in both U.S. and European productions. Brook won Mexico's equivalent of the Oscar for both Best Actor and Best Supporting Actor, and his fantasti-film credits span the decades; in addition to starring roles in both this film and *La Mano Que Aprieta*, he was in the first Neu-trón movie, as well as the U.S. productions *The Bees* and *The Devil's Rain*.

Santo vs. el Estrangulador (*Santo vs. the Strangler*, 1963)

(Estudios Americas) *Prod*: Alberto López; *Dir*: René Cardona, Sr.; *Scr*: Rafael García Travesi; *Photo*: Alfredo Uribe; *Music*: Enrico Cabiati; *Film Ed*: J. J. Munguia; *Art Dir*: Arcadi Artis Gener; *Prod. Mgr*: Luis García De León; *Makeup*: Antonio Ramírez.

Cast: El Santo, Alberto Vasquez (Javier), María Duval (Laura), Begonia Palacios (Irene), Ofelia Montesco (Lilian), Roberto Cañedo (the Strangler), Carlos López Moctezuma (Ville-gas), Eric Del Castillo (Marcos), Nothanael "Frankenstein" León, Gerardo Zepeda (Tor).

El Espectro del Estrangulador (*Spectre of the Strangler*, 1963)

(Estudios Americas–Cinematográfica Norte) *Prod*: Alberto López; *Dir/Scr*: René Cardona, Sr.; *Story*: Rafael García Travesi; *Photo*: Alfredo Uribe Jacome; *Mus. Dir*: Enrico C. Cabiati; *Prod. Mgr*: Luis García De León; *Asst. Dir*: Tito Navarro; *Film Ed*: José J. Munguia; *Art Dir*: Arcadi Artis Gener; *Camera Op*: Roberto J. Jaramillo; *SPFX*: Javier Sierra; *Makeup*: Antonio Ramírez.

Cast: El Santo, Alberto Vasquez (Javier), María Duval (Laura), Begonia Palacios (Irene), Roberto Cañedo (the Strangler), Carlos López Moctezuma (Villegas), Julián de Mereche (Don Julián), Gerardo Zepeda (Tor), "Picoro."

Well, it's all downhill from here, folks. No, seriously, with *Vampire Women*, Santo ushered in the "Golden Age" of both his own films and the genre's, and there were many fine efforts all around in the years to follow, although none ever seemed to attain the lofty creative heights achieved by that singular effort. The effect is some-what akin to musicians or bands who plays for decades—the early efforts are usually the hungriest, songs that have been build-ing up for years that need to come out. And while they may grow into better mu-sicians and are still capable of great work, the intervening years bring on a different perspective, and they just can never be at that same place again. And so it went with El Santo. It only took a couple of films to find his groove, but he found it fast and starred in his masterpiece in short order. The next few years brought a steady flow of highly entertaining product, and there are many grand moments to be found. In the mid–1970s, however, the genre started to lose steam, and Santo did as well, al-

Two more Aztecas from early Santo efforts. *Top*: A nice shot of El Santo's secret crime lab. *Bottom*: El Santo gets ready to rumble with old pals Nothanael "Frankenstein" León and Fernando Osés, while mad doc Claudio Brook looks on.

Another striking one-sheet from an early El Santo film. This one in particular seems to encapsulate the genre — masked wrestler, monster, beautiful woman, and music. Too bad there were no midgets in the movie, or they would have had it all.

though he stuck it out longer than the rest (and maybe even longer than he should have). But even up to the end he was still in there pitching, and the world was a better place for having him there.

Santo vs. the Strangler and *Spectre of the Strangler* were produced by the same man responsible for the previous two Santos, Alberto López, but here the directorial reigns were turned over to the "father" of the Wrestling Women, René Cardona, Sr. The results were not quite as edifying, although there's plenty of everything: music, wrestling, and horror. Again, a whiff of the serials survives in *Spectre*, when Santo is caught in the vise-like grip of a giant drill-press. Whether or not the two movies were shot back-to-back or concurrently remains open to conjecture, but one thing's for sure: about the only people who didn't work on the second one were those who were "killed" in the first entry! *Santo vs. the Strangler* is sort of a "Phantom of the Nightclub," with the scarred Strangler (reliable Roberto Cañedo) stalking and dispatching sexy women; and in *Spectre*, it's not his ghost, but rather the Strangler in the flesh (or, more accurately, his victims' flesh ... yeee!) back for revenge. Assisting him is the also-reliable Gerardo Zepeda, who earns points for simply being called "Tor."

Roberto Cañedo (b. 1918) has a history of genre roles dating all the way back to the "Fu Man Chu" series, and gave two of the best portrayals of Mad Mexican Médicos in *Las Luchadoras vs. el Médico Asesino* and *La Mujer Murciélago*. He has a grand time as the Strangler, and later displayed his considerable ability in *La Loba, La Hija del Frankenstein*, and the *Leones del Ring* series.

Atacan las Brujas (*The Witches Attack*, 1964)

(Fílmica Vergara–Cinecomisiones) *Prod*: Luis Enrique Vergara; *Dir*: José Díaz Morales; *Scr*: Rafael García Travesi; *Story*: Raúl García Travesi, Fernando Osés; *Photo*: Eduardo Valdéz; *Music*: Jorge Pérez Herrera; *Prod. Mgr*: Roy Fletcher; *Prod. Chf*: José Rodríguez; *Film Ed*: José J. Munguia; *Camera Op*: Dagobied Rodríguez; *Makeup*: Armando Islas; *Sound Rec*: Danieal Mercado Díaz; *Music/Re-Rec*: Salvador Topete.

Cast: El Santo, Lorena Velázquez (Elisa/ Mayra), María Eugenia San Martín (Ofelia), Ramón Bugarini (Arturo), Fernando Osés (Henchman), Crox Alvaredo (Lawyer/henchman), Edaena Ruiz (Medusa), Guillermo "Lobo Negro" Hernández (Henchman), Altia Michel, María Montiel, Alma Pichardi [a.k.a. Alma Rojo], Rita Romero, Juan Garza.

This was the first of four features that El Santo made for producer Luis Enrique Vergara, who was also responsible for a quartet of thrilling Blue Demon screamers. It was also the second — and final — time Santo would do a block of four pictures for one producer at a time; after this series, it was no more than two in a row for anyone, although there would be return customers (along with Santo co-producing from time to time). The Vergara films are of a somewhat lower budget than Santo's previous efforts; but what they lack in funds, they more than make up for with a wealth of bizarre characters and situations.

Atacan las Brujas is the first unofficial remake of an earlier Santo effort; okay, it's pretty much a carbon copy — just take *Mujeres Vampiro* and substitute Witches for Vampire Women (since screenwriter Rafael García Travesi worked on both, it's not surprising). *Witches*, however, lacks the verisimilitude of its predecessor. Lorena Velázquez reappears as an evil Queen, but doesn't cut nearly as memorable a figure here as her Vampire Woman Zorina. On the whole, though, *Atacan las Brujas* offers a splendid time for all.

A note on the poster art: as previously mentioned, the Mexican genre film distributors loved to utilize existing ideas; in

Top: The poster design from the Barbara Stanwyck film *The Night Walker* features prominently in the lobby card for this remake of *Vampire Women*. *Bottom:* El Santo's most able screen antagonist, Fernando Osés, as the brutish Baron Brákola.

this particular instance, they appropriate the central design from the Barbara Stanwyck thriller *The Night Walker*, which has nothing to do with witches attacking (but is nonetheless a great image — the devil looming over a fainted woman in a nightie).

El Hacha Diabólico (*The Diabolical Hatchet*, 1964)

(Fílmica Vergara–Cinecomisiones) *Prod*: Luis Enrique Vergara; *Dir*: José Díaz Morales; *Scr*: Raúl García Travesi; *Story*: Raúl García Travesi, Fernando Osés; *Music*: Jorge Pérez Herrera; *Makeup*: Armando Islas; *Costumes*: Bertha Mendoza; *Prod. Mgr*: Roy Fletcher; *Asst. Dir*: Angel Rodríguez; *Film Ed/Sound Ed*: José Juan Munguia; *Photog*: Eduardo Valdéz; *Dialogue Rec*: Jesús Sánchez; *Prod. Chief*: José Rodríguez; *Rec*: Daniel Mercado Díaz.

Cast: El Santo, Lorena Velázquez (Isabel de Arango), Fernando Osés (Encapuchado), Bety González (Alicia), Mario Sevilla (Abraca/Dr. Zanoni), Guillermo "Lobo Negro" Hernández, Juan Garza, Carlos Suárez, Mario Orea, José Alvarez Valdéz, Mario "Colocho" Zebadua, Martha Lasso Renteria, Emilio Garibay, Victor Velázquez, Juan Garza, Jorge Mateos, Roy Fletcher.

Lorena Velázquez is back to cement her claim as Santo's leading Lady in this second Vergara, as is Fernando Osés — this time in a flashy leading role as the "Encapuchado," a black-hooded scoundrel who wields a mean axe (not a guitar, but the hatchet of the title) and can appear out of nowhere at any time to attempt some hideous head-choppin'. Not only does he pop up right in the middle of Santo's wrestling matches, but, in one of the best scenes, right in the middle of the sleeping enmascarado's bedroom. What makes the scene so memorable is that Santo is sleeping in his mask(!) and also in his tights and boots(!!); so either Santo is exceptionally paranoid, or he's just always ready for action!

Profanadores de Tumbas (*Grave Robbers*, 1965)

(Fílmica Vergara–Cinecomisiones) *Prod*: Luis Enrique Vergara; *Dir/Scr*: José Díaz Morales; *Story*: Rafael García Travesi; *Music*: Jorge Pérez Herrera; *Asst. Dir*: Angel Rodríguez; *Makeup*: Armando Islas; *Prod. Mgr*: Roy Fletcher; *Asst. Dir*: Angel Rodríguez; *Film Ed/Sound Ed*: José Juan Munguia; *Cam. Op*: Dagobied Rodríguez; *Dialogue Rec*: Jesús Sánchez.

Cast: El Santo, Gina Romand (Marta), Mario Orea (Dr. Toicher), Jorge Peral (Carlos), Fernando Osés, Guillermo "Lobo Negro" Hernández, Nothanael "Frankenstein" León, "Quasimodo," Juan Garza, Los Chavales, Jesús Camcho, Jessica Munguia, Bigoton Castro, Martha Lasso Renteria, Fernando Saucedo, Julio Ahuet, Leonor Gómez.

Third time's the charm in this third Vergara Santo; although not as satisfying on the whole as, say, *Vampire Women*, it contains some of the wackiest scenes and most bizarre inventions ever to find their way into the Santo mythos. A killer lamp. A killer wig. A killer violin. A painting that drips blood. All these devices are created life by a certain Dr. Toicher, a nutcase in the grand tradition of Dr. Krupp from the Aztec Mummy movies; it is he and his henchmen who are the grave robbers of the title. Dr. Toicher's experiments require human hearts, but time and again he fails. He decides that the hearts they've used so far were not strong enough, and his next subject should be sturdier ... say, along the lines of a pro wrestler! (The Shadow knows what you're thinking, and, yes, it does sound an awful lot like *Las Luchadoras vs. el Médico Asesino*, and no, it wasn't written by Alfredo Salazar.)

El Barón Brákola (1965)

(Fílmica Vergara–Cinecomisiones) *Prod*: Luis Enrique Vergara; *Dir/Scr*: José Díaz Morales; *Story*: Rafael García Travesi, Fernando Osés; *Photo*: Eduardo Valdéz; *Music*: Jorge Pérez Herrera; *Asst. Dir*: Angel Rodríguez; *Makeup*: Armando Islas; *Film Ed*: José Juan Munguia; *Cam.*

Op: Dagobied Rodríguez; *Music/Re-Rec*: Salvador Topete.

Cast: El Santo, Fernando Osés (Barón Brákola), Mercedes Carreño (Silvia), Antonio de Hud (Eduardo), Ada Carrasco (Aurora), Susanna Robles, Miguel Macia, Manuel Arvide, Rosa Vinay, Jorge Fegan, César Gay, Enrique Ramírez, Jorge Mateos, Roberto Porter, Margarito Luna, "Quasimodo," Benny Galan, Juan Garza, "Picoro."

This may be the pinnacle of the Vergara Santo series. As stated elsewhere, Fernando Osés was Santo's best screen adversary, and he was never better than in this film. He plays the title character, a brutish vampire straight out of a Jack Kirby comic book (the "Transylvain" issues of *Jimmy Olsen*). Brákola and Santo mix it up numerous times cover the course of the movie, and they really go at it hard (as opposed to the usual listlessly-staged brawls in wrestler/monster films).

Like *Hacha Diabólico*, among others, *El Barón Brákola* makes extensive use of the "Colonial-era" Santo, "El Caballero del Plata" (or some variation thereof). And, like in the former film, Santo makes an enemy in the past who comes back to cause him grief in the present. In the by-now expected scene, Brákola disguises himself as Santo's wrestling opponent (funny how quickly these centuries-old monsters acclimate themselves to modern wrestling techniques!). But when he loses the match, he merely accepts defeat and starts to scheme anew. (The one time it would seem logical for a guy to change into a bat, and they don't follow through!)

Santo vs. la Invasión de los Marcianos (*Santo vs. the Martian Invasion*, 1966)

(Producciones Cinematográficas) *Prod*: Alfonso Rosas Priego; *Dir*: Alfredo B. Crevenna; *Scr*: Rafael García Travesi; *Photo*: Jorge Stahl, Jr.; *Music*: Antonio Díaz Conde; *Makeup*: Margarita Ortega; *Prod. Mgr*: Mario García Camberos; *Film Ed*: Alfredo Rosas Priego; *Prod. Mgr*: Mario García Cambreros; *Prod. Chief*: José Alcalde Gamiz; *Sub-Dir*: Felipe Palomino; *Asst. Ed*: Ramón Aupart; *Dialogue Rec*: Jesús González Gancy; *Sound Ed*: Abraham Cruz.

Cast: El Santo, Wolf Ruvinskis (Argos), Maura Monti (Afrodita), Belinda Correll (Diana), Eva Norvind (Selene), Gilda Miros (Artemisa), Ham Lee, "El Nazi," Benny Galan, Eduardo Bonada, Nothanael "Frankenstein" León (Martians), Yolanda Guzmán, Antonio Montoro, Manuel Zozaya, Consuelo Frank, Alicia Montoya, Roy Fletcher, Mario Sevilla, Niclas Rodríguez, Rosa Furman, Sergio Ramos, Aaron Hernan, Ramón Menéndez, Demetrio González, José Loza, Pepito Velázquez, Juan Antonio Edward.

Had this absolutely marvelous mid-period Santo been dubbed into English, it would probably be as popular as *Vampire Women*. It possesses all the wonderful elements in spades; were it not for legal reasons, it could be called "Mars Attacks Santo." Ostensibly, these alien invaders attack the whole earth, but most of their fighting, it seems, is directed at the silver masked-man. Oh, they manage to disintegrate a few citizens of Mexico City, although not in as gory a fashion as the original "Mars Attacks" card series; but the "Invasión" seems rather small-scale. Perhaps this was just an advance patrol? No doubt when the head Martians got wind of the mighty Santo, they realized that if Earth had such champions, it would be useless to waste any more green men!

Well, actually, they're not green, they look just like you and me, if you and me look like Wolf Ruvinskis and Maura Monti! As is typical of futuristic civilizations, the men run around in tights, and the women wear very short skirts. They're supposed to have a "third eye," but this is represented by a blinking light on a helmet, and is not part of their physiognomy per se. As is also typical of alien invaders, the men spend a lot of

SANTO, EL ENMASCARADO DE PLATA en
LA INVASION DE LOS MARCIANOS
WOLF RUBINSKIS
MAURA MONTI · GILDA MIROS · EVA NORVIND

EL VAMPIRO
Y EL SEXO
SANTO - NOELIA NOEL
ALDO MONTI
ROBERTO G. RIVERA - CARLOS AGOSTI
niña PILI GONZALEZ
ALBERTO ROJAS
A COLORES

time trying to take down the hero, and the women spend a lot of time seducing earthmen. Of course, they succeed in every case but Santo's. One scene has the Martian girls, in seductive sixties fashions, crash a party — and the claws really come out on the women already in attendance!

But by far the most intensely psychotronic sequence in the whole movie comes when the Martian girls don sexy showgirl outfits and perform a musical number! Like all such scenes, it must be "scene" to be believed! And, of course, like ancient vampires and executioners, the Martian males are well-versed in modern wrestling moves. This notion in itself is pretty outré, and part of what makes this genre so special. Other monster fighters used silver bullets and stakes ... the employed wrestler-heroes not only these, but drop-kicks as well! Wrestling Martians. Only in Mexico, baby.

Santo vs. los Villanos del Ring (*Santo vs. the Villains of the Ring*, 1966)

(Producciones Cinematográficas) *Prod*: Alfonso Rosas Priego; *Dir*: Alfredo B. Crevenna; *Scr*: Rafael García Travesi; *Story*: Rafael García Travesi, Mario García Camberos; *Photo*: Jorge Stahl, Jr.; *Music*: Antonio Díaz Conde; *Prod. Mgr*: Mario García Camberos; *Film Ed*: Alfredo Rosas Priego; *Sub-Dir*: Felipe Palomino; *Prod. Coord*: Alfonso Rosas Priego, Jr.

Cast: El Santo, Wolf Ruvinksis (Rodolfo), Silvia Fournier (María Elena Ramos), Graciala Lara (Rebecca), Eduardo Bonada (Fernando), Jean Safont, Ramiro Orci, Francisco Jambrina, Consuelo Frank, Carlos Nieto, Marco Antonio Arzate, Enrique Cárdenas, Rosa Furman, Benny Galan, Dick Medrano, Ray Mendoza, Ham Lee, "El Nazi," "Picoro."

The last Santo film in glorious black-and-white is somewhat of a letdown, especially after all of the zany shenanigans of *Martian Invasion*. It's not that the film lacks action — in fact, the action is almost constant — but practically all of said action consists of the listlessly-staged brawls mentioned in the *Barón Brákola* section. In addition, *Villanos del Ring* is one of the few Santo films with practically no "fantastic" content (unless you count seances). It seems that some fake spiritualists (are there any other kind?) are trying to rook El Santo's god-daughter out of six million pesos; El Santo fakes his own death and then exposes the charlatans. But this (one would think main) plot takes a back seat to drawn-out action choreography.

Operación 67 (*Operation 67*, 1967)

(Estudios América–Cina Films) *Exec. Prods*: Mauricio Walerstein, J. Fernando Pérez Gavilan; *Dirs*: René Cardona, Sr., and Jr.; *Scr*: Rafael García Travesi, Mauricio Walerstein; *Photo*: Raúl Domínguez, Fernando Colin; *Music*: Enrico Cabiati; *SPFX*: Javier Sierra; *Asst. Dirs*: Tito Novarro, Fernando Duran; *Prod. Mgrs*: Antonio Rodríguez, Jacobo Derechin; *Film Ed*: José Juan Munguia; *Art Dir*: Arcadi Artis Gener; *Underwater Photog*: Genaro Hurtado; *Sound Op*: Ricardo Saldivar.

Cast: El Santo, Jorge Rivero (Jorge Rubio), Elizabeth Campbell (Ruth Taylor), Noé Murayama (Suki), Midori Magashiro, José Luis Carol, Miguel Gómez Checa, Gerardo Zepeda, Juan Garza, Manuel "El Vikingo" Galavis, Ray Mendoza, Tony Sugar, Olga Morris, María Salome, René Barrera, Fernando Yapur, Armando Acosta, Jean Safont, Manuel Donde, Ruben Marquez, Julián de Meriche, Antonio Raxel.

Opposite, top: **Wolf Ruvinskis and a fellow martian go up in flames in this underrated El Santo camp-fest. Though it doesn't show in black-and-white, on the Azteca lobbies El Santo's silver mask was often overlaid with bizarre colors, making it look more like a ski-mask. In this case, it was green and red!** *Bottom*: **Azteca lobby for one of the notorious "El Sexo" films; graphics from the film are readily available, unlike the movie.**

El Tesoro de Moctezuma (*The Treasure of Montezuma*, 1967)

(Technical credits are the same as *Operación 67*)

Cast: El Santo, Jorge Rivero (Jorge Rubio), Noé Murayama (Suki), Amadee Chabot (Estela "Flor de Loto" Ruiz), Maura Monti, Alfonso Torres, Antonio Raxel, Vincente "Indio Cacama" Lara, Miguel Gómez Checa, Ray Mendoza, Henry Pelusso.

Following the momentary lapse of reason known as *Santo vs. the Villains of the Ring*, Santo returned in a big way — as a full-fledged Secret Agent (and, for the first time, in full color)! The "spy craze" was at its peak around this time, with not only the pioneering James Bond series at its apex, but other popular variations, like James Coburn's *Flint*, Dean Martin's *Matt Helm*, and TV's *Man from U.N.C.L.E.* proliferating, along with serious thrillers like *The Spy Who Came in from the Cold*. But although that latter work presented a more accurate picture of the real spy business, as far as the public was concerned, it was all guns, gadgets, and bikinis — and these two Santos had them to spare!

Seeing as how they were the first two Santos to be filmed in color, and since they were taking on the James Bond concept as a whole, the budget was appropriately expanded, and includes a number of well-mounted and picturesque set pieces — there's even a nod to *North by Northwest* (itself a Bond-like film), in which Jorge Rivero is stalked by a plane. Rivero had begun his career as a pseudo–Santo ("El Enmascarado de Oro," the Gold-Masked Man in *El Asesino Invisible*), and, although he and Santo play well off each other, one wonders why was he there in the first place. Did the producers think that the public, who had already accepted masked wrestlers fighting monsters, would be unable to embrace a masked secret agent? Regardless, Rivero does play his role well, and as a Bond-like agent, he at least does better than George Lazenby.

In fact, Santo and Rivero's introduction scene in the first movie is a wonderfully clever send-up of the whole affair. The world is in trouble, and a call comes through to the only men who can save it, secret super-agents El Santo and Jorge Rubio! The call is received by the heroes while entertaining bikini-clad lovelies on the beach … or so it seems. As the camera pulls back, we see it's only the "Beach Room" of Santo and Rubio's spacious headquarters! They toss off the lovelies like Bond tosses off "Dink" in his first scene in *Goldfinger*, and they roll into action against evil Elizabeth Campbell, herself a "Golden Rubio" in the Wrestling Women series. Campbell herself receives a memorable introduction in the same film, rising out of the surf, *à la* Ursula Andress in *Dr. No*, in her own breathtaking bikini.

Although it is not a "sexo" film, *Operación 67* is one of the few existing examples of the genre to feature nudity. Jorge Rubio goes to a night club to check out the dancing girl (a favorite spy endeavor), and goes Bond one better by watching her dance topless. The dancer (sexy Midori Magashiro) also has an extended sequence in which she dons stockings and lingerie before being surprised by Rubio (whom she thought the aforementioned plane had put out of commission), bringing to mind another similar sequence in *Dr. No*. Of course, there's beefcake, too, as Jorge exploits every opportunity to take his shirt off, but he did this in virtually every one of his films, so that's no surprise.

The *Treasure of Montezuma* offers the same team-up of Santo and Rubio, along with the returning Moe Nurayama, and another pair of gorgeous gals: Amadee Chabot, who played double agent "Lotus Flower," and starred in her own swingin' spy spoof, *Agente 00-Sexy* (which she certainly was); and Maura Monti as a bad girl spy (likewise, Maura had played a secret agent in the unforgettable *La Mujer Murciélago*, and also co-starred with Blue Demon in his pair of secret agent films). Miss Chabot had been 1964's Miss California, and appeared in two Hollywood films, *For Those Who Think Young* and *Three on a Couch*, before coming to Mexico in 1966. Her last genre role came in the 1972 Colombian production *Campeones del Ring*. Amadee's character falls in love with Rubio, and her tragic death brings to mind another Bond scene, the climax of *On Her Majesty's Secret Service*, with Lazenby and Diana Rigg. And, come to think of it, all of the actresses in this superior pair of Santo movies would have made great Bond Girls.

Santo en el Tesoro de Drácula (*Santo in the Treasure of Dracula*, a.k.a. *El Vampiro y el Sexo*, 1968)

(Cinematográfica Calderón) *Prod*: Guillermo Calderón Stell; *Dir*: René Cardona, Sr.; *Scr*: Alfredo Salazar; *Photo*: Raúl Martínez Solares; *Music Dir*: Sergio Guerrero; *Film Ed*: José W. Bustos; *Sound Sprvsr*: James L. Fields; *Makeup*: María Del Castillo; Eastmancolor.

Cast: El Santo, Aldo Monti (Drácula), Noélia Noel (Luisa), Carlos Agosti (Dr. Sepulveda), Jorge Mondragón (Prof. Soler), Carlos Suárez, Guillermo "Lobo Negro" Hernández, Jessica Rivano, Diana Arriga, Magali, Sonia Aguilar, Paulette.

As noted before, I occasionally take the opportunity to present a movie synopsis provided by the original pressbook for a film, translated by the producers to encourage distribution in other countries. This lusty piece is of particular interest, as it is from the "lost" version of the film *El Vampiro y el Sexo* (and, as in all other instances, is quoted and punctuated verbatim). And, somewhere, Ed Wood is smiling.

"The Saint has a time machine into which he puts lovely and luscious Luisa, sending her back through time and space to become the sweetheart of Count Alucard.

"The Count, when night falls, is none other than Drácula, the evil nobleman with the unquenchable thirst for the blood of young maidens. These priestesses of sex, shut up in the depths of his castle, officiate over sensual and exciting rites in which pleasures of the flesh are brought to thrilling climaxes.

"Through Luisa, The Saint finds out where Drácula's legendary treasure is hidden. The search for this treasure, which could be of such benefit to the poor of the world, plunges Silver Mask and his beautiful ally into a vortex of wild orgies in which Drácula, his fiendish mind driven berserk, bursts all bounds sweeping our heroes along with him to share a stanic adventure with 13 gorgeous and shapely women, frenzied priestesses of pleasure, who offer a new gamut of lustful emotions in which nothing... absolutely nothing... is held back from the spectator, who keeps a close watch."

Of all the films to lose ... but while the "El Sexo" version is indeed lost, *Santo en el Tesoro de Drácula* is alive and available. And, truthfully, the additional scenes, while no doubt titillating, could not have added that much, although you can pretty much tell where they would have been inserted. Without them, the existing film is entertaining enough, a sci-fi/horror tale with Aldo Monti as Drácula, a role he would reprise in *Santo y Blue Demon vs. Dracula y Hombre Lobo*. Santo invents a time machine (!) and sends the professor's hot young daughter back in time. She is vampirized by Drac, who has a treasure, but Santo brings her back before she can be staked through the heart. (Why didn't he bring her back before she got bit?)

For some reason, despite the fact that he's already suceeded in conquering time travel, El Santo believes his machine doesn't work, and he wants to use it to find that treasure. The oppostion just revives Dracula himself, and the battle is joined. Drac has El Santo and crew trapped in a grotto, and all looks lost, but just then, a hole opens up, and the rays of the sun decimate the Vampire King and his minions. Must have been the first grotto in film history to come equipped with a skylight! A color Santo film that managed to retain the spirit of the black-and-whites.

Santo contra Capulina (*Santo vs. Capulina*, 1968)

(Producciones Zacarias) *Prod*: Alfredo Zacarias; *Dir*: René Cardona, Sr.; *Scr*: Alfredo Zacarias; *Photo*: León Sánchez; *Music*: Manuel Esperón; *Prod. Mgr*: José Llamas Ultreras; *Film Ed*: Gloria Shoemann, Eufemio Rivera; *Sound* (Sprvsr): James L. Fields.
  Cast: El Santo, Gaspar "Capulina" Henaine, Liza Castro, Crox Alvaredo, Carlos Agosti, Nothanael "Frankensten" León, Juan Garza, René Cardona III, Jorge Guzmán, Carlos Suárez, Guillermo "Lobo Negro" Hernández, Angel Di Stefani.

In El Santo's first "team-up" film, he is paired not with another wrestler, but with Capulina! Gaspar "Capulina" Henaine was born on January 6, 1930, and his family moved to Mexico City in 1933. He entered show business in order to buy a dog(!), and rose quickly on the ladder of fame. Starting out as a musical comedy performer, he then became the "Lou" half of the Abbott & Costello–like comedy team Viruta and Capulina, and then went on to make a successful series of solo pictures, many involving monsters.

By now there had already been many sinister and downright bizarre moments in El Santo's films; this time the emphasis is on laughs, pure and simple — and in that modest regard, the film succeeds (even El Santo joins in as a jokester). Though more cheaply done than usual, *Santo contra Capulina* is carried by its stars' personalities.

The plot, such as it is, concerns diamond smugglers and robot doubles (of nearly every principal), so there is plenty of opportunity for comedic confusion. One of the children's roles is played by Jorge Guzmán, who was not only Santo's real-life son, but would grow up to become the "official" El Hijo del Santo. Another "unmasking" is provided by Angel Di Stefani as Capulina's boss— Di Stefani had played the Aztec Mummy in the classic trilogy eleven years earlier.

Santo contra Blue Demon en el Atlántida (*Santo vs. Blue Demon in Atlantis*, 1968)

(Producciones Sotomayor) *Prod*: Jesús Sotomayor Martínez; *Dir*: Julián Soler; *Scr*: Rafael García Travesi; *Story*: Rafael García Travesi, Jesús Sotomayor Martínez; *Photo*: Raúl Martínez Solares; *Music Dir*: Gustavo Ceasar Carrión; *Makeup*: Delores Camarillo; *SPFX*: Raúl Martínez Solares; *Prod. Suprvsr*: Miguel Sotomayor Martínez; *Prod. Chief*: Armando Espinosa; *Film Ed*: Jorge Bustos; *Cam. Op*: Cirilo Rodríguez; *Sound Suprvsr*: James L. Fields.
  Cast: El Santo, Blue Demon, Jorge Rado (Aquiles/Hugo Ulrich), Rafael Banquells (Prof. Gerard), Silvia Pasquel (Juno), Carlos Suárez, Juan Garza, Olga Guillot, Augustín Martínez Solares, Magda Giner, Rosa María Pineiro, Griselda Mejia, Héctor Guzmán.

"The Commission on World Safety is deeply worried: The man called Aquiles has threatened the destruction of the earth, and has given proof of his ability to carry out his threat, has been recognized as Ulbrich, who, along with his wife, is more than 100 years old, and both appear in vigorous health. Fearful that the dangerous activities of Aquiles can bring on the Third World War, The Commission seeks the help of Prof. Gerard, who has invented a bomb interceptor and they send Agent Duval to Mexico for a meeting with X21 who will put him in contact with Gerard. These plans are immediately made known to Aquiles and he gives orders to eliminate the Professor.

"Along with these secret movements, Santo the formidable fighter and Secret Agent X21 have an electrifying battle against Blue Demon, accompanied by the strangest circumstances: mysterious hands try to liquidate Santo but appear to find Blue Demon, who on falling victim, is picked up by an ambulance. Santo notices something strange amidst the stretcher bearers and a terrible battle ensues. They all wear mysterious rings with the symbol 'A' which is able to disintegrate any opponent. After following the ambulance and then losing it, Santo finds himself in the home of a beautiful woman who tries to seduce him. He eludes this trap planned by Duval, who is attempting to take over Gerard. Duval meets his death, falling from a high window. At the same time, Aquiles discovers the elixir of Eternal Youth, which with the use of hypnosis, he is able to attract Blue Demon and orders him to seize Santo.

"Santo is in contact with Gerard when Blue Demon appears unexpectedly and makes a date with him. Santo believes him, but on noticing the ring of Aquiles, a fiery battle takes place and he frees himself. At once another agent, X25 appears. She is a beautiful girl who expresses interest in meeting Gerard. In order not to fall into a possible trap, Santo puts her to a test. She proves herself and takes him to a place called Atlántida, refuge of Aquiles. This is a submerged city where evading a mortifying attack, Santo descends by parachute and follows some frogmen to the refuge. He falls into their hands and discovers to his great surprise that X25 is in the service of Aquiles.

"Aquiles takes Santo to the hypnosis chamber, ordering him to find Gerard and destroy his laboratory and bring him the professor. Within a short time, Santo arrives at Gerard's laboratory and begins to destroy his instruments. But another identical masked man enters the scene and stops the destruction, fighting until victory. The second masked man is our real hero Santo, who had liberated himself from the hypnosis with the help of Juno, a disappointed agent of Aquiles, who had also brought about a reaction in Blue Demon. Santo takes Gerard and Blue Demon to Atlántida, and while the two wrestlers distract and get the watchmen out of the way, the Professor disables the bombs which were ready. Meanwhile, Juno is discovered and she gives the alarm so that Santo and his friends can get out of the fortress refuge before the explosion prepared by Gerard.

"A ferocious battle takes place. Aquiles orders the bombs exploded and is about to kill Santo but Blue Demon intervenes and Aquiles is killed instead. But before his death, he reverts to his true physical condition as an old man. Attempting to rescue Juno, they find her dead, having given her life to save her friends. As Santo and his friends leave by helicopter, a tremendous explosion destroys Atlántida … The End!"

Santo y Blue Demon contra los Monstruos (*Santo and Blue Demon vs. the Monsters*, 1969)

(Producciones Sotomayor) *Exec. Prod*: Heberto Dávila Guajardo; *Prod*: Jesús Sotomayor Martínez; *Dir*: Gilberto Martínez Solares; *Scr/Story*: Rafael García Travesi; *Photo*: Raúl Martínez Solares; *Mus. Dir*: Gustavo C. Carrión; *Makeup*: María Del Castillo; *Suprvsr*: Miguel Sotomayor Martínez; *Prod. Mgr*: Julio Guerrero Tello; *Asst. Dir*: Mario Llorca; *Film Ed*: Jorge Bustos; *Cam. Op*: Cirilo Rodríguez.

Cast: El Santo, Blue Demon, Alejandro "Black Shadow" Cruz ("Bad" Blue Demon), Jorge Rado (Dr. Hadler), Hedy Blue (Gloria Hadler), "Resortes," Vincente Lara (Wolf Man), Manuel "Tinieblas" Leal ("Franquestain" Monster), Gerardo Zepeda (Cyclops), Fernando Rosales (Mummy), David Alvizu (Vampire), Elsa María Tako, Yolanda Ponce (Vampire women), Carlos Suárez, Juan Garza.

An El Santo highspot highlights this lobby card from the All-Star game of Mexican monster/wrestler movies.

Though one of the more famous non-dubbed Santos, *Santo y Blue Demon contra los Monstruos* really doesn't deserve its rep (acquired mostly because of its "all-star" cast of monsters, which is both its blessing and its curse). It does indeed feature the "big four" of monsterdom (Frankenstein monster, vampire, werewolf, mummy), plus the Cyclops from *Ship of Monsters*(!), assorted vampire girls and sinister midgets (not to mention an "evil" Blue Demon), but the monster makeups are so poorly executed that it really makes one wish that for such an "all-star" event (wrestlers as well as monsters) a little more care had been taken with the fiends. Sometimes this enhances the outré mood, as in the unforgettable scene which the Frankenstein Monster (sporting a moustache and goa-

tee!) drives a sports car; but in the extended fight scenes ... well, if they can't fight good, they might as well look good! Manuel Leal, who played the Monster, later became masked wrestling star Tinieblas.

Sequences like the one just described indeed prove memorable and keep the film moving at a brisk pace, and there's even one truly terrifying moment when the werewolf murders a family in bloody style. If the makeup had been even half as impressive as, say, Steven Ritch's in *The Werewolf*, it could have become a standout scene in the annals of screen horror; as it is, one simply recalls that the lycanthrope looked like Gabby Hayes. The other makeups are equally disappointing on the colorless actors playing the "classic" monsters—Drácula is a slickster in a top hat, while the mummy is a spindly fellow whose bandages are much too clean for a 3000-year-old walking corpse. Gerardo Zepeda's recycled Cyclops probably comes off the best, but you already knew what you were getting with that one.

El Mundo de los Muertos (*The World of the Dead*, 1969)

(Cinematográficos Sotomayor) *Exec. Prod*: Heberto Dávila Guajardo; *Prod*: Jesús Sotomayor Martínez; *Dir*: Gilberto Martínez Solares; *Scr*: Rafael García Travesi; *Story*: Rafael García Travesi, Jesús Sotomayor Martínez; *Photo*: Raúl Martínez Solares; *Mus. Dir*: Gustavo C. Carrión; *Makeup*: María Del Castillo.

Cast: El Santo, Blue Demon, Pilar Pellicer (Alicia/Dona Damiana Velázquez), Carlos León, Carlos Suárez, Juan Garza, Antonio Raxel, Guillermo Bianchi, Mary Montiel, Betty Nelson, Eduardo MacGregor, Fernando Yapur.

"THE COLONIAL ERA. Exorcisms, macabre legends, pacts with the Devil. An epoc filled with terror and superstition when Damiana, a beautiful witch and dangerous ally of the Prince of Darkness, fights against goodness. Using the occult sciences, she forms an army of monstrous super-beings: The Unburied. With their help, she tries to get control of the Silver Masked Hero.

"A pure and noble love unites Santo to the forces of goodness, the love of the gentle Aurora. The Church, the feared tribunal of the Inquisition and the Silver Masked Man fight against the evil powers of Damiana, until they trap her at great sacrifice: the death of Aurora. The beautiful witch is condemned to the stake, from where she leaves her evil oath, which will be fulfilled after five generations: 'The last of my descendants will avenge me against the last descendants of each of the men who have condemned me.'

"THE PRESENT TIME. Alicic, the last descendant of Damiana, visits an old colonial convent with her fiancé, Enrique. This is the same place where the witch had been burned. The young girl feels a strange presence, and upon returning home, tells her impressions to her father, Don Alfonso. He is mortified and terrorized, as he notices his daughter is prisoner of a strange state of being, a kind of trance which comes over her in the night.

"Alfonso is quite right. Alicia is subject to the ghost of Damiana, who in order to fulfill her curse, takes possession of the girl's body, who with the aid of a cabalistic dagger, goes in search of Santo, the last descendant of the Silver Masked Hero.

"Santo finds himself bound up in a macabre adventure. Crime after crime takes place which leaves everyone stupefied and in fear for their lives. From the ancient tombs, The Unburied spring forth and come to life once again.

"Horrifying danger followed by increasingly terrifying events plus a titanic battle occurs to save the beautiful Alicia from the evil curse of Damiana. And Enrique, Don Alfonso and Santo face the forces of the powers of Darkness and Evil.

"Desperately searching throughout ancient books, they discover the motive of the terrible plot threatening them. Fighting against superstition and looking for the logic of the macabre, Santo and his allies are at the point of succumbing before the almost indestructible power of Damiana. Only at the very end are the incredible powers and intelligence of Santo able to dominate his diabolical enemies, destroy them and end the vicious curse of the centuries."

Santo contra los Cazadores de Cabezas (*Santo vs. the Head Hunters*, 1969)

(Producciones Zacarias) *Prod*: Miguel Zacarias; *Dir/Scr*: René Cardona, Sr.; *Story*: Adolfo Torres Portillo; *Photo*: Rosalio Solano; *Music*: Luis

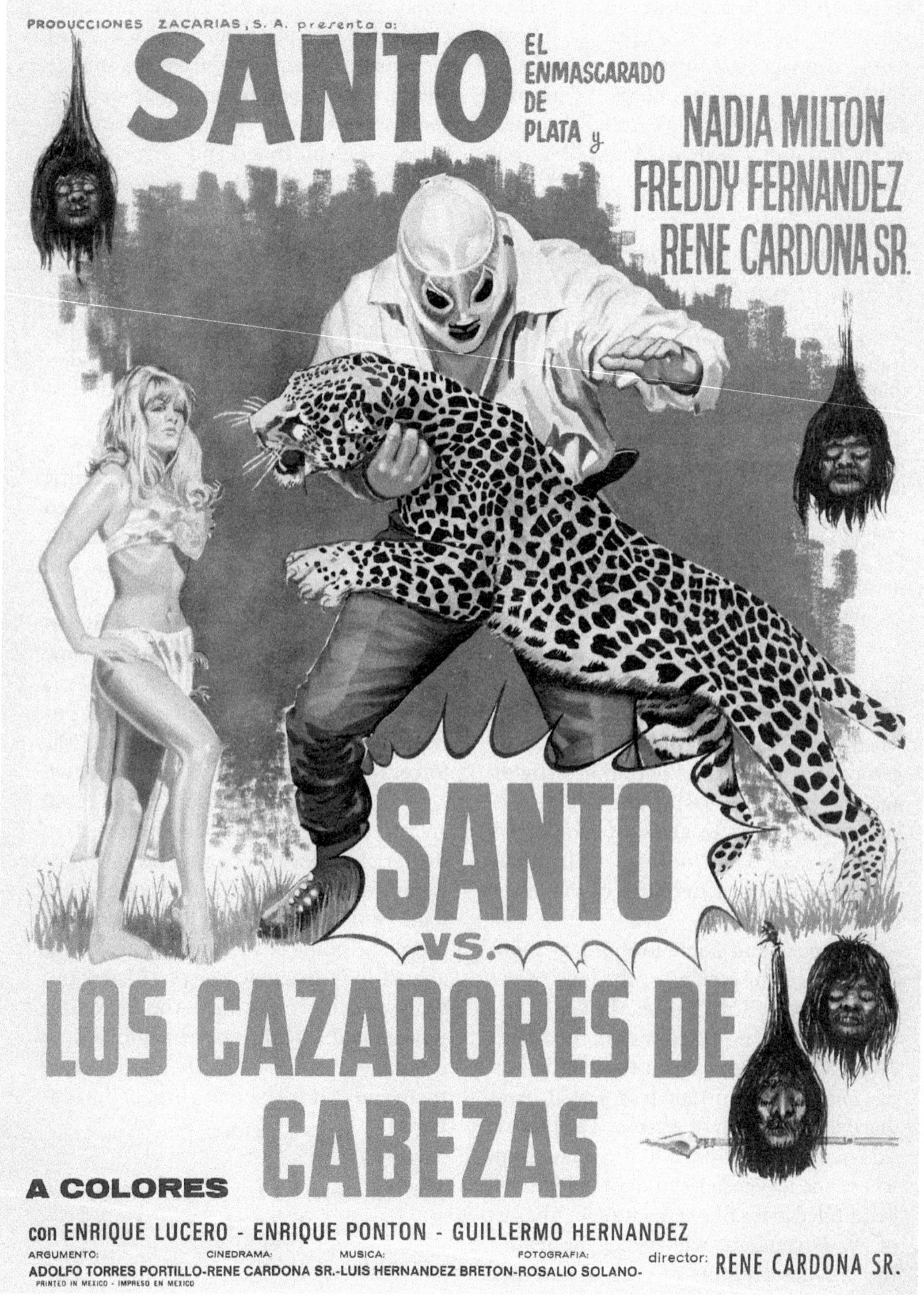

You'll get far more enjoyment out of this one-sheet than the film itself. While it looks like all the right elements are present, none are sucessfully exploited within the film itself.

Hernández Breton; *Asst. Dir*: Felipe Palomino; *Makeup*: Carmen Palomino; *Film Ed*: Eufemio Rivera; *Sound Ed*: José Li-Ho.

Cast: El Santo, Nadia Milton (Mariana de Grijalva), Freddy Fernández (Carlos), René Cardona, Sr. (Don Alfonso Grijalva), Carlos Suárez, Enrique Lucero, Enrique Ponton, Gillermo "Lobo Negro" Hernández, Margarito Luna, Antonio Miranda, Sergio Llanes, Victor Almazan, René Barrera, Caroline Barrett, Gloria Chávez, Arturo Silva.

I'm not going to mince words here, amigos. This one is boring with a capital "B," offering long stretches of Santo in a safari outfit endlessly trekking through the jungle searching for a pretty blonde who has been captured, crowned a princess, and is now about to be sacrificed (some perk!). The producers (literally) throw in a stuffed alligator, a leopard, and a jungle wrestling match in a vain attempt to liven things up. But check it out anyway to see Santo making like Marlon Perkins of TV's *Wild Kingdom*. Actually, he dresses like that in *The Vengeance of the Mummy*, too, so, honestly, you don't really need to see this unless you're a completist and/or writing a book.

Santo Frente a la Muerte (*Santo Faces Death*, 1969)

(Fonexsa Films— Tusisa Films) *Prod/Dir/Scr*: Fernando Orozco; *Photo*: Juan Manuel Herrera; *Music*: Daniel White; *Makeup*: Alvaro Bernal; *Prod. Mgr*: Pedro A. Rivera; *Co-Dir*: Fernando Osés; *Film Ed*: Reynaldo Portillo; *Prod. Mgr*: Pedro A. Rivera; *Chief of Staff*: Miguel Rincón; *Film Ed*: Reynaldo Portillo; *Cam. Op*: Enrique de la Rosa; *Sound Techs*: Jesús Jimenez, Luis Gutierrez.

Cast: El Santo, Elsa Cárdenas (Alicia), Mara Cruz (Lina), César Del Campo (Lt. Valle), Fernando Osés, Angel Menéndez, Celia Roldan, Johana Aloha (Agent X-25), Frank Brana, Antonio Pica, Ramiro Corso, Jimeno González, Luciano Merchan, Nelson Cuellar, Fransisco Tejada, Antonio Granados, Guillermo Morales, Manuel Velázquez.

Four El Santo films were released in 1969; the first two (*Santo y Blue Demon vs.*

Los Monstruos and *El Mundo de los Muertos*) were pretty good, but the quality dropped drastically with the other two, *Santo vs. the Head Hunters* and this one, *Santo Faces Death*. Well, didn't he in every picture? Everything from the title on out is uninspired; *Santo vs. Capulina* was an "A" production compared to *Faces Death* (oddly enough, the plots of both deal with diamond smugglers). Even Elsa Cárdenas proves lackluster in her usually tailor-made role of good/bad girl, here playing a female wrestler named Alicia who is only helping the smugglers because they are holding her father prisoner. El Santo is called in by the Colombian police to help with the case, and goes undercover as ... a masked wrestler. Every character except El Santo double-crosses everybody else, and just about every character except El Santo either winds up dead or in the pokey; so maybe it should have been called *Santo Wrestles a Few Times, but Everybody Else Faces Death*.

Santo contra los Jinetes del Terror (*Santo vs. the Riders of Terror*, a.k.a. *Los Leprosos y el Sexo*, 1970)

(Cinematográfica Calderón–Santo) *Prod*: Guillermo Calderón Stell; *Dir*: René Cardona, Sr.; *Scr*: René Cardona, Sr., Jesús Velázquez Quintero; *Story*: Jesús Velázquez Quintero; *Photo*: Raúl Martínez Solares; *Music Dir*: Gustavo César Carrión; *Prod. Mgr*: Carlos Suárez; *Makeup*: Felisa L. de Guevara; *Film Ed*: Jorge Bustos; *Sound Suprvsr*: James L. Fields; Eastmancolor.

Cast: El Santo, Armando Silvestre (Dario), Julio Aldama (Camerino), Mary Montiel (Carmen), Gregorio Cassals (José), Ivonne Govea (Lupe), Carlos Agosti (Dr. Ramos), Carlos Suárez, Nothanael "Frankenstein" León, Gloria Chávez, René Barrera, Margarito Luna, Victorio Blanco, Regino Herrera, Jesús Gómez, Alfredo Gutierrez, Armando Acosta.

It's a good thing that there was a "Sexo" version of this film, because, in its released form, it sure doesn't have much to recommend it — when all else fails, add nudity! Of course, *Los Leprosos y el Sexo* is "lost," so we have no way of knowing how much excitement this would've added, but it's a relatively tame story effort from "Bat" Velázquez, the same man who delivered the deliriously psychotronic Blue Demon film *La Sombra del Murciélago*. No monsters appear, unless one considers lepers to be monsters (though depicted in the ad art and selected camera angles as "monstrous," they are not portrayed in the film as such). It's actually a Western, with a masked wrestler instead of a cowboy hero, and even though that sounds like it has possibilities, it doesn't — El Santo's role could have (and probably *should* have) been played by the "other" Santo(s), Gaston. Like in *Santo vs. the Head Hunters*, Santo plays a straight action hero who just happens to be wearing a wrestling mask, and very little of his unique persona transfers to the setting.

La Venganza de las Mujeres Vampiro (*The Vengeance of the Vampire Women*, 1970)

(Películas Latinoamericanas — Cinematográfica Flama) *Prod*: Lic. Jorge García Besné; *Dir*: Federico Curiel; *Adapt/Dialogue*: Lic. Jorge García Besné, Fernando Osés; *Story*: Fernando Osés; *Photo*: José Ortiz Ramos; *Music*: Gustavo César Carrión; *Prod. Mgr*: Reynaldo Puente Portillo; *Prod. Chief*: Enrique Morfin; *Asst. Dir*: Manuel Ortega; *Film Ed*: Juan José Marino; *Cam. Op*: Felipe Mariscal; *Makeup*: Felisa Ladrón de Guevara; *Sound Suprvsr*: James L. Fields; Eastmancolor.

Cast: El Santo, Norma Lazareno (Patty), Gina Romand (Countess Mayra), Aldo Monti (Lt. Robles), Victor Junco (Dr. Brancov), Patricia Ferrer, Yolanda Ponce, Beto "El Bocario," Fernando Osés, Carlos Suárez, Nothanael "Frankenstein" León, El Rebelde Rojo, Federico Curiel, Alfonso Munguia.

After three lackluster efforts, El Santo made a comeback, aesthetically speaking,

with *The Vengeance of the Vampire Women*, another strong directorial effort from Fredrico Curiel that is actually *not* a sequel to *Santo vs. las Mujeres Vampiro*. The vampire queen, named Mayra this time around (and sensuously portrayed by Gina Romand), is revived by a mad scientist for his own purposes, but she winds up taking over the whole show. Apparently, the Santo family can't stay away from messing with vampires; yet another ancestor of El Santo has destroyed yet another coven, and, like Lorena Velázquez, Mayra takes it out on this year's model of the Silver-Masked Man. She also meets with the same amount of success as Lorena. Once more, the sexy vampires are put in their place by fire; all except for Mayra, who receives the honor of being personally staked by El Santo and returning to the state from whence she came. Meanwhile, the mad scientist who revived her from that state has grown tired of her honing in on his territory, and has decided to create a monster who'll obey him — but those man-made monsters never learn, and the ungrateful wretch polishes off his creator in the end.

Santo contra la Mafia del Vicio (*Santo vs. the Vice Mafia*, 1970)

(Películas Latinoamericanas — Cinematográfica Flama) *Prod*: Lic. Jorge García Besné; *Dir*: Federico Curiel; *Scr*: Fernando Osés, Lic. Jorge García Besné; *Story*: Fernando Osés; *Photo*: Alex Phillips; *Music*: Gustavo C. Carrión; *Prod. Mgr*: Luis Quintanilla Rico; *Film Ed*: José W. Bustos; *Cam. Op*: Ernesto Urbano Vazquez.

Cast: El Santo, Elsa Cárdenas (Elsa), Patricia Ferrer (Patricia), Mabel Luna (Mabel Moon), Victor Junco (Dr. Moon), Carlos Suárez, Jimmy Santy, Sonia Fuentes, María Fernanda, Rebelde Rojo, El Jaibo, Dagoberto Rodríguez, Rolando Valentino.

Made by most of the same team responsible for the preceding picture, *Santo contra la Mafia del Vicio* suffers from a lack

El Santo grapples with Gina Romand in this publicity photograph from *La Venganza de las Mujeres Vampiro* (1970).

of monsters, but it makes up for it in other ways. To begin with (literally), the pre-title prologue is almost a "music video"—but you've never seen anything like this on MTV! Popular junior lounge-lizard Jimmy Santy performs a jaunty number while attractive starlets do the hippy-hippy-shake in bikinis—and are joined in the fun by El Santo! Yes, it's a psychotronic treat to see the Silver-Masked Man swaying behind the wheel of an old clipper ship while the beach bunnies do the frug (in and of itself worth the price of admission). The beach bunnies are just a prelude to what seems to be the film's main selling point—showing (like *Santo in the Hotel of Death*) as many attractive women as possible wearing as lit-

tle as possible as often as possible (whether the actress played lead or support, if she appeared in this movie, she spent at least half of it in a bikini, or something very close). Which leads to another fine scene: Santo is snooping in the room of beautiful Elsa (Cárdenas) when she returns. Santo hides behind a curtain as she begins to disrobe; she spots the spy in her mirror, but a slight smile crosses her lips and she nonchalantly continues her striptease before going to bed. El Santo then sneaks out. Hey, why rock the boat, right? Jimmy Santy does another number for the road, and Patricia Ferrer prances around in a sexy showgirl outfit. The basic plot has something to do with drug smuggling, but that fact is apt to get lost amid all the jiggling.

Santo en la Venganza de la Momia (*Santo in the Vengeance of the Mummy*, 1970)

(Cinematográfica Calderón–Santo) *Prod*: Guillermo Calderón Stell; *Dir*: René Cardona, Sr.; *Scr*: Alfredo Salazar; *Photo*: Raúl Martínez Solares; *Prod. Mgr*: Carlos Suárez; *Music Dir*: Gustavo C. Carrión; *Makeup*: Margarita Ortega.

Cast: El Santo, Eric Del Castillo (Sergio Morales), Mary Montiel (Susana), César del Campo (Prof. Romero), Carlos Ancira, Tio Placido, Alma Rojo, Amada Zumaya, René Barrera, Rebelde Rojo, Gori Casanova, Goliat Ayala, Enrique Llanes, Carlos Suárez, Jorgito* (Agapito).

Not to be confused with the Spanish Paul Naschy film *La Venganza de la Momia*, this is actually a well-done Santo entry, and prophetic in regards to his next screen adversaries. Santo joins a mummy-finding expedition, and, just like in the Universal entries, no sooner is the mummy discovered than he starts polishing off the interlopers. And this is not your grandfather's mummy — no useless arm and dragging leg for him; no sir, this mummy is mobile, not only riding horses, but employing a bow and arrow! Margarita Ortega's makeup is one of the best ever done for a Mexican mummy — so it's doubly disappointing when the monster turns out to be a fake. In this sense, *Santo en la Venganza de la Momia* is the *Mark of the Vampire* of the Seventies (the 1935 Bela Lugosi chiller contained some of the most effectives scenes in any horror film of the Thirties, but likewise revealed its monster[s] to be mere mortals). Santo, Jr., Jorge Guzmán, returns as the son of the expedition's Indian guide, and features prominently on one of the Azteca lobby cards for the picture, his face contorted in a scream

of horror, with the mummy's head laying right in his lap! As far as the "Santo in a safari outfit" subgenre goes, *La Venganza de la Momia* is infinitely superior to *Vs. the Head Hunters*.

Las Momias de Guanajuato (*The Mummies of Guanajuato*, 1970)

(Películas Latinoamericanas) *Prod*: Rogelio Agrasánchez, Sr.; *Dir*: Federico Curiel; *Scr*: Rafael García Travesi; *Story*: Rogelio Agrasánchez, Sr.; *Photo*: Enrique Wallace; *Music*: Gustavo César Carrión; *Makeup*: Carmen Palomino; *Prod. Mgr*: Luis Quintanilla Rico; *Asst. Dir*: Manuel Muñoz; *Film Ed*: José W. Bustos.

Cast: Blue Demon, Mil Máscaras, El Santo, Elsa Cárdenas (Lina), Patricia Ferrer (Alicia), Jorge Pinguino (Pinguino), Manuel Leal ("Satán"), Carlos Suárez, Mabel Luna, Yolande Ponce, Martha Angelica, "Picoro," Federico Curiel.

You'll read more about this particular entry in the Blue Demon chapter, and rightly so; the film belongs to him and Mil Máscaras. A classic genre entry, this first teaming of the "Big Three" is usually thought of by the public as a "Santo" film. In truth, Santo has very little screen time compared to the other two, basically engaging in a wrestling match with the head mummy before he became a mummy, and showing up to distribute flame pistols(!) to the others at the climax. It's as if he was brought in at the last minute; and, in truth, he was, creating a resentment in Blue Demon that lasted until the day he died. Blue Demon was extremely angry that he and Mil did all the "work," while Santo came in at the end to reap all the glory. Personalities aside, though, this is, as stated, classic stuff. The pace is brisk, the performances assured, and the Mummy makeup well-done and creepy (and based on an actual real-life exhibit in the city of

---

**Jorgito (or "Little Jorge")— Jorge Guzmán, a.k.a. El Hijo del Santo.*

From the Mummies, More Mummies Department. *Top*: The coolest lobby card from one of the coolest genre films ever — how can any mere supernatural mummy hope to stand up against the flame pistol of El Santo? *Bottom*: Some photographs just say it all by themselves. This is one (*Santo en la Venganza de la Momia*).

Guanajuato, which remains on display to this day). There's the usual zany musical interlude (this time it's just downright weird — some sort of madrigal played by a bunch of guys dressed like Robin Hood!). And to top it off, all the assorted wrestlers, wrestlers' girlfriends, kids and general populace on hand get into the act! Despite Blue Demon's petulance, the climax really is grand, as the three heroes make a seeming last stand against the rampaging horde of mummies, until Santo has Mil fetch those trusty flame pistols out of Santo's convertible! (Doesn't everybody keep one in their glove compartment in case of mummy attacks?) And seeing the three of them together, taking down the mummies with said pistols, is undeniably exciting because it's the three of them; by this point, the original audiences must have been on their feet.

(See Mil Máscaras chapter for additional information.)

Santo vs. la Hija de Frankenstein (*Santo vs. the Daughter of Frankenstein*, 1971)

(Cinematográfica Calderón) *Prods*: Guillermo Calderón Stell, Santo; *Dir*: Miguel M. Delgado; *Scr*: Fernando Osés; *Photo*: Raúl Martínez Solares; *Music*: Gustavo C. Carrión; *Prod. Mgr*: Carlos Suárez; *Makeup*: Román Juárez; *Prod. Chief*: Jorge Cardeña; *Asst. Dir*: Felipe Palomino; *Film Ed*: Jorge Bustos; *Art Dir*: José Rodríguez Grananda; *Sound Suprvsr*: James L. Fields; *Sound Ed*: José Li-Ho; Eastmancolor.

Cast: El Santo, Gina Romand (Freda Frankenstein), Roberto Cañedo (Dr. Yanco), Sonia Fuentes (Elsa), Anel (Norma), Carlos Agosti (Don Elias), Carlos Suárez, Gerardo Zepeda (Ursus, Truxon), Jorge Casanova, Carlos Bravo y Fernández, Domingo Bazan, David Ayala, Goliat Ayala, Ismael Ramírez, Vincente Lara, Enrique Llanes.

Hot on the heels of his triumph in *Las Momias de Guanajuato*, El Santo finally meets a Frankenstein proper. Considered lost for many years, bootleg copies of this film began to circulate around the start of the new millennium, and a legitimate edition appeared shortly thereafter. Lost films have a nasty habit of acquiring reputations that often prove disproportionate to the actual thrills delivered when and if they're rediscovered; but, thankfully, *Santo vs. the Daughter of Frankenstein* does not disappoint. In fact, it's one of the better El Santo films of the 1970s, and no, it has absolutely no connection to the 1958 Allied Artists feature *Frankenstein's Daughter*, itself a small miracle of psychotronica.

Gorgeous Gina Romand makes her second appearance as a major villainess, and, fittingly for the Daughter of Frankenstein, she is mad scientist and monster all in one! This doesn't stop her from creating two more of her own (both played by the maestro, Gerardo Zepeda)—one a creature that bears a suspicious resemblance to the fiend that Gerardo portrayed in *Night of the Bloody Apes*, the other a more conventional Karloff-type monster (called "Ursus"). Zepeda even manages a few Karloff-like moments of pathos when he is befriended by Santo (who has just beaten the crap out of him *and* impaled him), and convinced to—you guessed it—turn on his mistress.

Misión Suicida (Suicide Mission, 1971)

(Puerto-Mex Films/Jorge Camargo) *Prod*: Jorge Camargo; *Assoc. Prod*: Carlos E. Camacho; *Co-Prod*: Roxana Bellini, J. Díaz Santiago; *Dir*: Federico Curiel; *Scr*: Rafael García Travesi; *Story*: Fernando Osés; *Photo*: Augustín Jimenez; *Music*: Gustavo C. Carrión; *Makeup*: M. Ortega.

Cast: El Santo, Lorena Velázquez (Ana Silva), Elsa Cárdenas, Dagoberto Rodríguez, César del Campo, Juan Gallardo, Pola Sanders, Angela Rodríguez, Carlos Hennings, Margarito Luna, Roxana Bellini, Patricia Ferrer, Fernando Osés, Carlos Suárez, "The Teen-Agers."

Well, you can't win 'em all. *Misión Suicida* proved a bit of a let-down after the

SANTO CONTRA EL DOCTOR MUERTE

Top: El Santo squares off against the titular physician in this rare Spanish lobby card; while (*bottom*) Gina Romand, as Frankenstein's daughter, goes nuts again.

previous few, although it does have some perks—El Santo looks rather spiffy in a black leather jacket, and Lorena Velázquez is along for the ride (only this time, she's on El Santo's side). She plays a secret agent who teams up with El Santo, and she infiltrates a squad of female assassins who wear bikinis, mini-skirts and go-go boots (always recommended as fighting attire). So where's Pussy Galore? After Lorena works her way into the gang, she gets to wear go-go boots, too, and even sings a song, though it's not quite as rockin' as her number in *Ship of Monsters*. The assassinesses (assassinettes?) work for the Ratzi Nazis, who work for the Commies, and they've all kidnapped a plastic surgeon to change the face of a Ratzi scientist. Naturally, Interpol and its vast resources are ill-equipped to handle the job, so they call in El Santo. He and Lorena save the plastic surgeon (and his daughter, who had been kidnapped for good measure), and the climax reveals that he'd operated on the Ratzi all right—he carved swastikas into his cheeks!

Misión Suicida was one of the last roles for Dagoberto Rodríguez, who died in 1974. Primarily a Western star, his first movie was *The Ghost Rider* (1946). He co-starred with all three major wrestling film stars, making three films with El Santo, two with Mil Máscaras, and one with Blue Demon.

Asesinos de Otros Mundos (*Killers from Other Worlds*, 1971)

(Filmadora Chapultepec) *Prod*: Pedro Galindo Aguilar; *Dir*: Ruben Galindo; *Adapt*: Ramón Obón; *Story*: Ramón Obón, Ruben Galindo; *Photo*: Raúl Martínez Solares; *Music*: Jesús Zarsosa; *Makeup*: Margarita Ortega; *Asst. Dir*: Jesús Marin; *Film Ed*: Jorge Bustos; *Prod. Mgr*: José Luis Orduna Guzmán.

Cast: El Santo, Sasha Montenegro (Karen Bernstein), Juan Gallardo (Licur), Carlos Agosti (Malkosh), Carlos Suárez (Dr. Bernstein), Gerardo Zepeda, Marco Antonio "Viruta" Campos, Sonia Fuentes, César Valentino, Armando Acosta, Marcelo Villamil, Patricia Borges.

Asesinos de Otros Mundos is lifted from the routine by one of the cheesiest monsters ever committed to film in any language. Technically a Blob from Outer Space, in reality it's three or four guys waddling along underneath a huge spray-painted tent or sheet or something. When it "eats" somebody, they merely lift up the edge of the sheet, and the "victim" crawls underneath! This other-worldly creature is so terrifying that its victims can barely contain their hilarity as it descends upon them. Another psychotronic sequence has El Santo captured by one of the tag-team of villains, and forced to face off against three goons in gladiator(!) gear—one of them even goes after the Saint with a flame thrower! Finding that it's taking much too long to subdue the gladiators with the usual wrestling moves, El Santo just grabs a tommy gun from one of the security guards and mows 'em down! So much for good sportsmanship! This brings back fond memories of Captain Marvel burp-gunning baddies (in the back!) in *The Adventures of Captain Marvel* (1941). Another serial, *The Crimson Ghost* (1946), is evoked by the use of poison-gas collars that keep henchmen and kidnapees alike in line. At the priceless climax, the blob chases El Santo and pals into the mountains, where El Santo traps it in a cavern, thereby saving the world from death by laughter.

El Águila Real (*The Royal Eagle*, a.k.a. *Santo y la Tigresa en el Águila Real*, 1971)

(Producciones Raúl Portillo-Luis Quntanilla) *Exec. Prod*: Luis Quintanilla; *Dir*: Alfredo B. Crevenna; *Scr*: Raúl Portillo; *Story*: Raúl Portillo, Luis Quintanilla; *Photo*: Rosalio Solano;

Music: Gustavo César Carrión; *Makeup*: Margarita Ortega; *Asst. Dir*: Mario Lorca; *Film Ed*: Rafael Ceballos; *Sound Ed*: Raúl Portillo.

Cast: El Santo, Irma Serrano (Irma Morales, La Tigresa "The Tigress"), Jorge Lavat, Juan Gallardo, Fernando Osés, Carlos Suárez, Soledad Acosta, Jorge Patiño, Domingo Bazan, Carlos León, Guillermo Galvez, Ines Murillo, Angela Rodríguez.

An alternate title for this one could've been "Santo Meets the Big Valley," because the heroine is a no-nonsense woman who owns a ranch (that someone wants control of, naturally)—and wields a mean bullwhip, besides! "The Tigress" is portrayed by big, sexy brunette Irma Serrano, who had co-starred with El Santo ten years earlier in *Santo vs. the Zombies*. In the intervening years, Ms. Irma became sort of the Marilyn Monroe of Mexico—nose job, boob job, slept with the president—and became more famous for her exploits off-screen. *Tigresa* sports some surreal "romantic interlude" scenes with El Santo and Tiger-Lady, with them sharing horseback rides and a picnic lunch. There's not much in the way of monsters, except for one short hunchback and one fall mute; and we discover that "the Tigress" is neither attentive nor observant—the tall one turns out to be her bastard brother, and the hunchback works for her! These positives, however, are overshadowed by the number of animals killed or injured during the course of events (some of the offenses are implied, but others are all-too-obviously real), and these incidents happen with such frequency that it becomes not only distracting, but rather disheartening; El Santo might have been the champion of the people, but he sure didn't do much for his furry friends on this particular set. This was Juan Gallardo's last Santo; he had appeared in four of the previous five, as well as *Capulina contra los Vampiros*.

Santo y Blue Demon vs. Drácula y el Hombre Lobo (*Santo vs. Dracula and the Wolf Man*, 1972)

(Cinematográfica Calderón) *Prods*: Guillermo Calderón Stell, Santo; *Dir*: Miguel M. Delgado; *Scr*: Alfredo Salazar; *Photo*: Rosalio Solano; *Music*: Gustavo C. Carrión; *Prod. Mgr*: Carlos Suárez; *Makeup*: Margarita Ortega; Eastmancolor.

Cast: El Santo, Blue Demon, Aldo Monti (Drácula), Augustín Martínez Solares ("Rufus Rex," the Wolf Man), Nubia Marti (Lina), María Eugenia San Martín (Laura Cristaldi), Jorge Mondragón (Prof. Cristaldi), Wally Barron, Carlos Suárez, Angel Blanco, Renato el Hippie.

This was the last bona-fide classic that both Santo and Blue Demon would appear in, and the last (and most satisfying) time they would face the classic Universal-style monsters. (They would later meet up with another member of the Frankenstein family, but the monster was nothing like the Karloff conception.) Drácula is aptly portrayed by Aldo Monti, who had previously essayed the role in *Santo en el Tesoro de Drácula*, and would return to the series later in the year as director, for *Anónimo Mortal*. Augustín Martínez Solares, although no Lon Chaney, Jr., makes a good wolfman; his relationship to Drácula parallels the relationship between Bela Lugosi and Matt Willis in *Return of the Vampire* (1944), only Solares receives far more to do, and isn't as whiny. Some auxiliary werewolves and living dead girls further liven things up for the protagonists, and the result is pure, grand, comic book style.

Since Alfredo Salazar wrote the script, one has to expect scenes lifted from other movies, and he doesn't disappoint here. We get yet another Mexican version of the resurrection scene from *Dracula, Prince of Darkness* when Professor Cristaldi's throat is cut and the blood drips into Drácula's coffin to revive the Count. Salazar adds new spin to the old resurrection record by employing the same method to resuscitate the Wolfman. Salazar also harkens back to *El Mundo de los Vampiros* by having the title fiends meet their demise in a pit of stakes. Drácula should've consulted Count Subotai from that earlier film on the wisdom of such decor.

(See the Blue Demon chapter for additional information)

Santo contra los Secuestradores (*Santo vs. the Kidnappers*, 1972)

(Oro Films–Puerto-Mex Films–Juan Camargo) *Exec. Prod*: Eduardo de la Barcena; *Dir*: Federico Curiel; *Scr*: Alfredo Salazar; *Story*: Fernando Osés; *Photo*: Luis Medina; *Film Ed*: Reynaldo Puente Portillo; *Sound*: Enrique Rodríguez.

Cast: El Santo, Ernesto "Evaristo" Alban, Guillermo Galvez (Don César), Rossy Mendoza (Elsa), Elizabeth Sartore (Rosita), Fernando Osés, Carlos Suárez, Oscar Guerra, Carlos Guerra, Marcelo Guerra, Carlos Camcho Espiritu.

Santo y Blue Demon vs. Drácula y el Hombre Lobo was probably the last great Santo film. Despite a decent track record up through the early 1970s, the genre as a whole, as well as its most famous representative, was starting to lose steam; and even though Santo would continue making films for another ten years, the great moments, like the movies themselves, would come few and far between. El Santo had already met up with one funnyman (Capulina), and so did not really need to be paired with another, but was nonetheless stuck with Evaristo in this entry. Apart from Evaristo's unfunny shtick, *Santo contra los Secuestradores* is not a bad little film, although it has absolutely no fantasy elements (not even a seance). The producers would make up for this omission in the very next outing.

Perhaps not coincidentally, around this time the El Santo (and similar genre) movie poster art began to decline as well. Like with the films themselves, all hope was not lost, and some sparkling pieces would still be produced; but, in general, even less care was being taken with the graphics than with some of the productions.

Santo contra la Magia Negra (*Santo vs. Black Magic*, 1972)

(Películas Latinoamericanas–Cinematográfica Flama) *Prod*: Jorge García Besné; *Co-Prod*: Joseph W. Saliba; *Dir*: Alfredo B. Crevenna; *Adapt*: Rafael García Travesi; *Story*: Fernando Osés; *Photo*: Alfredo Uribe; *Music*: Henry Celestin; *Makeup*: Castaneda.

Cast: El Santo, Elsa Cárdenas (Lorna), Sasha Montenegro (Bellamira), Gerty Jones (Michelle), César Del Campo, Fernando Osés, Carlos Suárez, Guillermo Galvez, Lyne Williams Rouzier Ballet [with Nancy Saliba and Edmond Baily], "Les Deficilles de Petionville."

This offered fantastic elements aplenty, not the least of which was sexy Sasha Montenegro, who is both gorgeous and lethal as the voodoo priestess Bellamira. This Mexican *Live and Let Die* also featured zombies, an explosive more powerful than the H-bomb, and a lot of voodoo rituals and crazed fruggin'—all shot on location in Haiti (all, that is, except the wrestling scenes, which were lifted from *Santo en la Venganza de las Mujeres Vampiro*). Points, as always, are deducted for cruelty to animals (in this case, a live goat is sacrificed), but this is almost made up for by the sight of Elsa Cárdenas flouncing through the jungle in a baby-doll nightgown. The harrowing climax offers "the Test of Damballah," in which both El Santo and Bellamira but their hands into a basket of snakes. Both are bitten, but apparently Sasha wasn't in as good with Damballah as she thought, as only Santo passes the test.

The poster art and lobby cards for *Santo contra la Magia Negra* are a good ex-

Top: "Comedian" Evaristo impersonates our silver-masked hero in this bizarre scene from *Santo vs. los Secuestadores* (1973). *Bottom*: A group shot from El Santo's next-to-last movie, *El Puño de la Muerte* (1982), surrounded by Grace Renat, Tinieblas, and the tuft-monster.

ample of the series' decline, graphics-wise. All of the standard elements are there — El Santo, a girl in flimsy nightgown about to be burned at the stake by villagers, etc.— but the composition is off; the elements are poorly-placed, and weakly rendered at that. By contrast, the poster for the Spanish release is gorgeous, and should have replaced the homefront design.

Las Bestias del Terror
(*The Beasts of Terror*, 1972)

(Películas Latinoamericanas) *Exec. Prod*: Fernando Osés; *Dir*: Alfredo B. Crevenna; *Scr*: Fernando Osés; *Photo*: Minervino Rojas, Rafael J. Remy; *Music*: Rafael H. Lima; *Makeup*: María Antonia del Rio; *Assoc. Prod*: César Del Campo; *Film Ed*: Jorge W. Bustos; *Prod. Mgr*: Francisco del Busto; *Asst. Dir*: José G. Prieto; *Cam. Asst*: Manuel Jimeniz.

Cast: El Santo, Blue Demon, Elsa Cárdenas (Nora), Victor Junco (Dr. Matthews), César Del Campo (Tony Carelli), Fernando Osés (Sandro), Alma Ferrari, Carlos Suárez, Antonio de Hud, Quintin Bulnes, Indania del Canal, María Antonia del Rio, Ismael Ramírez, Ivan Curiel.

"Lucky's men give Pedro a terrible beating, for he owes them money. Nora, Pedro's mistress, talks him into kidnapping Susy, for whom they can get a high ransom. After the kidnapping, Nora kills a man in order to take his car and escape. At that point, she, Susy and Pedro are attacked by men in the pay of Dr. Mathius, a scientist experimenting with dead bodies. Nora's beauty impresses the aloof scientist, who momentarily interrupts the project of transmitting the blood of the young people to the dead bodies, in order to study the cerebral hormones of these corpses. The two girls are locked up together with several women who behave like Zombies. Rocco, the doctor's mute servant, has fallen in love with Susy.

"Susy's sister goes for help to Tony, a private investigator who in turn requests the assistance of Santo and Blue Demon.

They each start investigating on their own. Santo is the first to discover a connection between the kidnapping of the young girl and the stealing of dead bodies. Tony is helped by the information received from Alma, his sweetheart, a dancing girl in Lucky's nightclub. However, Tony falls in a trap set by Sandro, the doctor's main assistant. Tony is set free by Santo and Blue Demon. The doctor ships the zombie women out, while Pedro is attacked by a pack of dogs who tear him to pieces. Sandro, believing himself in danger, sells his secret to Lucky and escapes to Puerto Rico. He is followed by Blue Demon, who beats him mercilessly, thus obtaining the information he is after. Sandro dies suddenly and mysteriously.

"At Nora's suggestion, Susy flirts with Rocco and he saves their lives when they are caught by the doctor in their search for Pedro, whom they find dead. At the cost of his life, Rocco prevents the two girls being covered in paraffin, which would have turned them into wax figures. When the doctor is on the point of throwing them into a piranha-infested pool, Santo, Blue Demon, and Tony arrive. A fierce battle takes place with the doctor's men, who are beaten by the wrestlers. To avenge the death of Pedro, Nora pushes the doctor into the deadly pool, but as he falls, the doctor takes hold of her dress and they both disappear in the water. Susy is set free and Santo and Blue Demon once again emerge victorious from a dangerous adventure."

The Beasts of Terror was the last genre picture for Victor Junco (1917–1988), who played the mad scientist. Twenty years earlier, he helped usher in that very genre as one of the leading men of *El Enmascarado de Plata*. He worked with Blue Demon and Mil Máscaras as well, appearing in *Blue Demon contra Cerebros Infernales*, and with Mil in *Enigma de Muerte*.

Santo vs. las Lobas (*Santo vs. the She-Wolves*, 1972)

(Estudios Jimenez Pons Hermanos) *Exec. Prod*: Jaime Jimenez Pons; *Dirs*: Jaime Jimenez Pons, Ruben Galindo; *Scr*: Ramón Obón, Jaime Jimenez Pons; *Photo*: Raúl Domínguez, Victor Gaitin; *Makeup*: Irene Bustos, Antonio Ramírez; *Prod. Mgr*: Héctor Luna; *Asst. Dir*: Javier Duran; *Cam*: Armando Castillon, Rafael Chávez, Carlos Cuenca.

Cast: El Santo, Rodolfo De Anda (César/Eric Harker), Gloria Mayo (Adriana), Jorge Russek (Lican), Federico Falcón (Jaime Pons [!]), Nubia Marti, Carlos Suárez, Rosa Furman, Bruno Rey, Tamara Garina, Carlos Jordán, Nora Wolf, Silvia Mowat, Marga Dunhill, Guillermo Ayala, Patricia Borges, Luis Ruvalcaba, Leticia Ochoa, Manuel Moreno, Miguel Lara.

A Mexi-film without Fernando Osés is like a Hammer film without Michael Ripper; it feels just slightly … off-center. But despite Oses' absence, *Santo vs. the She-Wolves* is one of the brighter spots in the mid-seventies Santo series. In fact, it would work well as a straight horror film without Santo's presence, and so his role comes as a bonus. *Santo vs. las Lobas* looks eerily like a mid-seventies' TV movie, and it indeed belongs to a group of his and Blue Demon's films that appear as though the small set was their original destination, but were instead blown up to 35mm and released theatrically. Despite this apparent handicap, *She-Wolves* (not connected to the '64 Kitty De Hoyos classic, by the way) generates a genuinely creepy atmosphere and some gripping shock moments.

The dual role(s) of twin brothers César and Eric Harker (nice touch) is essayed by Rodolfo de Anda, son of actor/director/producer Raúl de Anda. Though involved with very few genre films, Rodolfo proved to be a chip off the old block, as he, too, had a long and respected career as an actor/director/producer.

Anónimo Mortal (*Anonymous Death Threat*, 1972)

(Producciones Jimenez Pons Hermanos) *Exec. Prod*: Jaime Jimenez Pons; *Dir*: Aldo Monti; *Scr*: Carlos Enrique Taboada; *Photo*: Ricardo Carretero; *Asst. Dir*: Jorge Santoyo; *Makeup*: Irene Bustos; *Film Ed*: Marcelino Aupart; *Lighting*: Alfonso López.

Cast: El Santo, Armando Silvestre (Ponce), Tere Velázquez (Yvette), Sasha Montenegro (Ester), Geregorio Cassals, Carlos Suárez, Jorge Rado, Jorge Mondragón, El Polaco, El Nazi [you just knew he had to be in this one!], Raymundo Capetillo, Xavier Masse, Fernando Wagner, Antonio Raxel, Armando Arreola, Margarita Herman, José Mora, Manolo Calvo.

This intended-for-TV feature was directed by Aldo Monti, who had played Drácula twice opposite El Santo, and now had his chance for revenge! Monti, born in Rome in 1929, began his acting career in 1952 in Venezuela, and came to Mexico in 1955. His other genre films include *Misterios de la Magia Negra* and *Santo en la Venganza de las Mujeres Vampiro*, in which he, oddly enough, didn't play a vampire. El Santo once again goes up against Nazis, although there aren't nearly as many fantastic elements here as in his previous close encounters of the Ratzi kind — *Santo vs. Blue Demon en el Atlántida* and *Misión Suicida*. Sasha Montenegro and Lorena V's sis Tere are on hand to provide spice, and Armando Silvestre repeats the "Inspector Ponce" role he had previously played in two Blue Demon films from the same time period, *La Mafia Amarilla* and *Noche de Muerte*. The Nazis this time are neither immortal nor working for Commies, but are simply up to their old tricks of trying to reestablish their fan base, which, by the looks of them, is minuscule to begin with (and is even smaller by the time El Santo finishes mopping up the place with their Aryan butts). The climax is fitting, ironic, and shudder-inducing, as the Head Kraut meets his demise in his personal gas chamber.

Santo y Blue Demon contra el Dr. Frankenstein (*Santo and Blue Demon vs. Dr. Frankenstein*, 1973)

(Cinematográfica Calderón–Santo) *Prods*: Guillermo Calderón Stell, Santo; *Dir*: Miguel M. Delgado; *Scr*: Francisco Cavazos, Alfredo Salazar; *Story*: Alfredo Salazar; *Photo*: Rosalio Solano; *Music*: Gustavo César Carrión; *Prod. Mgr*: Carlos Suárez; *Makeup*: Román Juárez; *Film Ed*: Jorge Bustos; *Sound Sprvsr*: James L. Fields.

Cast: El Santo, Blue Demon, Sasha Montenegro (Alicia), Jorge Russek (Dr. Irving[!] Frankenstein), Ivonne Govea, Carlos Suárez, Jorge Mondragón, El Angel, Ray Mendoza, Enrique Vera, César Valentino, El Gran Markus, José Rojas y Marhala.

I have just two words to say about this movie: Alfredo Salazar. As you know by now, Abel's brother was a prolific genre screenwriter who had some good ideas—and just loved to recycle them. Having written the stone-classic *Las Luchadoras vs. el Médico Asesino*, he then proceeded to write it again and again, and this entry is one of those times. Not that there's anything wrong with that, but the results could have been a lot more lively, considering the source. That being said, *Santo and Blue Demon vs. Dr. Frankenstein* still offers some great scenes. The opener, for instance, is a dead ringer for the opening of *El Médico Asesino*, but with a twist. A woman is abducted from the street and taken back to a secret lab for a brain transplant, which fails. Now here's the twist ... instead of transplanting the brain into a monster, Dr. Frankenstein transplants it into another woman, who also dies—and then both are revived by the doc, who orders them to wipe out their families! It becomes rather tough sledding after that, but there *is* that operating room scene (see the Blue Demon chapter). The climax is right out of *Médico Asesino* again: Doc F. dons a wrestling mask to pose as a promoter; his

creation wrestles; and they both fall to their deaths from a tower. That's no twist. Though a decent effort, *vs. Dr. Frankenstein* could have been so much more.

Trivia note: El Gran Markus, a "name" wrestler in his own right, essayed the part of El Médico Asesino in the Blue Demon outing *Los Campeones Justicieros* (1971).

Santo contra el Dr. Muerte (*Santo vs. Dr. Death*, 1973)

(Cinematográfica Pelimex) *Exec. Prod*: Joaquín Mortera Díaz; *Prod*: Manuel Torres; *Dir*: Rafael Romero Marchant; *Scr*: Rafael Romero Marchant, José Luis Navarro Basso; *Photo*: Godofredo García Segura; *Makeup*: Mariano García; *Film Ed*: Antonio Gimeno; *Art Dir*: Jaime P. Cubero; *Cam. Op*: Domingo Solano.

Cast: El Santo, Carlos Romero Marchant (Paul), Helga Line (Sara), Jorge Rigaud (Dr. Mann), Antonio Pica, Marta Miller, Carlos Suárez, Maribel Hidalgo, Frank Brana, Eduardo Calvo, Lorenzo Robledo, Eulalia del Pino, Betsabe Ruiz.

The last of the four Santo films that have been English-dubbed, *Santo vs. Dr. Death* is the only one in color. In retrospect, it seems like a rather odd choice; not that it's a bad one, but it just seems more logical to go with a little higher-profile subject, like *Santo and Blue Demon vs. Dracula and the Wolf Man*. The choice probably had something to do with the fact that it was a Spanish production rather than a Mexican one, and therefore was subject to a different set of contractual rules. Consequently, the dubbing was not done by the expected K. Gordon Murray crew (it was possibly dubbed in Canada, although Santo never says "Eh," so it's hard to tell).

There's a twist in the mad doctor's tale this time; not only is he a surgeon, but an art thief! He steals famous paintings, kidnaps beautiful models, and then forges the paintings by extracting tumors from the models, thereby killing them in the process ... eh? But wouldn't it have been far easier to have had somebody simply *paint* a copy? Though a weird premise, it's handled well, especially at the wild climax in which the art-doc makes his escape by speedboat. Santo leaps into the craft, a furious battle ensues, and the Saint makes a well-timed exit as the boat splinters on the shore.

On a fashion note, apparently nobody in Spain ever told Santo that wrestling masks and cardigan sweaters don't mix.

Santo en el Misterio de la Perla Negra (*Santo in the Mystery of the Black Pearl,* 1974)

("Juan J. Ortega presents a Film by Luisa María Fernández") *Dir/Scr*: Fernando Orozco; *Photo*: Juan Manuel Herrera; *Music*: Gustavo César Carrión; *Asst. Dir*: Javier Carreño; *Prod. Mgr*: Pedro Rivera; *Film Ed*: Reynaldo Portillo; *Cam. Op*: Enrique de la Rosa.

Cast: El Santo, María Eugenia San Martín (Wu-Li), Guillermo Galvez (Che Dávila), Fernando Osés, Carlos Suárez (Puerto Rican policeman), Antonio Pica (Andrés Cortes), Juan Garza, Mara Cruz, Frank Brana (Julio), Orlando Velez.

The only real mystery in this film is what it's actually supposed to be about, because there's nary a black pearl in sight. It *is* about diamond smuggling, so why didn't they just call it "The Mystery of the Black Diamond?" There's none of those either, but at least that way they could have featured Kiss on the soundtrack. On the other hand, it could've been called "The Mystery of the Shark," since said fish features prominently on the one-sheet; but, by Jorge, there's none of those in the film either! Did I mention this was Burt Reynolds' first appearance in a Santo movie? Yep, sure is, courtesy of stock footage. In fact, there's a lot of stock footage, swiped from various movies, and the attempt to integrate this flick's performers into it remains half-hearted, at best.

Santo y Mantequilla en la Venganza de la Llorona (*Santo and Mantequilla in the Vengeance of the Crying Woman,* 1974)

(Cinematográfica Calderón) *Prods*: Guillermo Calderón Stell, Santo; *Dir*: Miguel M. Delgado; *Scr*: Francisco Cavazos; *Photo*: Jorge Stahl, Jr.; *Music*: Gustavo César Carrión; *Prod. Mgr*: Carlos Suárez; *Makeup*: Carmen Palomino.

Cast: El Santo, José "Mantequilla" Napoles, Kiki Herrera Calles (Dona Eugenia Ezparza), Alfonso Castano (Prof. Lira), René Cardona, Sr., Ana Lilia Tovar (Lilia), Carlos Suárez, Jorge Guzmán, Sonia Fuentes, Kid Rapidez, José Rojas, Roberto Palacios, Octavio Menduet, Alejandra Meyer, El Greco, Tony Salazae, Marco Antonio Arzate, Alfonso Romero.

Legend meets legend, as the Silver-Masked Man encounters the Crying Woman, although "meets" and "encounters" are relative terms in this movie, for although the plot indeed revolves around the murderous machinations of La Llorona, she never comes into direct contact with the heroes. This time around, Santo's action-chum is pro boxer "Mantequilla" Napoles (insert extraneous boxing match to showcase his skills, along with the mandatory wrestling matches), who's no Blue Demon (but at least he isn't Evaristo). The legend of the Crying Woman remains pretty much the same, only now the Devil element has been added: When the Dona finds her lover will marry another, she plans to kill their children and herself to frame the bastard—but now it's Satán doing the prompting, and it is he who will bring back Dona Eugenia as La Llorona if the frame fails to hang. Of course it does, and so does he. It is the lover's accumulated riches that become the object of a treasure hunt by the principals, and La Llorona is defeated by the act of giving the treasure to charity! This was the last legend that Santo would meet—too

A vintage (1970s) Santo comic book with a cover by the man responsible for El Santo's comic-book career, José G. Cruz. The inside stories were told fumetti-fashion.

bad he never got a chance to face off against El Chupacabra!

Santo en Oro Negro, a.k.a. *La Noche de San Juan* (*Santo in Black Gold*, a.k.a. *Night of San Juan*, 1974)

(Jorge Camargo) *Prod*: Camargo; *Dir/Scr*: Federico Curiel; *Story*: David Sergio Pérez Gallardo, Carlos Suárez; *Photo*: J. Antonio Ruiz Juárez; *Co-Prod*: Juan Mariano Ruiz Noriega; *Sub-Dir*: Luis Quintanilla; *Film Ed*: Max Sánchez; *Cam. Op*: Lorenzo Contreras; *Sound/Re-Rec*: Ricardo Saldivar; *Makeup*: Lula's Beauty Salon [yes, really!].

Cast: El Santo, Rossy Mendoza (Vanessa del Valle), Luis Daniel Rivera, Gilda Haddock (Marta Cristal), Carlos Suárez (Enrique Artigas), Roberto Rivera Negroni, José Geajales, Hijo, Federico Curiel, Luis Quintanilla, Jimmy Bou, Tigre Pérez, Barrabas, Huracán Castillo.

La Venganza de la Llorona was more or less the last time El Santo would fight monsters. Oh, he runs into a pair of robots in this film, and his last two movies featured a man-beast, but these were merely window-dressing rather than featured creatures. The rest of El Santo's screen epics would concentrate on straight adventure stories, with a few mildly fantastic elements thrown in. Oil propels the adventure this time, as robot terrorists threaten to sabotage oil supplies. Naturally, the oil barons can't let this happen, and so call upon El Santo. The Saint splits his time between wrestling, donning disguises, and romancing Gilda Haddock, a statuesque beauty who still seems somewhat fishy. She spends most of the movie in various states of undress, but this does not hamper her ability to mix it up with the robots.

Misterio en las Bermudas (*Mystery in the Bermudas*, 1977)

(Producciones Agrasánchez) *Exec. Prod*: David Agrasánchez; *Prod*: Rogelio Agrasánchez; *Dir*: Gilberto Martínez Solares; *Idea*: Rogelio Agrasánchez; *Photo*: Adolfo Martínez Solares; *Music*: Ernesto Cortazar, Jr.; *Prod. Crew*: Jorge Moreno, Ernesto Fuentes, Luis Tovar; *Film Ed*: Jorge Bustos.

Cast: El Santo, Blue Demon, Mil Máscaras, Silvia Manriquez (Rina), Sandra Duarte (Spy), Carlos Suárez (Spy), Gaynor Cote (Princess Sorieda), Ernesto Solis (Ramiro), Humberto Cabanas, Julio César Agrasánchez, Rebeca Sexton, Leticia Montemayor, José Luis Elizondo, Marco Antonio Marin.

(See the Blue Demon and Mil Máscaras chapters for additional information)

Santo en la Frontera del Terror (*Santo on the Frontier of Terror*, 1979)

(Producciones Geminis–Cinematográfica RA) *Prod/Dir/Scr*: Rafael Pérez Grovas; *Story*: Sergio David, Carlos Suárez; *Photo/Assoc. Prod*: Alfredo Uribe; *Prod. Mgr*: Fernando Uribe; *Asst. Dir*: José Amezquita; *Film Ed*: Alfredo Jacome; *Cam. Op*: Guillermo Bravo; *Mus. Dir*: Francisco Salcido; *Makeup*: Estla Sánchez; *Sound Op*: Jorge Guerrero; *Re-Rec*: Salvador Topete.

Cast: El Santo, Gerardo Reyes (Gerardo), Carmen del Valle (Azucena), Carlos Suárez (Carlitos), Federico Falcón (Fernando), Miguel Angel Fuentes (Monk), Sarita Gómez (Florecita), Fernando Yapur, César Gómez, Roberto Gómez, Sixto Hinojosa, Angelica Sierra, Lilia Landua, Armando García Vaca, Cien Caras, Bobby Lee, Ringo Mendoza, Karloff Lagarde, Mocho Kotta, Jungla, Congre Chicana, Carnicero Aguilar.

Santo el la Frontera del Terror is not, as the title might suggest, a western — although part of the action does take place in Texas, which I'm sure is considered a frontier of terror by some. That it's not more terrifying is testament to the directorial skills of Rafael Pérez Grovas, who also helmed El Hijo del Santo's maiden efforts in the same uninspired manner. *Frontera del Terror* takes the travails of illegal aliens to a whole new level — they've been betrayed by promises of better money and living conditions before, but not so they could be used as subjects for a mad doctor! Santo actually doesn't have much to do, except tangle with a pair of pseudo-zombies and help a little blind girl obtain a sight-restoring operation (which you know he does, the big softie); most of the action is handled by pudgy Gerardo Reyes, who also gets to warble a couple of numbers. A few bits of business with a jar of eyeballs is a welcome, er, sight, but they're simply employed as background props, and they don't wind up in the youngster's head. *Frontera del Terror* is the best of the Grovas Santo/Son of Santo pics, but that's not really saying much.

Santo contra el Asesino de la T.V. (*Santo vs. the Television Killer*, 1981)

(Producciones Geminis–Cinematográfica RA) *Prod/Dir/Scr*: Rafael Pérez Grovas; *Story*: Sergio David, Carlos Suárez; *Photo/Assoc. Prod*: Alfredo Uribe; *Mus. Dir*: Rafael Carrión; *Makeup*: Estela Sánchez; *Asst. Dir*: José Amezquita; *Film Ed*: Fernando Uribe; *Cam. Op*: Guillermo Bravo; *Sound Op*: Consuelo Jaramillo; *Re-Rec*: Ricardo Saldivar.

Cast: El Santo, Gerardo Reyes (Himself), Rubi Re (Diana), Carlos Agosti (Magnus), Rosalia Montero, Carlos Suárez (Carlitos), Jean Safont, Nelson Juárez, Coloso Colosetti, El Polaco, El Vikingo, Ham Lee, Fernando Yapur, Jesús Velázquez, Oscar Arredando Asuara, Jorge A. García Zubieta, Johnny Barahona, El Mago Yeo.

El Santo's last starring role for Grovas couldn't have come a minute too soon. El Santo was limping, rather than marching, towards the end of his film career, and if he was going to make any more decent features, he would have to look beyond producer-director-screenwriter Rafael Perez Grovas; and he did. The mix here is the same as in his previous Grovas "epic"— not enough Santo, and too much Gerardo Reyes and musical tomfoolery. The villain of the piece is Magnus, a rogue arms dealer who wears a black wrestling mask and appears on TV to announce his crimes. Not only that, but the pioneer of "Reality TV" broadcasts the crimes as they happen. Naturally, this will not do, so Santo and Gerardo bust his chops—which is something of a stretch, since El Santo is obviously past his prime, and Gerardo is a pudgy goofball; but it's two against one, so that can pass. What's really a stretch is that we're supposed to believe that Gerardo is a secret agent of the government! While these films require a willing suspension of disbelief, that's about as hard to swallow as Smiley Burnette being an FBI man in *Dick Tracy* (1937). There's also a magician along for the ride, and after the wrap-up, he's joined by El Santo and the other characters on stage for his act — an eerie foreshadowing of the events surrounding El Santo's death three years later.

Chanoc y el Hijo del Santo contra los Vampiros Asesinos (*Chanoc and the Son of Santo vs. the Killer Vampires*, 1981)

(Cinematográfica RA) *Prod/Dir/Scr*: Rafael Pérez Grovas.

Cast: El Santo, El Hijo del Santo, Nelson Velázquez (Chanoc), Arturo "Cobitos" Cobo (Tzekub), Carlos Suárez (Carlitos), "Marcos Vargas" (Marcos).

This is yet another Grovas, but since it stars El Hijo, I'll save slamming it as a whole until the last chapter. El Santo appears in only one scene, and it comes during the prologue, so you can watch that and then skip the rest. The scene in question, however, is not only well-done, but actually rather touching. El Santo and son stand in a cavern. Santo, of course, is resplendent in mask and cape, but Son is in his dweeby "Marcos" get-up. Santo says the time has come to pass on the Silver Mask; will "Marcos" accept the honor, responsibility, and danger that go with it? (Well, of course he does, or there's no movie!) El Santo pops a pellet, and in a cloud of smoke "Marcos" is replaced by (the now also resplendent) El Hijo del Santo! They embrace, and the credits roll. Lunchtime!

El Puño de la Muerte (*The Fist of Death*, 1982)

La Furia de las Karatecas (*The Fury of the Karate Men*, 1982)

(Technical credits are the same for both films)

(Victor Films–Cinematográfica Jalisco) *Exec. Prod*: Victor Herrera; *Dir*: Alfredo B. Crevenna; *Adapt*: Alfredo B. Crevenna, Sergio Alvarez; *Story*: Ramón Obón; *Photo*: Juan Manuel Herrera; *Makeup*: María Luisa Carrasco; *Prod. Mgr*: Eduardo Martínez.

Cast: (*Fist*): El Santo, Grace Renat (Kungyan/Quiera), Tinieblas, César Sobrevals, Steve Cheng, Carlos Suárez, Gilberto Trujillo, Sandra Duarte, "Franky," Ismael Ramírez.

Cast: (*Fury*): El Santo, Grace Renat (Kungyan/Quiera), Tinieblas, César Sobrevals, Steve Cheng, Carlos Suárez, René Cardona, Edgardo Gazcon, Sandra Duarte, "Franky," Ismael Ramírez.

These represent El Santo's last pair, and that term is not to be taken lightly, especially since the obvious main feature of both films is the sultry Grace Renat. The buxom vixen plays twin sisters, one good and one evil. As the evil twin, attired in a very skimpy black outfit, she engages in several dance numbers that threaten to melt the film stock. These are definitely two steps up from the previous Grovas snooze-fests, with veteran director Alfredo B. Crevenna calling the shots. Fellow genre vet and Wrestling Woman daddy René Cardona is also on hand, but as an actor (in the last one). The two films offer plenty of wrasslin', karate, and even a monster, and although El Santo needed younger wrestlers and actors to carry the action scenes, his presence is still solid as a rock. He had come to the end of his cinematic line, and would tragically pass away only two years later (while performing in a magician's act on stage). Neither picture is *Vampire Women*, but then, not many are. All in all, *Fist* and *Fury* make for a good send-off.

FIVE

"Devil with a Blue Mask On"
The Life and Films of Blue Demon

Blue Demon (Born Alejandro Muñoz in April 1922) could be called the "Avis" of Mexican Wrestling Heroes—he was number two, so he tried harder. Or to couch the analogy in monster movie terms, he was "Lugosi" to El Santo's "Karloff"—rivals, co-stars, one the bigger celebrity, but the other always giving 100 percent, each developing his own towering presence. Although he only made about half as many films as Santo, and never quite attained the somewhat mythical aura which surrounds the Silver-Masked Man, Blue Demon could be content with the knowledge that he was a better technical wrestler than the Saint (he always pointed out in interviews that he had taken two out of three championships from Santo). And while none of Blue's movies have attained the mythical aura that surrounds *Santo vs. las Mujeres Vampiro*, they are consistently psychotronic, and a few have almost reached those rarified heights.

While employed in his teens by the railroad in Monterrey, Muñoz acquired the nickname that would stick with him throughout his career — Manos de Pala, or "Shovel Hands." He married in 1947 (the union lasted throughout his lifetime), and made his pro-wrestling debut in 1948. He quickly became very popular in Mexico, and often teamed with Black Shadow as half of "the Shadow Brothers." In Septem-ber of 1953 Blue Demon won the welterweight championship from El Santo. Like Santo, he became a star of not only the ring, but of movies and comic books. He made his last feature film, *Misterio en las Bermudas*, in 1977, with El Santo and Mil Máscaras, and retired with great ceremony from the ring in 1989, upon which occasion he produced a video documentary entitled *Blue Demon, el Campeón*. He owned his own gym, and trained many wrestlers, including the son (one of three) who wrestles as Blue Demon, Jr., Blue Demon died of a heart attack on December 16, 2000, while returning home from a workout at his gym.

Blue Demon, el Demonio Azul (1965)

(Fílmica Vergara Cinecomisiones) *Exec. Prod*: Jorge García Besné; *Prod*: Luis Enrique Vergara Cabrera; *Dir*: Chano Urueta; *Scr*: Rafael García Travesi; *Story*: Rafael García Travesi, Fernando Osés; *Photo*: Alex Phillips, Jr.; *Music*: Jorge Pérez Herrera; *Prod. Chief*: José Rodríguez; *Asst. Dir*: Angel Rodríguez; *Film Ed*: Juan José Munguia; *Art Dir*: Gerardo Aguilera R; *Camera Op*: Dagobied Rodríguez; *Masks/Special Makeup*: Antonio Niera; *Makeup*: Armando Islas; *Dialogue Rec*: Guillermo Mateos; *Music Re-Rec*: Heinrich Henkel; *Rec*: Ricardo Saldivar; *Sound Ed*: J.J. Munguia.

Cast: Blue Demon, Jaime Fernández (Lauro Carral), Rosa María Vasquez (Marina Gruber),

One of the very best Blue Demon posters, known affectionately as *Blue Demon and the Flamin' Brain*!

Mario Orea (Prof. Gruber), Ceasár Gay (Prof. Rafael), Fernando Osés (El Sanguinario), Altia Michel (Waitress), Guillermo Hernández [a.k.a. "Lobo Negro"] (Ursus), Margarito Luna (Matias), Carlos Suárez (Inspector).

The first Blue Demon–starring film, for better or worse, illustrated both the future series' strong points and shortcomings. (This was not, however, the first Blue Demon film appearance; he had appeared in two "sports dramas" previously — titled *Asesinos de la Lucha Libre* [*Killers of Wrestling*] and *La Furia del Ring* [*The Fury of the Ring*] — but only in wrestling sequences, not in dramatic roles.) Both El Santo's and Blue Demon's film debuts were low-budget affairs, but El Santo was sailing in relatively uncharted cinematic waters, and the low budget was more indicative of the "chance" taken by the producers. Plus, the combination of wrestling heroes and the fantastic had not yet been clearly defined when Santo first strode across the screen. Made several years after the heady artistic and financial successes of gems like *Santo vs. las Mujeres Vampiro* and *Las Luchadoras contra la Momia*, the first Blue Demon outing already had its parameters of expectations defined. It was just a question of how they went about it.

Santo and the Wrestling Women were monster-fighting "super-heroes" by the time of *El Demonio Azul*, and so Blue would follow suit. But whereas Santo came fully-equipped with a secret lab and snazzy sports car, Blue just sort of appears on the scene of any given crime, has no appreciable home base, and even makes his entrance (in *Blue Demon vs. the Shadow of the Bat*) driving a Mustang with a missing tail-light! And that set the tone — always second banana. The most important difference between the two wresling super-heroes, though, was their respective pesonalities. Santo was certainly a capable action star, but his tone was wise, reasoned, and somewhat paternal. Blue Demon was a more impulsive, no-nonsense type; he was there to kick ass and take names, and that was that.

This difference of presentation is especially notable in the "Holy Moley, my opponent is a *werewolf!*" scene, used both in *Mujeres Vampiro* and *Blue Demon, el Demonio Azul*. (And, yes, that is the actual film title, which translates as *Blue Demon, the Blue Demon*. Don't ask me why.) Santo's Vampire Women are the real deal, truly undead and in league with Ol' Scratch. Blue Demon's werewolf is scientifically-fabricated. And whereas in the Santo scene the suspense builds slowly, culminating in the Great Unmasking and Revelation, Blue's opponent, the bare-faced Fernando Osés, simply changes in full view of the audience. Plus, *Vampire Women* takes it to the next level by having the werewolf then turn into a bat to escape. Fernando-wolf simply scares the crap out of everyone and then runs (or lopes, if you will) out of the arena.

This is not to say that the first Blue Demon movie is bad; no, far from it. We actually get two werewolves for the price of one, and even though Blue is a little stiff, the supporting actors are fine, including the always-dependable Osés and Jaime Fernández. A waitress, portrayed by Altia Michel, is very sexy, and may have been sexier still, but we may never know. Although the film posters and many publicity shots portray her in black lace bra and panties being menaced by a werewolf, the film itself only offers a couple of shots of Fernández' wolfman peering in her window before switching to the police discussing her murder the next day. Obviously, some cuts appear to have been made.

And speaking of the poster art, *El Demonio Azul* features one of the more blatant rip-offs in film-monster (and film-monster magazine) history, as it not only "borrows" the image of Oliver Reed as the werewolf from Hammer's *Curse of the*

Werewolf (which in no way do the werewolves on the screen resemble), but the image used is taken from the cover of *Famous Monsters* magazine!

Overall, *El Demonio Azul* was a solid opener (actually more solid than Santo's first feature), and, like Santo's initial efforts, gave a hint of better things to come.

Blue Demon vs. el Poder Satánico (*Blue Demon vs. the Satanic Power*, 1965)

(Fílmica Vergara Cinecomisiones) *Exec. Prod*: Jorge García Besné; *Prod*: Luis Enrique Vergara Cabrera; *Dir*: Chano Urueta; *Scr*: Rafael García Travesi; *Story*: Rafael García Travesi, Fernando Osés; *Photo*: Alex Phillips, Jr.; *Music*: Jorge Pérez Herrera; *Prod. Chief*: José Rodríguez; *Asst. Dir*: Angel Rodríguez; *Film Ed*: Juan José Munguia; *Art Dir*: Gerardo Aguilera R; *Camera Op*: Dagobied Rodríguez; *Masks/Special Makeup*: Antonio Niera; *Makeup*: Armando Islas; *Dialogue Rec*: Guillermo Mateos; *Music Re-Rec*: Heinrich Henkel; *Rec*: Ricardo Saldivar; *Sound Ed*: J.J. Munguia.

Cast: Blue Demon, Martha Elena Cervantes, Jaime Fernández (Gustavo), El Santo, Fernando Osés (Inspector Andrade), Mario Orea (Judge), Lobo Negro (Prisoner), Margarito Luna (Detective), "El Nazi" (Raúl), Ray Mendoza (Himself), Carlos Suárez (Prison warden), Ruben Marquez (Prison doctor), Picoro (Ring announcer).

The second Blue Demon movie is middling. In some ways better, in some ways not, it almost seemed to be biding time until the first really *great* Blue Demon, which would be the next one —*La Sombra del Murciélago*.

Reliable Jaime Fernández plays Gustavo, a murderer who escapes execution by placing himself in a cataleptic state and returning 50 years later. His chief power seems to be picking up women, having them dress in sexy lingerie, seducing them, and then throwing them into a furnace. This he does until Blue tracks him down

and pulls out the prerequisite can of whoop-ass. Though there's less action here than in *El Demonio Azul*, *Poder Satánico* offers more in the way of atmosphere (certainly as much as, if not more than, some American cheapsters— such as the highly-touted *Strangler of the Swamp*).

Blue Demon vs. el Poder Satánico is also notable for being the first film in which El Santo and Blue Demon appear together. It's not really a team-up, but more like a Santo cameo, as he stops by Blue's dressing room after a match to congratulate and encourage him in his role of crime-fighter. He tells Blue: "I'll always be there by your side, if you need me." But it would be another few years before their first real partnership. Interestingly, the Santo match seen in *Poder Satánico* is lifted lock, stock and barrel from *Santo vs. el Rey del Crimen*. Perhaps Vergara, who was producing both Santo's and Blue's series at the time, was anticipating a picture with both of them which never materialized; or perhaps he simply thought it would help boost Blue's profits by featuring the already-established star.

A respectable follow-up to *El Demonio Azul*, *Poder Satánico* merely set the stage for zanier things to come, the first of which would be Blue's first truly great cinematic adventure, in which he would fall under the shadow of the Bat.

La Sombra del Murciélago (*The Shadow of the Bat*, 1966)

(Fílmica Vergara) *Prod*: Luis Enrique Vergara; *Dir*: Fredrico Curiel; *Scr*: Jesús "Mucielago" (Bat) Velázquez, from an original idea by Vergara; *Photo*: Eduardo Valdéz; *Music*: Jorge Pérez Herrer; *Prod. Mgr*: Raúl Manjarrez; *Asst. Dir*: Angel Rodríguez; *Art Dir*: Artis Gener; *Makeup*: Armando Islas; *Music Re-Rec*: Salvador Topete; *Dialogue Rec*: Jesús Sánchez; *Musical Arranger*: Armando Manzanero; *Costumes*: Bertha Mendoza López.

Cast: Blue Demon, Jaime Fernández (Daniel), Marta Romero (Marta), Fernando

Top: The second Blue Demon movie. *Bottom*: More beautiful female aliens try to take us over in this winner, which was also released in a "Sexo" version as ***Blue Demon vs. las Seductoras***.

Osés (El Mucielago), Mario Orea (Inspector), Gerardo Zepeda (Gerardo), "Bat" Velázquez (Trainer), René Barerra (Henchman), Marco Antonio Arzate (Henchman), Enriqueta Reza (Cirila Campos), Eduardo Bonada (Kidnapped wrestler), José Loza (Mario).

It took Santo a while to find his cinematic legs, and the same held true for Blue Demon. While his first two starring vehicles proved perfectly acceptable, his third, *La Sombra del Murciélago*, begins to breathe the rarified air of true psychotronica. It's *Phantom of the Opera*, only with masked wrestlers! And that's where the ride *starts*.

The movie takes its name from screenwriter Jesús Murciélago Velázquez, himself a Mexican wrestling legend, who also makes an appearance as a trainer that helps Blue prepare to fight "the Bat." The Bat is a mentally and physically scarred former wrestling idol who kidnaps wrestlers to stage private Texas-style Death-cave matches. He also takes a fancy to nightclub singer Marta Romero. Fernando Osés, truly the all-purpose man of Mexican monster/wrestler cinema, portrays the Bat—and he chews the scenery most enjoyably and effectively, ranting and raving and rassling up a storm.

And speaking of chewing, special accolades go to Gerardo Zepeda as the Bat's right-hand goon, Gerardo. Zepeda is a delight, conjuring up visions of Frank Moran in Monogram's *Return of the Ape Man* as he vacantly gnaws on a turkey leg while the Bat outlines his evil plans. In another scene, a leaf provides a clue, and Blue visits the Mexican version of María Ouspenskya to uncover its origin. There Blue chews on some of her witches' brew, and then takes what can only be classified as a "trip!" He doesn't learn anything from her, but he sure has fun!

These are but a few of the many wacky moments that *The Shadow of the Bat* has to offer, and it's a damn shame that absolutely *no* Blue Demon movies were ever released dubbed in English (*à la* the K. Gordon Murray Santos). *Shadow* is certainly just as deserving of cult status as the classic Neutrón films, which became more well-known because they *did* get dubbed. That's the kind of injustice Blue and Santo needed to fight!

Arañas Infernales (*Infernal Spiders*, 1966)

Exec. Prod.: Reynaldo Puente Portillo; *Prod*: Rafael Pérez Grovas; *Dir*: Chano Urueta; *Scr*: Antonio Orellana, Fernando Osés; *Photo*: Alfredo Uribe; *Music Dir*: Gustavo C. Carrión; *Asst. Dir*: José Luis de León; *Film Ed*: Sergio Soto; *Art Dir*: Octavio Ocampo, José Mendez; *Camera Op*: Carlos Morales; *Makeup*: María Eugenia Luna; *Script Clerk*: José Delfos; *Sound Op*: Victor Rojo; Eastmancolor.

Cast: Blue Demon, David Reynoso (Lt. Reyes), Ana Martin (María), Noé Murayama (Dr. Sanders), Victor Junco (Dr. Kadar), Dagoberto Rodríguez (Randall), Barbara Angeli (Katia), Victor Alcocer (Dr. Jiminez), Fernando Osés (Henchman), Burdett Zia, Jesús Valaquez (Oso; Himself) Julie Janssen, Martha Arlett, Reyes Olivia, Iliano Urieta, Mario Texas [also billed as Mario Tejas in the same film], Lina Marin ("Robot"), Glira Chávez, Jorje [sic] Casanova (Medical examiner), Linda Renger, Carlos Suárez ("Robot"), Margarito Luna (Dr. Robles), Gerardo Zepeda and Pedro Ortega ("Robots"), José Alvarez V., Alejandro Cruz ("Black Shadow"), Eduardo Bonada, Rodolfo Falinda ("El Cavernario"), Juan Garza ("Robot"), Eduardo MacGregor (Doctor in hospital), Miron Levine.

Starting with *La Sombra del Murciélago*, the Blue Demon movies really started to hit their stride—and managed to maintain it. In a way, Santo had reached his peak with *Vampire Women*. Certainly Santo had some great adventures after that (like in *Martian Invasión*, and *vs. Dracula and the Wolf Man*, among others), but everything in *Vampire Women* proved so defining of the genre that each film that followed, no matter how good, was destined to come off as second-best. Consequently, no Blue Demon movie could ever reach the heights of *Vampire Women* or *Wrestling Women vs. the Aztec Mummy*; but then, neither could any subsequent Santo feature. And while the really right-on Santo films became fewer and farther between, Blue, with half as many to his credit, didn't have as many chances to squander, and so therefore made the most of his opportunities. You wouldn't catch Blue yukking it up with Capulina!

While the first two Blues offered up their fair share of fantastic elements, it wasn't until the third feature that these elements began to gel into that steady surreal atmosphere that proved so important for films of this type. *Sombra* had it in spades, and happily the trend continues in *Arañas*. Alien spiders in search of human brains to feed their queen makes for a good start; then toss in stock footage from *Plan 9 from Outer Space* and *Teenagers from Outer Space*, and mix in musical cues taken from the *Themes from Horror Movies* record, and you've got yourself one mighty satisfying piece of psychotronica. The spider puppets are really hokey, but that only adds to the surreality of it all, much like the "suit-mation" effects in Japanese giant-monster films.

Arañas Infernales was the last Blue movie in glorious black-and-white, and also the last he would do for Vergara. Long thought to be "lost," a print turned up on Mexican television in 1999.

Blue Demon vs. las Diabólicas (*Blue Demon vs. the Diabolical Women*, 1966)

Cast: Blue Demon, David Reynoso, Ana Martin, Martha Cisneros, Griselda Mejia, María Salome, "special appearance" by Barbara Angeli; Color.

The first Blue Demon movie for Cinematográfica RA, and the first in color, is considered to be "lost"—that is, like *Arañas*, until somebody finds a copy. Clips from it featured in *Blue Demon, El Campeón* (1989), so it may eventually turn up. And it seems like it would be a worthy find, if one judges from those few clips, and available posters and lobby cards. Op-art, go-go boots, and bright primary colors abound, making it seem as though the influence of the *Batman* television show was already starting to make itself felt. (That in itself is not bad. People who complain that the TV show "ruined" Batman simply don't get the joke.)

Blue Demon contra Cerebros Infernales (*Blue Demon vs. the Infernal Brains*, 1966)

(Estudios America/Cinematográfica RA) *Exec. Prod*: Reynaldo Puente Portillo; *Prod*: Rafael Pérez Grovas; *Dir*: Chano Urueta; *Scr*: Antonio Orellana, Fernando Osés; *Photo*: Alfredo Uribe; *Music Dir*: Gustavo C. Carrión; *Asst. Dir*: José Luis De León; *Film ed*: Sergio Soto; *Art Dirs*: Octavio Ocampo, José Mendez; *Camera Op*: Carlos Morales; *Makeup*: María Eugenia Luna; *Script Clerk*: José Delfos; *Sound Op*: Victor Rojo; Eastmancolor.

Cast: Blue Demon, David Reynoso (Lt. Reyes), Ana Martin (Marta), Noé Murayama (Dr. Sanders), Victor Junco (Dr. Kadar), Dagoberto Rodríguez (Randall), Barbara Angeli ["Angely" on the posters] (Katia), Victor Alcocor (Dr. Jiminez), Fernando Osés (Henchman), Jesús "Murciélago" Velázquez (Oso; and Himself), Lina Marin (Robot), Carlos Suárez (Robot), Margarito Luna (Dr. Robles), Gerardo Zepeda (Robot); wrestlers: Alejandro Cruz "Black Shadow," Eduardo Bonada, and Rodolfo Galindo "El Cavernerio" ("The Caveman").

Unlike *Blue Demon vs. las Diabólicas*, Blue's second color adventure *is* available, and it continues with the "mod" mood and wacky antics. Eminent scientists are being kidnapped and having their brains extracted (and then replaced with different ones!) so that Foreign Powers will have access to the secrets locked within them. Their henchmen are male and female robots; but the males are more robotic-looking than the females, who are much more human-looking (so that they can parade around in mini-skirts!).

Just like *La Sombra del Murciélago* featured (along with Marta Romero's lounge numbers) a rockin' Spanish-language version of "Wooly Bully," so does *Infernal Brains* offer up some rock and roll — in the form of several instrumentals by "El Klan"—(and, no, they're not dressed in white hoods; actually, they wear a queasy shade of yellow tuxedoes!). Nothing like frugging and twisting to take your mind off alien brain-snatchers!

On a graphic note (as in design, not violence), *Infernal Brains* features what may be the best ever Blue Demon poster art: a well-rendered painting of Blue in an action pose, against the backdrop of a huge flaming brain. In many cases, particularly with "fantastic" films, Mexican poster art (like that for many American b-films and serials) was hastily conceived and executed (though still managing to possess an air of vitality that their north-of-the-border counterparts lacked), but this example was right on the money.

Blue Demon, Destructor de Espías (*Blue Demon, Spy Smasher,* 1967)

Pasaporte a la Muerte (*Passport to Death,* 1967)

(Technical credits are the same for both films, except where noted)

Prod/Dir (*Espías*) and *Prod* (*Pasaporte*): Emilio Gómez Muriel *Dir* (*Pasaporte*): Alfredo Crevenna; *Scr*: Alfredo Ruanova; *Story*: Emilio Gómez Muriel, Alfredo Ruanova; *Photo*: Alfredo Uribe; *Music*: Antonio Díaz Conde; *Prod. Mgr*: Luis García de León; *Co-Dir*: José Luis González de León; *Film Ed*: Raúl J. Casso; *Art Dirs*: José Mendez, Octavio Ocampo; *Camera Op*: Carlos Morales; *Dialogue Rec*: Victor Rojo; *Rec*: Francisco Guerrero; *Music/Re-Rec*: Heinrich Heinkel; *Sound*

Op (Espías): Ricardo Saldivar; *Script Clerk* (*Pasaporte*): José Delfos; Union: STIC.

Cast (*Destructor de Espías*): Blue Demon, Carlos East (Julio), Maura Monti (Nora), Alma Delia Fuentes (Marcia), Héctor Gómez (Lafarge), Guillermo Zettina (Maj. Albert/Uncle Halsey), Jorge Rado (Hans), Bruno Rey (Col. Dawson), Carlos Nieto (Robles), Chuck Anderson (Prof. Garfield), Fernando Osés (Henchman), Cavernario Jalindo, "Picoro" (Ring announcer); Bands: The Rocking Stars, Los Johnny Jets.

Cast (*Pasaporte a la Muerte*): Blue Demon, Ana Luisa Peluffo (Laura), Maura Monti (Nora), Eric del Castillo (Android), Carlos East (Julio), Héctor Gómez (Lafarge), José Galvez (Marcus), Bruno Rey (Colonel), Mario Orea (Professor), Raquel Bardiza, Nothanael "Frankenstein" León (Troglodita), René Barrera (Henchman).

The *Batman* TV show had already made its presence felt in the world of the monster/wrestler movies; now producers in Mexico were looking across the Atlantic for inspiration — specifically, to Bond, James Bond. In both the Santo films *Operación 67* and *El Tesoro de Moctezuma,* and in this pair of Blue Demon movies, the masked wrestler becomes a Secret Agent Man, paired with a leading-man type as his "partner" (in the Santos, it was Jorge Rivero; in the Blues it was Carlos East).

The quartet exploits all the expected accoutrements of the super-spy genre — improbable gadgets, tons of gorgeous women in bikinis (and less), lavish setpieces and over-the-top action. The Santo pair are the superior efforts, but the Blues are not far behind (and both feature Maura Monti). One factor in Blue's favor was that he kept in great shape throughout his career, and so a partner proved superfluous; Santo, at times, looked like he was glad Jorge Rivero was around to handle the more strenuous sequences.

The posters for both Blue Demon productions were very attractive: *Destructor de Espías* features a painting of a large Blue Demon mask, along with other fan-

This Blue Demon one-sheet possesses the two most important elements of successful poster design — a strong central image, and Maura Monti in a bikini.

tastic elements (including Maura Monti in a bikini); while *Pasaporte* shows Blue and Carlos East being attacked by a huge robot that bears a striking resemblance to a fellow automaton by the name of Gort. Holy Klaatu Barada Nikto!

Blue and Maura Monti's co-star in these two "spy" epics, Carlos East, also made two films with Boris Karloff (see chapter nine), and another psychedelic spy spoof, *Cazadores de Espías*, with Ms. Monti. These were some of his few leading roles; he fell into the supporting ranks shortly thereafter.

Blue Demon y las Invasoras
(*Blue Demon and the Women Invaders*, a.k.a. *Blue Demon vs. las Seductoras*, 1968)

Prod/Story: Rafael Pérez Grovas; *Dir/Scr*: Gilberto Martínez Solares; *Photo*: Raúl Martínez Solares; *Music Dir*: Gustavo C. Carrión; *Prod. Chief*: Julio Guerrero; *Sub-Dir*: Manuel Muñoz; *Film Ed*: Gloria Schoemann; *Décor*: Carlos Granjean; *Camera Op*: Cirilo Rodríguez; *Lighting*: Horacio Calvillo; *Makeup*: María del Castillo; *Sound Suprvsr*: James L. Fields; *Dialog. Rec*: Francisco Alcayde; *Re-Rec*: Galdino Samperio; Eastmancolor.

Cast: Blue Demon, Gilda Miros (Nora), Regina Torne (Narda), Augustín Martínez Solares, Jr. (Raúl Cárdenas), Enrique Aguilar (Businessman/hostage), Gina Morett (Nadia), Raúl Martínez Solares, Jr. (Shepherd boy), Oscar Morelli (Scientist/hostage), José Marti (Van driver/hostage), Griselda Mejia (Nereida), Sandra Boyd (Nita), Carlos León (Impresario), René Barrera (Hotel employee), Dorrell Dixon (Wrestler).

With this 1968 feature, Blue came as close as he could (in his films sans other wrestlers) to matching holds with Vampire Women. Except in this case, the Diabolical Women don't have fangs, they're from Outer Space! And they've traveled across galaxies not to drink our blood, but to kidnap Earth Men to help them re-populate their planet. But why the kidnapping? One look at these space-vixens and I, for one, would gladly volunteer!

Not content to appropriate stock footage from an Ed Wood film, the producers of *Invasoras* went *Infernal Spiders* one better by appropriating Wood's budget-restricted style, including providing laughable flying saucers. But, once again, that's part of the fun. In fact, Ed might have actually done it a little better — at least his flying saucers had shape and form; in *Invasoras*, they're just round lights.

Blue Demon vs. las Invasoras was one of the chosen few to be released in an El Sexo version, which, like all the others except for *Night of the Bloody Apes*, is lost. It's especially a pity in this case, as all the alien females are drop-dead gorgeous, especially Regina Torne. Torne would become part of the Wrestling Women legend with her appearance in *Wrestling Women vs. the Killer Robot*, which, in turn, was also released in a "Sexo" version as *El Asesino Loco y el Sexo*. In the sexy *Seductoras* version of *Invasoras* the space-babes go to bed with their "victims"; in the cleaned-up version, they merely kiss them, whereupon the guys disappear and reappear on the girls' space ship. One of the seduction sequences — when Space Doll Number 3 does an incredible dance for a businessman — manages to be pretty erotic. And Enrique Aguilar as the businessman makes no secret of the fact that he's enjoying the scenery!

In short, if, for some odd reason, you've never seen a Blue Demon movie, this is one great place to start!

Santo contra Blue Demon en la Atlántida (*Santo vs. Blue Demon in Atlantis*, 1969)

(See Santo chapter for technical and cast credits.)

Both Santo and Blue Demon had more than a few movies under their belts before someone decided to team them up. (I'm deliberately excluding *El Poder Satánico* because Santo's role in that one was merely a cameo and not a true teaming.) In this respect, *Santo contra Blue Demon en la Atlántida* parallels the 1934 version of *The Black Cat*, which, of course, was the first pairing of Bela Lugosi and Boris Karloff. Not to belabor the Lugosi-Karloff analogy, but *Atlántida* also emulated that screen duo's films in a larger sense — in practically every picture Karloff and Lugosi made together (except for 1935's *The Raven*), Lugosi played a role subservient to Karloff's (in importance if not in actuality). In *Atlántida*, the producers subtly imply Blue's stature in relation Santo's by casting him as a villain for the majority of the picture. In fact, the "Blue Demon's Evil Twin" ploy became almost standard fare after this picture, with Blue either being cloned or hypnotized (or even having a mummy dress up like him!). One begins to understand why he held such a grudge against the Saint! Still, though, the hero vs. hero clash is fun in a Marvel Comics' Human Torch vs. Sub-Mariner way, and the Atlantis and ex–Nazi Mad Scientist elements only add to the comic-books-for-young-and-old atmosphere.

Arañas Infernales employed footage from two American B-movies; for *Atlántida*, they traveled across the big pond to raid the vaults of the Japanese, coming away with pieces of *Monster Zero* and *Atragon*. Far from being a mis-matched distraction, these sequences actually help give the film a more expensive look. This was a favored tactic of producer-writer Sotomayor, who went to other movies' wells far too often (a surprisingly lazy device for the same people responsible for *La Loba*).

Augustín Martínez Solares, Jr., co-starred in this and the previous Blue; and if the last name seems familiar, yes, he *is* related to all the other Solareses mentioned

in this book. His most famous genre role was that of Rufus Rex, the hirsute half of the monster team seen in *Santo y Blue Demon vs. Drácula y el Hombre Lobo*. Although presumed alive and well at the time of this writing, he has not appeared in a film for some time.

Santo y Blue Demon contra los Monstruos (*Santo and Blue Demon vs. the Monsters*, 1969)

(See Santo chapter for technical and cast credits.)

The second co-starring feature employing Santo and Blue Demon is also one of the most well-known (somewhat surprisingly, especially since it was never dubbed into English and has only been recently [2003] released with subtitles). No doubt this is due to the "all-star" cast of Universal-inspired monsters (plus the Cyclops from *The Ship of Monsters*). In a way, that's too bad, because it really falls short of its potential. Not that it isn't fun (it is), but it could have been so much more. And the fault lies mainly with those selfsame monsters.

In the Golden Age of Universal Horror, Jack P. Pierce created some of the most imaginative, realistic, and memorable monster make-ups of all time. Unfortunately, the same cannot be said for his south-of-the-border counterparts. But what they lack in skill, they make up for with sheer audacity. For instance, the Frankenstein Monster, here called Franquestain(!), not only sports a turtleneck and goatee(!!), but can drive a small foreign sports car(!!!). We're getting into *Munsters* territory now. The Monster is portrayed here by Manuel Leal, who played an assortment of other creatures, including the lead mummy in *The Mummies of Guanajuato*, and would go on to greater fame as the masked wrestler "Tinieblas."

The other monsters fare just as badly, with Drácula and the Mummy coming off the worst. The Wolf Man looks like a cross between Glenn Strange's hillbilly werewolf in *The Mad Monster*, and Gabby Hayes, but at least he's the catalyst for a couple of genuinely brutal, scary moments. And damned if we don't get *another* "Evil Blue Demon," who most of the time is fighting *with* the monsters rather than against them.

What plot exists does so only to link the monster scenes, which *are* plentiful. So in that respect, *Contra los Monstruos* certainly delivers the goods—too bad they couldn't have arrived in a nicer package. And that extends to the poster art: the monsters didn't look that great to begin with, and the painted renditions of them are rather sloppily executed.

El Mundo de los Muertos (*The World of the Dead*, 1969)

(See Santo chapter for technical and cast credits.)

By this point in his movie career, Blue Demon sure must have been glad he could whip Santo in the ring, because every time they co-starred on-screen, he just couldn't win. In *The World of the Dead*, Blue not only receives less screen time than usual, but *again* he's "evil" for most of the picture (a fact which doubtless not only galled *him*, but piqued his ardent fans who were used to seeing him as a hero)! Wasn't this getting old? This even carried over to his solo films—if you can't escape being an evil clone of yourself in a movie that you *star* in, what hope is there?

Though choppy, *El Mundo de los Muertos* remains interesting for the "colonial" sequences in which Santo and Blue portray 16th-century counterparts of themselves; and the weird "Dead World" scenes at the climax, which, true to Sotomayor form, contain footage from a for-

eign film (although nobody to date has discovered the source).

The poster art for *El Mundo de los Muertos* is simple, yet striking: Full-figure paintings of Santo and Blue Demon face off against each other, with only the title of the film holding them apart, while a Phantom of the Opera–type monster face looms over all. *Under* it all lay a girl in a coffin, who looks like she's struggling to get out from under the weight of all the above elements!

(For more on this film, see the El Santo chapter)

Los Momias de Guanajuato (*The Mummies of Guanajuato,* 1970)

(See Santo chapter for technical and cast credits.)

Blue Demon must have been pleased with the script for *Mummies of Guanajuato*; no longer a boot boy for Santo, he and Mil Máscaras had strong roles in a good monster movie with decent production values. At least, that's how it started out. As filming progressed, the producers decided they needed a little added oomph … and so they called in Santo, who basically comes in and saves the day after Blue and Mil have done all the dirty work (a fact which rankled Blue until the day he died; Mil Máscaras didn't mind nearly so much—the more stars on the card, the more money at the box office).

To add insult to injury, the picture offers yet *another* "evil Blue Demon." But there's a twist, which turns out to be the most unflattering of all. In *Guvanajuato* Blue's not merely hypnotized or his own ancestor; this time he is beaten up by one of the titular mummies, who steals the clothes right off his back! The mummy then puts on Blue's togs and proceeds to commit a series of crimes, which, of course, the dimwitted policemen blame on Blue! Poor Blue!

Blue Demon carping aside, this is a stone classic. The mummies are great, and possibly (along with *Night of the Living Dead*) helped inspire Amando de Ossorio's *Blind Dead* series. The ladies are gorgeous, there are some genuinely creepy moments (particularly when prominent characters meet their demise), and there's the by-now obligatory weird musical interlude (this time courtesy of a bunch of guys wearing frilly costumes and playing Mandolins!). There's plenty of physical action, too, but one begins to question why anybody would continually subject themselves to mummy beatings when thus far all such efforts have been for naught! (It's like in *Spooks Run Wild*: when all the efforts of the Bowery Boys have failed against the "vampire," Leo Gorcey's solution is "to get plenty tough with 'em, see?"

The impressive one-sheets used to advertise the film offers excellent photographic and painted renditions of not only the Big Three, but of the title creatures as well.

Los Campeones Justicieros (*The Champions of Justice,* 1970)

(Prodduciones Fílmicas Agrasánchez) *Prod*: Rogelio Agrasánchez; *Dir*: Fredrico Curiel; *Scr*: Rafael García Travesi.

Cast: Blue Demon, Mil Máscaras, Elsa Cárdenas, David Silva, La Sombra Vengadora [Fernando Osés], Tinieblas [Manuel Leal], El Médico Asesino, Black Shadow.

Los Campeones Justicieros (*The Champions of Justice*) is often referred to as "The Justice League of Mexico," a favorable comparison to the DC Comics superhero team. And this south-of-the-border team certainly was super, comprised of some of the most famous wrestlers this side of Santo: Blue, Mil Máscaras, La Sombra Vengadora, El Médico Asesino, and newcomer Tinieblas. Santo, in fact, *was* slated to appear, but had to bow out due to other obligations, a fact that relieved Blue to no end. With Santo's abdication, Blue would receive the lion's share of screen time, and would be the undisputed leader of the group. Not only that, there was no evil Blue Demon this time!

Champions is chock-full of all the elements that make Mexican monster/wrestler movies so special, starting with its inherently bizarre premise — the mad scientist wants revenge on the wrestling heroes, and goes about it by creating an army of super-powered midgets! (When the midgets finish their treatment in the power-magnifying machine, they all emerge in tights emblazoned with a big "M" on the chest!) The evil scientist also kidnaps all the wrestlers' girlfriends, who all just happen to be beauty contestants (in fact, we are treated to a beauty pageant right in the middle of the film!). Our heroes then give chase — in hot rods, on motorcycles, and in speedboats.

And would you believe that, of the three *Champions* movies, this one is the most mundane?!

For the "So Many Wrestlers You Need a Scorecard Dept.": La Sombra Vengadora and Huracán Ramírez were wrestlers that became wrestlers only after those characters had been created for the screen. However, the man who had played Sombra on-screen, Frenando Osés, was not the man who wrestled under that mask; but Osés returned to the screen role for *Champions*. David Silva, Huracán's original alter ego, did not wrestle as him either; he pops up as a villain in *Champions*—one by the name of Mano Negra (Black Hand), the moniker of another real-life wrestler. El Médico Asesino was a wrestler first, but he isn't the original, who had passed away; instead he is portrayed by Juan Chavvarria, a wrestler who was better known as Gran

Markus. Alejandro Cruz, "Black Shadow," was also on hand for *Champions*; Cruz had doubled as Blue's evil twin previously (but thankfully did not repeat that ruse here).

In 1998 plans were announced for the release of a dubbed version of the film, to be produced by Steve Ross, creator of the *Chesty Sánchez* comic book, but nothing ever came of it.

La Invasión de los Muertos (*Invasion of the Dead*, 1971)

(Producer Fílmica Re-Al–Prods. Nova) *Prods*: René Cardona, Jr., Enrique Rosas; *Dir/Scr*: René Cardona, Sr.; *Story*: Cardona Jr.; *Photo*: José Ortiz Ramos; *Music*: Raúl Lavista; *Prod. Chief*: Fidel Pizarro; *Asst. Dir*: Winfield Sánchez; *Film Ed*: Alfredo Rosas Priego; *Art Dir*: Alberto de Guevara; *Décor*: Carlos Arjona; *Lighting*: Fernando Calvillo; *Camera Op*: Manuel González; *Makeup*: Ana María Soriano; *Sound Op*: Manuel Topete; *Sound Ed*: Abraham Cruz; *Re-Rec*: Salvador Topete.

Cast: Zovek, Blue Demon, Christa Linder (Erika), Raúl Ramírez (Prof. Bruno Volpi), Carlos Cardan (Rancher), Polo Ortin (Blue Demon's assistant), Roberto Y. Palacios (Cemetery watchman), Armando Acosta (Police official), Ramón Menéndez (Helicopter pilot), Gerardo Zepeda (Werewolf).

This is the Mexican version of *Night of the Living Dead* (in spirit) and *Plan 9 from Outer Space* (in execution). In spirit, it's the standard zombie story that proliferated after *Night of the Living Dead* had made its indelible mark — an army of the un-living rise from their graves and besiege mankind. (These, however, are not your garden-variety zombies — they aren't content just to shamble and kill; they can drive pickup trucks and fly helicopters!) In execution, however, *Invasión* fell into the *Plan 9* camp: the star of the film, Zovek, like Bela Lugosi, died during production (the victim of a helicopter crash), and the filmmakers went ahead and completed the movie anyway. Though instead of employing an unconvincing double, like

Dr. Tom Mason in *Plan 9*, they simply kept the Zovek sequences already shot, and just added scenes featuring Blue Demon and assorted monsters. Ed Wood would have been proud!

In *Santo vs. la Venganza de la Llorona*, Santo and boxer "Mantequilla" Napoles never actually come face to face with the monster. And so it is with *Invasión*; but instead, it's the two heroes who never hook up. The makers of the film tried to alleviate this problem by having Blue "talk" to Zovek on the phone, but the deception is pretty transparent. Heck, Blue doesn't even fight the same monsters as Zovek! (Perhaps we didn't escape the spectre of Dr. Tom after all.) Zovek was a real-life magician and escape artist (sort of the Mexican Mister Miracle) who had one other movie to his credit, *El Incredible Prof. Zovek*. That one, and his scenes in *Invasión*, proved to be a promising start to a career that unfortunately never, er, materialized.

With all the allusions to Ed Wood, one might think this is a "bad" or cheap film. Far from it, once past the details delineated above, *Invasión* becomes an entertaining action/monster movie. How could a helicopter-flying zombie fail to arouse interest? (Unfortunately, the posters were disappointing, with Zovek painted sporting a silly headband and outfit that makes it look like the movie should be called "Blue [Sunshine] Demon and the Hippie Meet the Zombies!")

La Mafia Amarilla (*The Yellow Mafia*, 1972)

Prods: René Cardona, Jr., Enrique Rosas; *Dir/Scr*: René Cardona, Sr.; *Story*: Cardona Jr.; *Photo*: José Ortiz Ramos; *Music*: Raúl Lavista; *Prod. Chief*: Fidel Pizarro; *Asst. Dir*: Winfield Sánchez; *Film Ed*: Alfredo Rosas Priego; *Art Dir*: Alberto de Guevara; *Décor*: Carlos Arjona; *Lighting*: Fernando Calvillo; *Camera Op*: Manuel González; *Makeup*: Ana María

Top: Bad-to-the-Bone Biker Blue! *Bottom*: Blue's second team-up with Zovek (pictured in the insert), who died during filming.

Soriano; *Sound Op*: Manuel Topete; *Sound Ed*: Abraham Cruz; *Re-Rec*: Salvador Topete.

Cast: Blue Demon, Armando Silvestre (Inspector Ponce), Tere Velázquez (Yvette), Germán Valdés "Tin Tan" (Germán), Jorge Arvizu (Chang Lo), Polo Ortin (Rocha), Noé Murayama (Selim), Lupita Lara (Laura Lander), Amada Sumaya (Yi Kao), Oscar Moreeli (Fernando Tellez), Ivonne Govea (Magda Tellez), Juan Allende (Mario Lander), René Barrera (Jaibo Montiel), Roberto I. Palacios (Ling), Juan Garza (Henchman), Armando Acosta (Bartender), Agustín Fernández (Narc).

Noche de Muerte (*Night of Death*, 1972)

Exec. Prod: Jaime Jiminez Pons; *Dir*: René Cardona, Sr.; *Scr*: Carlos E. Talboada; *Photo*: Ricardo Carretero, Raúl Domínguez, Alberto Arellano; *Co-Dir*: Angel Rodríguez; *Film Ed*: Alfredo Rosas Priego; *Art Dir*: Rogelio Jiminez Pons; *Camera Asst*: Roberto Rivero; *Sound Ed*: Sigfrido García; *Makeup*: Victoria Celis; *Prod. Mgr*: Alberto Camilli; *Prod. Chief*: Héctor Luna; Eastmancolor.

Cast: Blue Demon, Armando Silvestre, Tere Velázquez, "Tin Tan," Gina Romand (Mabel), Fredrico Falcón (the Count), Carlos Vendrel (the Cossack), Jorge Patiño (Johnny Rengo), Leticia Robles (Mrs. Rengo), Carlos Rotzinger (Bank employee), Humberto Valdepena (Hotel dick), Agustin Fernández (Agustin), "Black Shadow."

With these two films (listed together because they were shot back-to-back by the same crew) and the next, *Las Bestias del Terror*, Blue Demon took a break from fighting monsters and sci-fi midgets to tangle with mostly run-of-the-mill thugs. Possibly shot as TV movies, but then released theatrically, *Mafia* and *Night* resemble (in both spirit and execution) American detective shows of the same period think (*The Streets of San Francisco* with Blue instead of Karl Malden).

Yellow Mafia showcases some fine action sequences and hot babes (one of which is Tere Velázquez, the sister of Lorena), but the best thing about it is the title (which they could *not* get away with these days).

Tere Velázquez was also in the follow-up, *Night of Death*, along with dependable pros like Armando Silvestre, Germán "Tin Tan" Valdés, and Gina Romand. *Night* also features the return of that well-worn plot device — an evil Blue Demon (only this time he's just a palooka in Blue's clothing). The poster art really played up the two Blue Demons angle, but they only tangle once in the whole movie, and then for about as long as Lugosi (actually Eddie Parker) and Chaney battled in *Frankenstein Meets the Wolf Man*.

Unusual for the fact they *don't* have any monsters, *Mafia* and *Night* are nonetheless solid pieces of work, as are both films' posters, with *Yellow Mafia* featuring an excellent painting of a shackled Blue Demon entwined by a Chinese dragon, and *Night of Death* a Blue Demon vs. Blue Demon rendering that looks like it was inspired by a *Doc Savage* pulp cover.

This was the last genre appearance of blond bombshell Gina Romand, whose association with said genre stretched all the way back to Santo's second feature, filmed in her native Cuba. Ms. Romand also provided El Santo with two of his best villainesses — in *Santo vs. the Daughter of Frankenstein* and *The Vengeance of the Vampire Women* — and appeared opposite wrestling-type heroes in *Mano Que Aprieta* and *Neutrón vs. the Maniac*.

Mafia and *Night* also finished the monster/wrestler game for Armando Silvestre. An all-purpose leading man, he appeared in many genre classics: the first two *Sombra Vengadoras*, the first Neutrón trilogy, and, of course, the immortal first two Wrestling Women films. Silvestre now lives in southern California.

Top: Fernando Osés has just insulted Blue's Hawaiian shirt. *Bottom*: Tere Velázquez (sister of Lorena) has just told Noe Murayama and friend what she's making for this movie.

Las Bestias del Terror (*The Beasts of Terror*, 1972)

(See Santo chapter for technical and cast credits.)

The Beasts of Terror was made along the same "shot on location in beautiful Miami Beach!" lines as the previous two Blues (and it actually was), complete with plenty of gangster double-crosses; but it transcends the straight crime feel of the previous entries by having some of its gangsters double as grave robbers for a boss who is not a "Don," but a mad scientist! Even better, the mad scientist takes blood from any captives he has handy to revive the corpses, who all happen to be bodies of gorgeous women, and creates zombie hookers!

Santo is back in the fold for *Beasts*, but this time the footing was more equal. (Apparently, the distributors felt that the two most famous masked wrestlers in Mexico weren't enough to draw patrons, and so added a completely anonymous wrestler in a black mask to the posters.) If this picture had been made a few years earlier, its weird elements would have made the movie; here, they are handled more routinely and matter-of-factly (as if there's anything matter-of-fact about zombie hookers!).

The title of *Beasts* makes it sound as if we're in for some monster chiller horror theatre, but the titular terrors turn out to be mere canines, and not very beastly ones at that. I've seen meaner-looking hounds on my old paper route!

Santo y Blue Demon contra Drácula y el Hombre Lobo (*Santo and Blue Demon vs. Dracula and the Wolf Man*, 1972)

(See Santo chapter for technical and cast credits.)

Santo y Blue Demon contra Drácula y el Hombre Lobo proved to be the last hurrah for Santo and/or Blue Demon fighting "classic" Universal-style monsters. Although each would go on to battle numerous other creatures, this was the final time they encountered anyone specifically named Drácula or the Wolf Man, and it really delivered the goods (the way *Santo and Blue Demon vs. the Monsters* couldn't, even with three times the fiends!).

Drácula thinks it's about time he ruled the world with armies of the undead, but, naturally, he has to go through Santo and Blue to accomplish that goal. He's assisted in his quest by the Wolf Man — not Larry Talbot, but Rufus Rex(?!?). There's a great donnybrook between Blue and Rufus at the climax, right before both monsters are impaled in Drácula's convenient pit of stakes. (Why do cinema vampires insist on keeping pits full of pointed sticks around? You spend your whole unlife avoiding sunlight, but you keep a pit full of fatal weapons in your lair. Go figure.)

Oddly enough, perhaps the most memorable scene in the film has nothing to do with the fiends. It occurs when Blue and Santo guard their girlfriends from imminent attack at their apartment. There the two lucha libre legends sit — across from each other at a table, in their masks, with matching turtlenecks and suits— playing chess. There is just something so innately surreal about this scene, so sublime, that it sticks in the mind long after many others sights have faded.

The film's only serious flaw comes in the form of Rufus' fashion sense, particularly when he sports a ridiculous frilly shirt (undoubtedly hoping to resemble Oliver Reed in *Curse of the Werewolf*, he winds up looking more like Jerry Seinfeld complaining, "But I don't wanna be a pirate!").

An Azteca lobby card for *Santo y Blue Demon vs. Drácula y el Hombre Lobo* (1972).

Vuelven los Campeones Justicieros (*The Champions of Justice Return,* 1972)

(Fílmicas Agrasánchez–Cin. Tikal Internacional) *Dir*: Federico Curiel; *Adapt*: Ramón Obón; *Story*: Rogelio Agrasánchez; *Photo*: Antonio Ruiz; *Music*: Bernardo Serrano; *Prod. Mgr*: Heberto Dávila; *Asst. Dir*: José Luis Urquieta; *Film Ed*: Jorge Rivera; *Camera Op*: Lorenzo Contreras; *Makeup*: Victoria Celis; *Dialogue Rec*: Roberto Muñoz; *Re-Rec*: Ricardo Saldivar; Eastmancolor.

Cast: Blue Demon, Mil Máscaras, El Rayo de Jalisco, El Fantasmo Blanco, El Avispón Escarlata, Yolanda Liévana (Sandra), Martha Angelica (Gatusy), Julio [Agrasánchez] César (Julio), Carlos Blanco (Himself, a singer and no relation to El Fantasmo), Santa Oviedo (Laura Jordan).

Blue Demon and Mil Máscaras return, but their crack squad of lucha com-mandoes has some new recruits in this second *Champions* epic. Gone are La Sombra Vengadora, El Médico Asesino, and Tinieblas; in their place are El Rayo de Jalisco ("The Light of Jalisco," whose costume was virtually identical to La Sombra's), El Fantasma Blanco ("The White Phantom," whose costume was virtually identical to El Médico's), and El Avispón Escarlata ("The Scarlet Scorpion," whose costume was identical to nobody's, and who was portrayed by Manuel "Tinieblas" Leal).

As stated previously, this and the next installment make the first zany *Campeones* movie look almost restrained. For instance, the midgets are back, but this time around they're not just super-midget-men, they're super-midget-*rat*-men, wearing outfits that resemble nothing so terrifying as a pair of jammies! The villain(ess) is not just a mad scientist, she's a masked beauty in hot pants! Moon rocks, toy robots, and "The Winner of the Tokyo Song Festival" (Carlos Blanco) also figure into the madness.

The Azteca lobby cards for this and the other *Campeones* films are among the most colorful and hero-filled of all the cards issued by that company. There's not too many "dead" cards in any of the sets, what with the number of heroes, villains and babes in each movie. The photos on the cards all prove memorable and the border artwork is crammed with wrestlers (and, of course, the hot pants–wearing, masked villainess).

Santo y Blue Demon contra el Dr. Frankenstein (*Santo and Blue Demon vs. Dr. Frankenstein*, 1973)

(See Santo chapter for technical and cast credits.)

Despite the promising title, *Santo and Blue Demon vs. Dr. Frankenstein* is actually a pretty slow-moving picture, even though the script was another re-working of *Wrestling Women vs. the Killer Doctor*, one of the shining examples of the genre. Also, even though they meet Dr. Irving(?!?) Frankenstein, they *don't* meet the famed monster of said Doc, but simply face off against a large black man with some barely-noticeable stitches on his forehead.

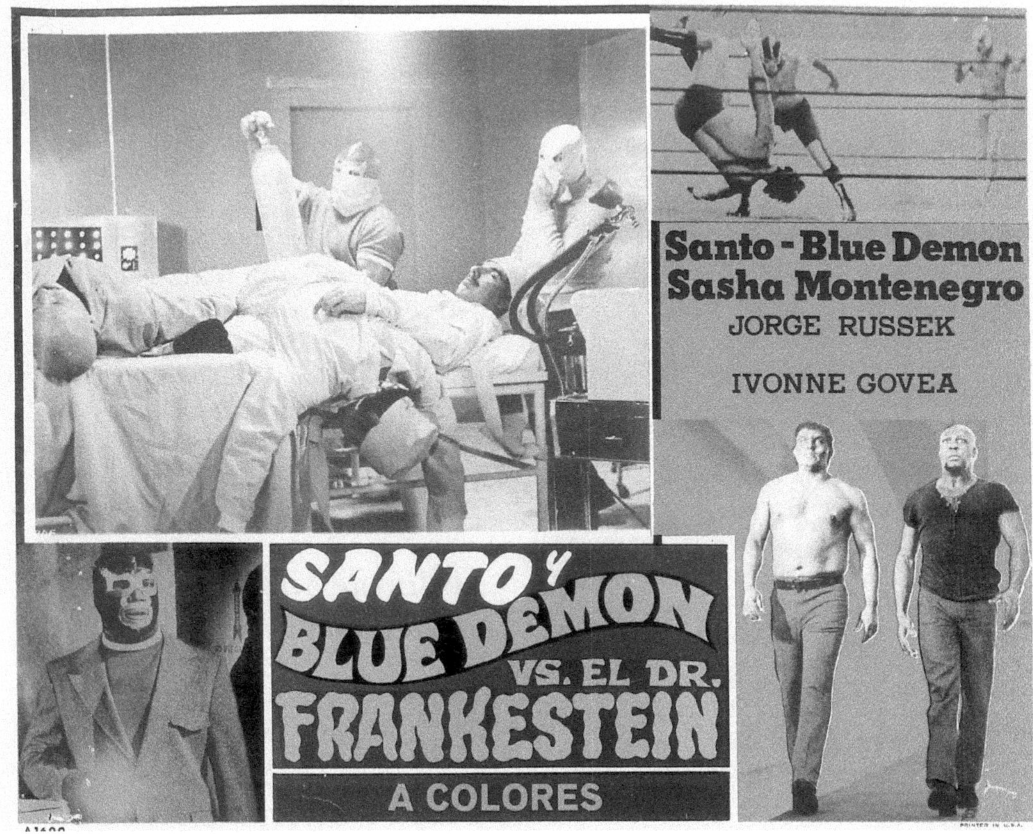

1973's *Santo y Blue Demon vs. el Dr. Frankenstein* (Azteca lobby card).

Of course, the Hammer films didn't use the classic monster either, but at least they had Peter Cushing. Cushing proved that the monster didn't have to be especially memorable as long as the good doctor was; but such was not the case with *vs. Dr. Frankenstein*. To Jorge Russek's credit (playing Dr. F.), however, he does pull off a few good lines, such as "When battling death, sometimes you have to kill."

But no movie featuring Santo and Blue Demon can be totally written off, although this one tries real hard. They too have some good lines, and there's one absolutely priceless scene in which they infiltrate the operating room with surgical masks and gowns covering their wrestling masks and tights! A fracas soon breaks out, and watching a fight scene involving masked wrestlers disguised as surgeons is worth the price of admission alone.

El Triunfo de los Campeones Justicieros (*The Triumph of the Champions of Justice, 1973*)

(Prods. Fílmicas Agrasánchez) *Dir/Scr*: Rafael Lanuza; *Photo*: Javier Cruz; *Prod. Mgr*: Carlos Lanuza; *Asst. Dir*: Damian Acosta; *Film Ed*: Nacho Chiu; *Makeup*: Antonio Castaneda; *SPFX*: José Amezquita; *Dialogue Rec*: Hugo Sánchez; *Re-Rec*: Enrique Rodríguez.

Cast: Blue Demon, Superzán, El Fantasmo Blanco, Elsa Cárdenas (Venus), Carol Lanuza (Lila), Jorge Abaunza (Head Midget).

The third and final installment in the Champions of Justice series again finds the "Justice League" changing and/or shortening its membership — except for Blue Demon. Mil Máscaras is gone, his place taken by Superzán — which is not at all a fair trade-off, for although his costume appears just as glittery as some of Mil's, Superzán has nowhere near the ability nor presence to replace Mil Máscaras, the third of Mexico's "Big Three" wrestling screen stars. (For more on why Superzán never really made it, see the "Under-Card" chap-

ter.) The only other wrestler on hand (the others must have been on solo missions) was the returning El Fantasmo Blanco, who demonstrates the previously-unseen ability to turn into a puff of smoke while entering and leaving rooms! (In this report, El Fantasma Blanco is sort of like "Nightcrawler" from the X-Men; but apart from the early Superzán films, Mexican wrestling heroes' powers were generally pretty down-to-earth.) The beautiful Elsa Cárdenas returns, but in a completely different role than in the first film. There she was a villain, but here she's a member of the team, and goes by the appropriate moniker of "Venus."

In the previous two movies, midgets had been the instruments of the main villains (super-powered midgets in the first, and rat-midgets in the second). Here they graduate to head honchos— midgets from outer space! They need a formula from a scientist who's now incognito as the owner of a circus(!). So instead of the usual musical acts, we see plenty of big-top action. The climax even takes place in the three rings. Said setting makes the poster art especially colorful and festive — at first glance, it's uncertain whether they're advertising a movie or a circus (which, in a way, seems appropriate)!

Director Rafael Lanuza is indeed related to Carol Lanuza and Carlos Lanuza; nepotism is just as rampant in the Mexican film industry as it is in the U.S. (they're just a little more honest about it there).

El Hijo de Alma Grande (*The Son of Alma Grande, 1974*)

(Prods. Fílmicas Agrasánchez–Belize International) *Exec. Prod*: Ernesto Fuentes; *Prod/ Adapt*: Rogelio Agrasánchez [Linage]; *Dir*: Tito Novarro; *Story*: Laura H. de Marchetti; *Photo*: Antonio Ruiz; *Music*: Gerard Garbuit; *Prod. Mgrs*: José Luis Urquieta, Rafael Rosares; *Film Ed*: Angel Camacho; *Sound*: Salvador Topete; Filmed in Belize.

"Peanuts! Popcorn! Get yer red-hot Masked Wrestlers and Space Midgets right here!" The circus setting of the film provided the inspiration for this colorful one-sheet for the third and last "Champions of Justice" film.

Cast: Blue Demon, David [Agrasánchez] Lamar (Alma Grande son), Ana Bertha Lepe (Mirca), Noé Murayama (Noé), Noelia Noel (Kira), Orlando Hernández (Orlando), José Luis Urquieta (José).

This modest (though worthy) picture was an Agrasánchez family affair. It was produced and adapted by Rogelio Agrasánchez (Linage), Sr. (the man responsible for the wildly-successful *Mummies of Guanajuato* and *Champions of Justice* series), and stars one of his sons, David (under the screen name David Lamar). Although not as large in scale or scope as Agrasanchez Sr.'s two most famous series, *Alma Grande* acquits itself nicely, as does David Agrasánchez.

Aliens, led by the ever-dependable Noé Muyryama, have set up shop in the Mayan ruins of Belize and have enslaved a bunch of puny flesh creatures, including Blue's (screen) brother, who's there on his honeymoon. When they don't come back, Blue goes a-lookin' for them, and frees the angry villagers, and the aliens that don't die, disappear.

Poor Blue, he just can't get a break. When Santo trotted off to the jungle in *Santo vs. the Head Hunters*, at least he sported some snazzy Daktari-style threads, including a stylish bandana. Blue just has a pair of boots and pants (along with his mask, of course). Geez, amigos, at least throw him a t-shirt!

La Mansión de las Siete Momias (*The Mansion of the Seven Mummies*, 1975)

(Cinematográfica Tikal–Fílmicas Agrasánchez) *Assoc. Prod*: Rogelio Agrasánchez; *Dir/Scr*: Rafael Lanuza; *Photo*: Armando Castillon; *Music*: Luis Hernández Breton; *Prod. Mgr*: Carlos Lanuza; *Asst. Dir*: José Luis Urquieta; *Film Ed*: José W. Bustos; *Makeup*: Antonio Castaneda; *Sound*: Febronio Tepozte; *Sound Ed*: José Li-Ho.

Cast: Blue Demon, Superzán, María Cardi-nal (Sofia de la Garza), Claudio Lanuza (Barón), Laura Fierro (Isabel), "Manolin" (Manolin), Enrique Bremermann.

This Cinematográfica Tikal–Fílmicas Agrasánchez co-production is more or less another installment in the *Mummies of Guanajuato* series, although the films were no longer employing that particular location. The mummies have the same look, though, and wrestlers battling them (Blue having not done so since the original *Mummies of Guanajuato*). Blue Demon is joined again by ex–Campeón Superzán (this was, after all, an Agrasánchez movie) and comedian "Manolin" as their sidekick.

Sofia de la Garza (María Cardinal) must perform three tasks to inherit her late father's fortune. Unfortunately, dead ol' dad made a deal with the Devil, and she has to go through the mummies to get to it. Of course, with Blue and Superzán's help, she does, but not before lots of weird and creepy action fakes placce, including a scene in which the mummies rise out of a swamp underneath a rope bridge, across which Sofia is walking! Once again, scenes like this were echoed by the subsequent Spanish *Blind Dead* series.

This would be the last time the Guanajuato-style mummies would appear on screen, and was the second-to-last theatrically-released feature for Blue Demon. The golden age of the masked wrestler vs. monster film was about to come to an end (although Santo would stick it out on his own for a few more years), but there was one last team-up left in the Big Three, who went out with a bang — literally.

Misterio en las Bermudas (*Mystery in the Bermudas*, 1977)

(See Santo chapter for technical and cast credits.)

This historic production from the

mexican wrestler/monster pantheon was the last movie to star "the Big Three" of the genre–El Santo, Blue Demon and Mil Máscaras. The days when a popular wrestler might do three or four picture a year were long gone; indeed, this was Blue's last, and Santo and Mil only had a few more left in them.

Like many of the latter-day classics of this genre, *Misterio en las Bermudas* was produced by Rogelio Agrasánchez. And while admittedly not in the same class as, say, *Las Momias de Guanajuato*, it's a fitting send-off— although, as usual, Blue got the short end of the stick. Still, it's a joy to see them all together one last time — and I do mean last (at least in this movie), as the film's climax suggests that either they disappear into the Bermuda triangle or (even more disturbing) (perish in an atomic explosion! At least the usual compliment of great wrestling, hot girls in bikinis, and snazzy sports cars and speedboats kept them occupied until the end (and what a way to go!).

All of the above elements are incorporated into the movie's striking one-sheet poster design as secondary themes, with the major portion taken up by a triangle that places photographic head shots of Santo, Blue and Mil at the corners, each with a telling expression: Santo (at the top, of course) looks, well, saintly; Mil looks regal; and Blue ... well, Blue is looking sideways at both of 'em, just waiting for the right word before he drops a suplex on them!

Misterio en la Bermudas producer Rogelio Agrasánchez was not only responsible for the Guanajuato and Campeones series, but also for many of the latter-day classics (he pretty much kept the genre afloat in the 1970s). For these films and all his other efforts, he earns our undying gratitude.

Blue Demon, el Campeón (*Blue Demon, the Champion,* 1989)

(Osbe S.A.–Videocom Empresarial) (Video) *Exec. Prods*: Alejandro Muñoz [Blue Demon], Juan A. Díaz; *Dir*: J.J. Hoyos; *Scr*: Muñoz, Alberto Munguia, Manuel Carbajal, Jorge Hoyos; *Photo*: Ariel Aviter, Vincente Bernal, Salomon Camacho, Héctor Guerrero, Jorge Hoyos, Rafael Melgoza, Mario Reyes; *Film Ed*: Guillermo Onate.

Blue Demon, el Campeón is not a movie per se, but rather a shot-on-video documentary produced by Blue when he retired from the ring in 1989. A good portion of the production is dedicated to his final match, and it provides great insight into just how revered a figure Blue was; his retirement was handled with the kind of ceremony that would, in this country, be reserved for someone like Michael Jordan, or, in Canada, Wayne Gretzky. His opponents go out of their way to make him look great, and treat him with all the respect due his truly legendary stature.

Blue's screen career is not ignored, but the amount of time may not satisfy fans looking for more movie-related information. Still, for what it is, the film segment is well-done, featuring still photos, movie posters and lobby cards (although offering clips from only two films, *Blue Demon vs. Cerebros Infernales* and, curiously, *Blue Demon vs. las Diabólicas*, proving that the movie *does* exist, but remains "lost" to the general public). The rest of the documentary consists of re-creations of events from Blue's life, and interviews with various producers, wrestlers, etc., who were associated with him at various times over the course of his long career.

Like Santo, Blue Demon had a son who continued his legacy in the ring as Blue Demon, Jr. (but, unlike El Hijo del Santo, not on the movie screen). And one other thing has endured — the rivalry be-

Luchas 2000 magazine cover with Blue at rest — "Adios, campeón."

tween their famous fathers has continued through to this generation (and, like the Hatfields and McCoys, it won't stop there). To this day, the very mention of the name Blue Demon (Senior *or* Junior) brings a pained expression to the face underneath the mask of the Son of El Santo.

Six

"Man of a Thousand Masks"

The Life and Films of Mil Máscaras

Mil Máscaras was born Aaron Rodríguez, and worked his way up through the ranks to become not only one of Mexico's greatest wrestlers, but one of the most famous grapplers on the international scene as well, winning numerous titles and becoming the first masked Mexican wrestler to work Madison Square Garden. The January 1980 issue of *Wrestling Superstars* magazine named him as one of "the Greatest Wrestlers of the '70s," alongside such legends as Bruno Sammartino and Andre the Giant. Mil had four brothers, two of whom would also forge stellar careers in the ring — as Dos Caras and El Sicodelico. Mil Máscaras didn't make as many movie appearances as his sometime screen partners El Santo or Blue Demon, and came into the game a bit later than they did, but his film and wrestling career spanned four decades, and he starred in some of the classics of the genre. Mil Máscaras, translated, literally means "one-thousand masks," and sometimes it actually seemed like there *were* that many, all of them colorful and flamboyant (just like his matching ring gear). Sometimes he would wear three or four different masks during the course of a single film! His mat technique was legendary, and his assortment of moves was as colorful as his costumes, both of which continue to provide inspiration to this

very day. This author had the privilege of meeting him, interviewing him, and watching him wrestle live (twice during the late 1990s). Not only did he acquit himself well in the ring, but he proved to be the proverbial class act, and showed beyond the shadow of a doubt why he is a legend.

Mil Máscaras (*Thousand Masks*, 1966)

(Fílmica Vergara–Cinecomisiones) *Prod*: Luis Enrique Vergara; *Dir*: Jaime Salvador.

Cast: Mil Máscaras, Malu Reyes, Dagoberto Rodríguez, Eric del Castillo, Juan Miranda.

What's a producer to do? Your biggest star, El Santo, has quit in a contract dispute, and your second biggest star, Blue Demon, is on the shelf after a serious injury, with no timetable for his return. Well, you go out and get a rookie (at least he comes cheaper), and cross your fingers. That's exactly the situation that Luis Vergara faced in 1966, and that's exactly what he did; only he didn't have to cross his fingers for long. The rookie he got was Mil Máscaras.

Mil's first screen effort is notable for two reasons. The first, and most important, was Mil Máscaras himself. Whereas it took Santo and Blue Demon a few

"The Man of a Thousand Masks": Mil Máscaras.

movies to grow comfortable on screen, Mil took to films like a fish to water (he had even taken acting lessons to prepare for a moment like this, and he wasn't going to blow it!). His masks and apparel also lent themselves to filmland — ornate and flamboyant, they virtually begged for a camera.

The second reason is Mil Máscaras' "origin," as laid out by this film. Though the movie as a whole is mostly in the mold of a Huracán Ramírez ring drama (only without the family restaurant), the first ten minutes or so are another story. Literally.

In 1933 (the same year that Salvadore Lutteroth introduced masked wrestling in Mexico), an American pulp magazine publisher, Street and Smith, issued *The Man of Bronze*, the first novel in a long-running series of adventures featuring a character by the name of Doc Savage. Doctor Clark Savage, Jr., was raised, virtually from the cradle, by the leading experts of every mental and physical field known to humanity, until he became a virtual (if not literal) super-man, and was a model for every variation on the theme that followed — including, it seems, a certain masked wrestler.

Now, keep in mind that, although they were portrayed by real-life wrestlers, the on-screen "characters" of El Santo, Blue Demon, etc., were just that — characters — and therefore subject to artistic interpretation. In the case of El Santo, different backstones crop up in different films, one drawing on Fawcett's *Captain Marvel*, but others emulating Lee Falk's *Phantom*, (and the idea that the mask — and the character — is ageless, passed on from generation to generation throughout time). Curiously, Blue Demon never received such a perk — he just appeared out of nowhere in his first film, and went on about his business. Come to think of it, that Blue Demon is one existential cat. Mil Máscaras only had one origin, and its similarity to the origin of Doc Savage is striking.

During the waning days of World War II, a group of scientists decide that a new breed of man should be developed, imbued from birth with a strong sense of justice. When they find a baby in its dead mother's arms, they have their test subject. Raised from the cradle by the leading experts of every mental and physical field

known to humanity, this orphaned infant grows into a virtual (if not literal) super-man. It is then decided that his incredible abilities can best be put to use as a … masked wrestler! Given such a build-up, it's curious that the rest of the film consist of (more or less) mundane ring/J.D. activity, but a personality as robust as Mil Máscaras' could not be contained for long.

Los Canallas (*The Evil Ones,* 1966)

(Fílmica Vergara–Cinecomisiones) *Prod*: Luis Enrique Vergara; *Dir*: Federico Curiel.

Cast: Mil Máscaras, Regina Torne, David Silva, Marolo Muñoz, Fredrico Falcón, Claudia Martell, Fernando Osés, Cavernario Gallindo.

Television's *Batman* series had more than its share of influence on the wrestler/monster genre. To wit: After *Batman*'s debut, it just wouldn't do to have superheroic types perform their feats in plain old black-and-white anymore. No, post–Caped Crusader, there had to be color — loud, spashy, "op-art" color, and lots of it. El Santo and Blue Demon had been around for a while, and had the black-and-white experience to prove it. But Mil Máscaras was the new breed, and had made only one black-and-white film before the color revolution. The timing was perfect — Mil's masks and costumes virtually cried out for full color, and it would have been a crime to keep the tones muted much longer.

Los Canallas moves us much closer to the promised land than *Mil Máscaras*; and, although we would have to wait until the next one, *Las Vampiras*, to achieve true psychotronic nirvana, Mil's second proved far more satisfying than the first. The J.D. angle is expanded from a gang of teen thugs in *Mil Máscaras* to a gang of *devil-worshipping* teen thugs (called "Hell's Angels!") in *Los Canallas*, and the fantastic, serial-like element is much more pronounced. Future Wrestling Woman Regina Torne is definitely not on the side of justice this time, as she spends much of her leader-of-the-pack time dressed in as little as possible — and wielding a whip! Mil survives numerous serial/spy-like perils involving tear gas canisters, machine guns, and lip poison. One of the main villains has a hook for a hand, and he escapes from prison using a toy piano! Of course, he also menaces Mil with that hook — in the secret underground library climax — and comes to an "Odd Job"–like end.

Mil had it pinned to the canvas with only his second film; the next one was a flying suplex off the ropes.

Las Vampiras (*The Vampire Girls*, 1967)

(Fílmica Vergara–Cinecomisiones) *Prods*: Jesús Frangoso, Luis Enrique Vergara; *Dir*: Federico Curiel; *Story*: Curiel, Adolfo Torres Portillo; *Music*: Gustavo César Carrión; *Cinematography*: Alfredo Uribe; *Film Ed*: Juan José Munguía; *Prod. Design*: José Méndez, Octavio Ocampo.

Cast: Mil Máscaras, John Carradine (Count Drácula), Pedro Armendáriz, Jr., Sara Bentz, Rossy Ceballos, María Duval, Manuel Garay, Elsa María, Maura Monti, Jessica Munguia, Dagoberto Rodríguez, Marta Romero.

Las Vampiras is Mil Máscaras' *Santo vs. las Mujeres Vampiro*— not because of similarities to its glorious ancestor (despite the similarity of the titles and the fact that they feature a bevy of female vampires), but because both were the high-water mark of their respective star's early solo adventures. WARNING: The nuttiness in this movie reaches extreme levels, and *Las Vampiras* would have become every bit as famous as the Santo effort had it had been dubbed into English. Despite the language barrier, it still carries a pretty hefty rep among genre fans, and it's easy to see why.

The link between the Universal classics and Mexican monster movies was es-tablished in *La Casa del Terror*, with Lon Chaney, Jr., playing both a Kharis-style mummy and Larry Talbot-esque were-wolf; it was solidified in this production, with the pivotal role of Dracula essayed by John Carradine, who had, of course, played the Count in both *House of Frankenstein* (1944) and *House of Dracula* (1945). "Pivotal" may be the wrong word, as Carradine spends most of the film locked in a cage, scheming to escape; but the action does revolve around him, and he is absolutely and completely over the top (there's so much ham in his performance, one wonders why pigs aren't extinct!).

In what is probably the movie's most famous scene (set in a canyon cavern), Mil Máscaras and cub reporter Pedro Armen-dariz, Jr., look on while Long John wails and caterwauls, locked in his cage by shapely, rebellious vampire girls (who wear green tights and sport bouffant hairdos to complement their fangs). And right now, they're having one heck of an undead cat-fight — with torches! As Sam Spade would say, "This is the stuff that dreams are made of." And it's all directed with extreme gusto by Fredrico Curiel.

As for reports over the years about Carradine being difficult to work with, let's hear what Mil has to say:

"In *Las Vampiras* with John Carradine, I have a terrific experience, because, when I start to make the movie, I don't know he's in the cast, and I see him before in American movies, especially with John Wayne. And it was interesting to do, you know. He's very professional — very good and very professional. After, I meet his son David, and years later, he became popular, too."

Enigma de Muerte (*Enigma of Death*, 1968)

(Fílmica Vergara–Cinecomisiones) *Prod*: Luis Enrique Vergara; *Dir*: Fredrico Curiel; *Scr*: Ramón Obón; *Cinematography*: Alfredo Uribe.

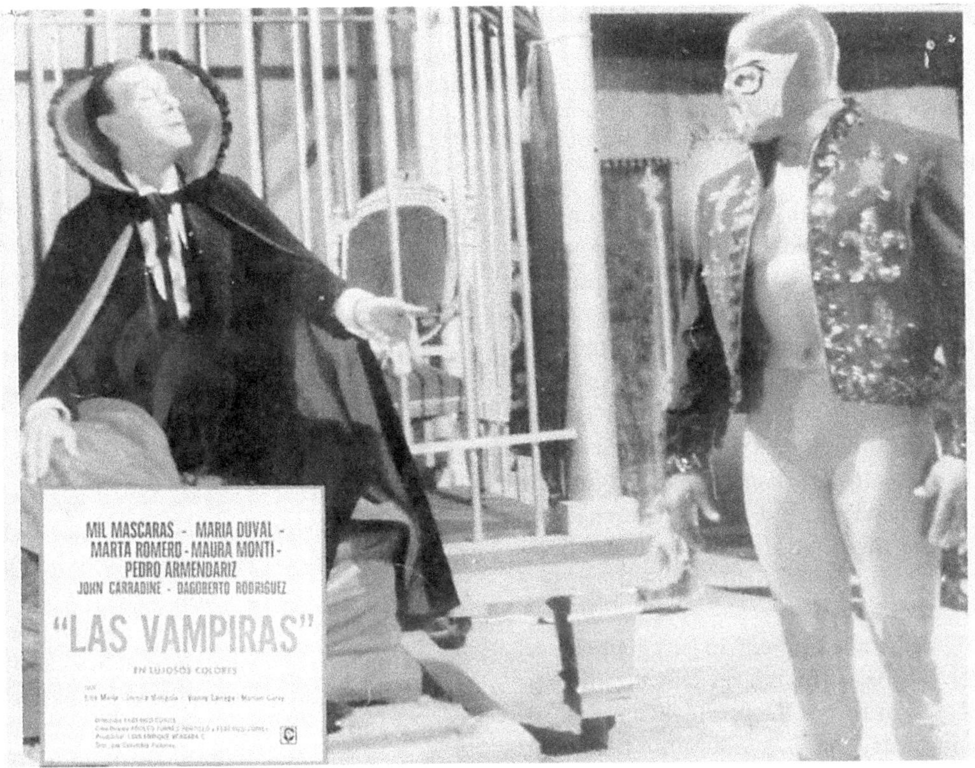

Two Mexican lobbies from Mil's most famous solo effort, *Las Vampiras*. *Top*: John Carradine holds court with Mil. *Bottom*: Mil offers a light to Maria Duval, who politely refuses.

Cast: Mil Máscaras, John Carradine, Eric del Castillo, María Duval, Víctor Junco, Nothanael "Frankenstein" León, Altia Michel, David Silva, Isela Vega.

With certain Mexican genre films, although scattered technical information and/or display art (lobby cards, posters, stills, etc.) are available, the movies themselves, unfortunately, are not. At the time of this writing, *Enigma of Death* just happens to be one of those films. Hope springs eternal, though; the Santo film *Santo vs. the Daughter of Frankenstein* long held a similar status, but a print turned up around the beginning of the new millennium, and so we still keep our fingers crossed.

This was the next-to-last genre credit for the beautiful María Duval, who appeared in two of the seminal vampire-girl films, *Las Vampiras* and *Santo contra Las Mujeres Vampiro*. She was also the girlfriend of superhero Rocambole in his two features. *Enigma de Muerte's* other female lead was model/singer Isela Vega, who bared all in *Playboy* magazine six years later to promote the Sam Peckinpah western *Bring Me the Head of Alfredo Garcia*.

Los Campeones Justicieros (*The Champions of Justice,* 1970)

(See Blue Demon chapter for technical and cast credits, and additional information.)

Los Campeones Justicieros was yet another winner in a string of successes for Mil. With *Las Vampiras*, he had arrived cinematically, and his pro wrestling career was continuing its meteoric rise. This position of respect and authority was reflected in his two *Champions of Justice* films, where he and Blue Demon played the leaders of wrestling's "Justice League." Mil wears the mantle well, and his performance is smooth and assured. He also owns the film's snazziest ride, a green metalflake dune buggy; and his wardrobe was at its peak, including a leopard-skin vest!

Las Momias de Guanajuato (*The Mummies of Guanajuato,* 1970)

(See the Santo chapter for technical and cast credits, and the Blue Demon chapter for additional information.)

Imagine the Interview.

Interviewer: "Do you have the same feeling about *Mummies of Guanajuato* that Blue Demon does? He resents Santo being brought in at the very last."

Mil Máscaras: "Well, let me tell you this. *Mummies of Guanajuato*, at first, supposedly, just Blue Demon and I make it, and, at the last moment, the last week before they start to make the movie, they change the script, they change everything because El Santo's coming. For me, it don't mean nothing, but Blue Demon — he don't like it! For me, it's not the same. The more stars in the movie, the more guarantee for the producer. It's the same in wrestling, you know, the more stars you have on the card, it's more guarantee, more people come. Last night I wrestle, and ... quién es quién? Who is who? Who's on the card? Nobody! Nobody knew the other wrestlers there. The more stars, the more guarantee of cash money."

El Robo de las Momias de Guanajuato (*The Theft of the Mummies of Guanajuato,* 1972)

(Producciones Fílmicas Agrasánchez–Cinematográfica Tikal) *Prod*: Rogelio Agrasánchez Linaje; *Dir*: Tito Navarro; *Adapt*: Francisco and Miguel Morayta; *Story*: Rogelio Agrasánchez Linaje; *Photo*: Antonio Ruiz; *Music*: Rafael Carrión; *Prod. Mgr*: Herbert Dávila; *Prod. Assts*: Lic. Rafael Rosales Duran, Ernesto Fuentes G; *Prod. Co-Ord*: Rafael Lanuza; *Asst. Dir*: José Luis Uruquieta; *Film Ed*: Angel Camacho;

Two lobbies from the first "Mexican Justice League" movie.

Cam. Op: Lorenzo Contreras; *Makeup*: Victoria Celis; *SPFX*: Eduardo Daniel; *Re-Rec*: Ricardo Saldivar; *Dialogue Rec*: Roberto Muñoz.

Cast: Mil Máscaras, Blue Angel, El Rayo de Jalisco, Julio César [Agrasánchez], Mabel Luna (Ana), Tito Novaro (Count Alejandro de Cagliostro), Carlos Figueroa, Rafael Rosales, Anabella Portilla, René García, Kyra Rosenhouse.

Mil's second and last stint as a mummy-fighter comes in this first sequel (filmed in Guatemala) to the 1970 classic *Mummies of Guanajuato*. Blue Demon and Santo couldn't make it this time, so Mil enlists the help of fellow Justice Champions Rayo de Jalisco, a sub for La Sombra Vengadora, and Blue Angel (no, not Marlene Dietrich, but a wrestler whose mask looked just like Captain America's cowl, minus the tiny wings above the ears).

The evil Count Cagliostro (played by the director, Tito Navarro) is on the prowl for a uranium-like substance called "ernia," but he has two problems: he doesn't know where it is, and, if he does find it, to touch it is fatal. Ergo, he raises the original miners from the dead (guess that's why they're in that condition), who not only know the location (Guanajuato, obviously, although the movie was shot in Guatemala), but can work unhindered by the dangerous substance (or the issue of wages, for that matter). Soon, he has enough of the explosive mineral for an ernia bomb, and sends a threat to the United Nations. But the threat is intercepted by Mil, who decides that he and two other wrestlers can handle it. They lay siege to the Count's stronghold, battling a horde of mummies who just don't know enough to stay down when they're punched, kicked, impaled or otherwise maimed. They do stay down, however, when Mil stumbles across the seemingly simple solution of removing their control devices. The creatures are helped on their way to mummy heaven by Cagliostro himself, who, in trying to reorganize their pri-

orities, simply short-circuits everything and blows up the entire shebang — except for the wrestlers and the pretty girls in mini-skirts.

El Robo de las Momias de Guanajuato made less impact (and money) than the first *Mummies of Guanajuato* movie; but with the absence of two-thirds of the Three Lucha-teers, and considerably less screen time for the mummies, that should have been expected. Particularly effective are the mummy resurrection scenes, always a high point of the *Guanajuato* films, and an obvious inspiration for similar scenes in the *Blind Dead* series that oozed out of Spain a few years later.

Vuelven los Campeones Justicieros (*The Return of the Champions of Justice*, 1972)

(See the Blue Demon chapter for technical and cast credits.)

Una Rosa sobre en Ring (*A Rose in the Ring*, 1972)

(Producciones Fílmicas Agrasánchez) *Prod*: Rogelio Agrasánchez Linaje; *Dir*: Arturo Martínez; *Story*: Rogelio Agrasánchez Linaje; *Photo*: Antonio Ruiz; *Music*: Bernardo Serrano; *Makeup*: Antonio Castaneda.

Cast: Mil Máscaras, Crox Alvarado, Irma Dorantes, Rogelio Guerra, David Silva, Arturo Martínez, Julio César [Agrasánchez], Claudio Lanuza, Antonio Almorza.

This Huracán Ramírez–style "ring drama" centers on a young boy, played by Julio César. César was in reality the son of producer Rogelio Agrasánchez, and essayed juvenile roles in many of his father's productions: the first two Mummies of Guanajuato movies, *Superzán el Invencible*, *Return of the Champions of Justice*, and the final team-up of Mil, Blue and El Santo *Misterio en las Bermudas*. Rogelio's other son, Rogelio, also tackled a youthful role or two in his father's productions; he is now

Mil and Blue's "Champions of Justice" series featured so many masked heroes, they could barely fit onto the lobby cards and stills!

the "Keeper of the Flame," housing the largest collection of Mexican film graphic material in the world (which he has displayed internationally), and co-authoring several fine books on Mexican poster art. (This author is cited in the dedication of Rogelio's *Mexican Horror Cinema*.)

Las Momias de San Angel (*The Mummies of San Angel,* 1973)

(Producciones Fílmicas Agrasánchez) *Prod*: Rogelio Agrasánchez Linaje; *Dir/Scr*: Arturo Martínez; *Story*: Rogelio Agrasánchez Linaje; *Photo*: Antonio Ruiz; *Music*: Bernardo Serrano; *Makeup*: Antonio Castaneda; *Asst. Dir*: José Luis Uruquieta; *Prod. Mgr*: Antonio Moreno; *Asst. Cam*: Lorenzo Contreras; *Sound*: Beto Muñoz.

Cast: Mil Máscaras, Tinieblas, El Fantasma Blanco, El Enmascarado Negro, Lorena Velázquez (Alicia), Rogelio Guerra (Manuel/Don Manuel de Monsivais), Alicia Encinas, Arturo Martínez (Comandante), Claudio Lanuza, Sacha Fredy Pecherelli, Elias Charur, Edgar Echeverria, Hugo Carranza, Enrique Breberman, Miguel Jimeniz.

This is the second feature (following *Capulina contra las Momias*) to utilize the Guanajuato bandage-brokers without using the name. Which begs the question: Why (since it seems like it would have been more profitable to maintain the connection)? And even if *Las Momias de San Angel* isn't in the same league as the first two "official" Guanajuato movies, there's still plenty of fun to be had. Mil wears his "dragon" mask (my favorite), a gold and red affair that looks like a cross between Spider-Man (the eyes) and a Flying Tiger plane (the huge grinning mouth filled with pointed teeth). Tinieblas gets a second go at the monsters after having played the head mummy in *Mummies of Guanajuato*. El Fantasma Blanco, however, is a non-entity—come to think of it, he barely registered even when he had something to do. The poster art makes El Enmascarado

Negro seem like a super-special guest grappler, but he's actually the villain of the piece! (The poster for this one proved especially striking, with half of the artwork dominated by a creepy close-up of a mummy's face.) El Enmascarado Negro and his gang participate in some impressive scenes, the gory climax (in which one of the thugs gets his eyes bloodily poked out). The mummy mayhem doesn't stop with the gangsters—a young couple making out in a car are zapped by a mummy who can shoot flames from his hands! (So much for Lovers' Lane.)

Las Momias de San Angel suffers from some haphazard construction, but, as noted in the Santo and Blue Demon chapters, by this time the genre was starting to lose a little steam, and not as much care was taken with the form (but then, that's true of any genre). At least they were still in there pitching!

Leyendas Macabras de la Colonia (*Macabre Legends of the Colony,* 1973)

(Producciones Fílmicas Agrasánchez) *Prod/Story*: Rogelio Agrasánchez Linaje; *Co-Prod*: Rafael Lanuza; *Dir/Adapt*: Arturo Martínez; *Photo*: Antonio Ruiz; *Music*: Bernardo Serrano; *Makeup*: Antonio Castaneda; *Prod. Mgr*: Antonio Moreno; *Prod. Chief*: Ignacio Padilla; *Asst. Dir*: José Luis Uruquieta; *Film Ed*: Ignacio Chiu; *Cam. Op*: Lorenzo Contreras; *Sound*: Enrique Rodríguez.

Cast: Mil Máscaras, Tinieblas, El Fantasmo Blanco, Lorena Velázquez (Luisa), Rogelio Guerra (Antonio de Talamantes), Dinorah Judith, Nancy Vega, Arturo Martínez (Inquisitor), Manuel Corquera (Diego de Velazco), Claudio Lanuza, Enrique Bremmermann, René Hernández, Edy Moreno, María Luisa Salazar "Magda," Alfonso Milan.

Leyendas Macabras de la Colonia is cut from the same cloth as *Las Momias de San Angel* (no small surprise, since the technical crew and cast are virtually the same). Like the Rayo de Plata feature *Campeones*

Mil shows off a variety of masks and moves in these stills from *Las Momias de San Angel*.

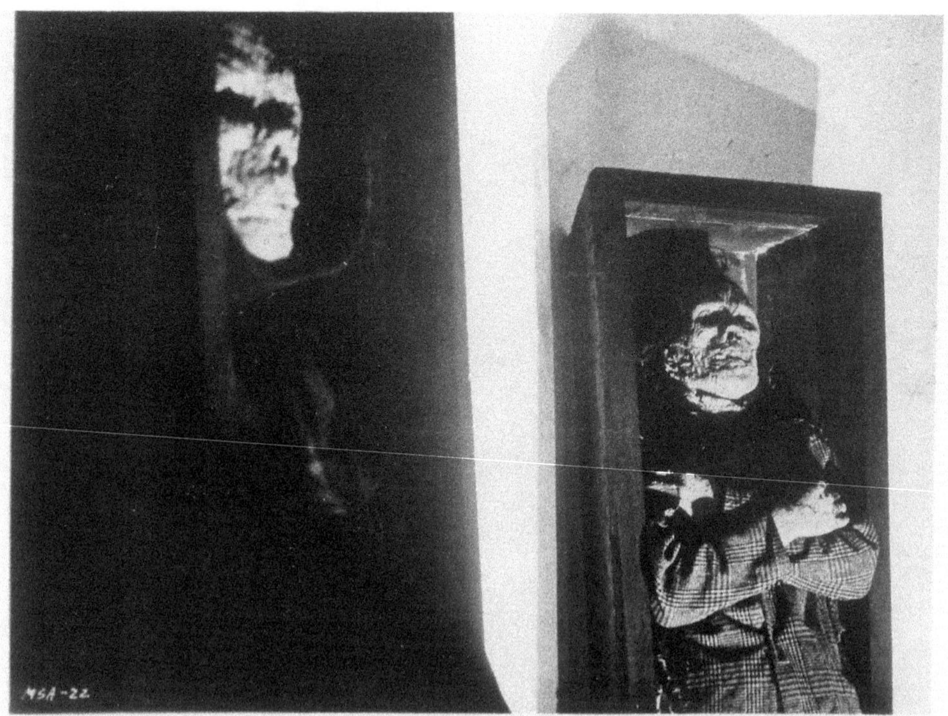

Two shots of the title monsters from *Las Momias de San Angel*. Guanajuato by another name?

del Ring (also made in Guatemala — was there something in the air?), *Leyendas Macabras* is a crazy quilt of scenes and characters, which, besides having very little relevance to the storyline, have very little relation even to each other! This is one of those movies that appear both astounding and incomprehensible at four a.m., but you could watch it at any time of the day and it still wouldn't make much sense. Fortunately, like *Momias de San Angel*, it doesn't need to—it's still fun. Just take what comes your way, enjoy it for what it is, and make sure you pick up your brain at the door on the way out.

Considered an unofficial part of the Guanajuato series, this outing, also filmed in Guatemala, offers only one mummy, but so many other odd characters and events populate the film — masked wrestlers, gorgeous women, beautiful witches, enchanted paintings, "the Mad Monk" (a popular radio, comic strip, and short-feature mystery character), La Llorona — that one bandaged beast is enough. What little plot exists has Tinieblas buying a supposedly cursed painting. He pooh-poohs the notion and takes it home, where, at a party, he and Mil Máscaras argue about art! At midnight the painting starts to release smoke, and the wrestlers and their girlfriends are suddenly transported to the 15th century! There they tangle with the evil Lorena Velázquez (and defeat her when—just as she's about to murder Mil—they hit her over the head with the painting[!] and return to the present). The Mad Monk (sort of a Mexican Crypt Keeper or Uncle Creepy) occasionally pops up out of nowhere to comment on the story, and then disappears again; and, for some reason, La Llorona shows up, utters her signature wail ("Ayyy, mis hijos!" [Aiee, my children!]) and disappears as well.

Los Vampiros de Coyoacán
(*The Vampires of Coyoacán*, 1973)

(Producciones Fílmicas Agrasánchez) Prod: Rogelio Agrasánchez; Dir/Adapt: Arturo Martínez; Story: Agrasánchez, Mario Cid; Music: Ernesto Cortazar, Jr.; Cin: Xavier Cruz; Film Ed: Angel Camacho; Camera Op: Alberto Arellanos [Bustamante]; Wardrobe: Esperanza Valerio.

Cast: Mil Máscaras, Superzán, Germán Robles (Dr. Wells), Sasha Montenegro (Nora), Carlos López Moctezuma (Dr. Thomas), Mario Cid (Barón Bradok), Nothanael "Frankenstein" León (El Espectro), Pura Vargas (Housekeeper), Tony Salazar, David Castañeda, Alfredo Gutiérrez (Detective), Judith Velasco, Jorge Victoria, Alfonso Quiroz, Gabriel Mondragón, Gerónimo Díaz, Armando Acosta (Baggage clerk), Luis Guevara, Humberto Elizondo (Ticket clerk).

It's another winner for Mil Máscaras. Following hot on the heels of his triumphs in the incredibly popular "Champions of Justice" and "Mummies of Guanajuato" series, this full-tilt funfest, again produced by Rogelio Agrasánchez, takes Mil and Superzán to a different city to square off against a different type of living dead.

The poster art for *Vampiros de Coyoacán* is not only one of the most striking examples of genre art, it's one of the most misleading. The central image is a well-done piece with four gradually-enlarging bats swooping downward over a large splatter of blood. (In the movie, these furry flying fiends turn into vampiric midgets!) Germán Robles stars in the film with Mil and Supe, although he goes against expectations by playing a heroic Van Helsing–type doctor. This did not stop the poster artist, however, who added a large rendering of a vampire about to put the bite on a sleeping beauty — with the vampire looking just like Robles! Also included, for no apparent reason, is what appears to be a swipe from one of the black-and-white Skywald gory horror comics of the 1970s—an incredible image featuring a wild-maned vampire about to stake a female vamp! (Exactly why would he want to do that?)

Mil Máscaras and Superzán play tag-team partners, and Mil carries the weight of the action (as well as the acting) in a l-o-o-o-ng wrestling sequence. When a fellow luchador is killed in the ring by bald stalwart "Frankenstein" León, our heroes pile into a convertible and head to Coyoacan, where they hook up with Robles. Robles suspects that the Barón in the castle just around back may be a vampire (he should know), so Mil and Supe invade the castle grounds, where the Barón has transformed somewhat—though still in tuxedo and cape, he now sports a huge bat-head! That's when he calls in the bat-midgets! They swoop in as bats and then turn into midgets with fangs; and when Mil or Supe smack them, they turn into bats again and go poof! The wrestlers needn't have bothered—the sun comes up and does their job for them. (Despite the vanquishing of the vampires, the operation was not *entirely* successful, as most of the people the good guys were supposed to protect bit the dust! Oops.)

Los Vampiros de Coyoacán proved to be a non-stop thrill-ride, one considerably enhanced by the presence of Robles. About his masked co-stars, Robles once said: "As actors, they made great wrestlers!" Ah, go bite somebody. This was the last genre film for the sassy Sasha Montenegro, who graced six genre entries in all from 1970 to 1973, and then turned her considerable talent and physical assets towards sexy comedies, where she truly made her name.

El Poder Negro (*Black Power*, 1973)

Prod: Roberto Rodríguez; *Dir*: Alfredo B. Crevenna; *Scr*: Roberto Rodríguez; *Adapt*: Alfredo B. Crevenna, Roberto Rodríguez; *Adapt.*

Asst: Alfonso Morones A; *Music*: Gustavo César Carrión; *Cin*: Ramón Carthy; *Film Ed*: Jorge Bustos.

Cast: Mil Máscaras, Héctor Suárez, Lila Morillo, Ignacio Navarro, Sergio Oliva, Sergio Torres, Francisco Ferrari, María José Picado, Enrique Soto.

It's blaxploitation, south-of-the-border style! Obviously, if you're this far into the book, you know that Mexican producers have never been shy about mixing genres, and so it should come as no surprise that they ventured into territory previously claimed by Blacula, Superfly and Shaft. *Poder Negro* primarily draws from *Hammer*, an American film starring Fred "the Hammer" Williamson (so named because of his punishing hitting style while a pro footballer) released the year before. Both stories concern a black man of considerable physical prowess who just wants to be left alone, but is constantly put upon by evil whiteys who just want him killed or maimed. Possessing every convention already set forth by the blaxploitation subset, *Black Power* doesn't add anything new or substantial to that genre or the wrestling one, and the weirdness that one would naturally expect from mixing the two just never materializes. Can ya dig it?

Misterio en las Bermudas (*Mystery in the Bermudas,* 1977)

(See Santo chapter for technical and cast credits.)

By 1973, the genre was near the end of its "golden age." Mil Máscaras realized this, and so, still at the top of his game in the ring, concentrated on his wrestling career. As a result, he didn't make another movie for four years, and the film, *Misterio en las Bermudas*, proved to be his (as well as Blue Demon's) virtual swan song. Their co-star, Santo, kept on until 1982, but by that point the genre's time had well

Lobby cards from two of Mil's 1970s efforts. *Top*: A solo Huracán Ramírez–style ring drama. *Bottom*: One of Mil's last, and the final time the "Big Three" of the genre would team up.

and truly passed. Mil would return to the screen only three more times—in 1983 he would step in and help Santo's son complete production of *Frontera sin Ley* when that effort ran into financial trouble; and Mil ended his screen career with two self-produced "serious" ring dramas, *La Verdad de la Lucha* (*The Truth About Wrestling*, 1988) and *La Llave Mortal* (*The Deadly Wrestling Hold*, 1990), both minor efforts that failed to cause much of a ripple.

Curiously, *Misterio en las Bermudas* offers only the second teaming of all three heroes; and while it's no *Mummies of Guanajuato*, it's still nice to see them fake one last turn together. And at least they go out in weird and apocalyptic style: Like some Mexican "Ragnarok," the heroes' boat races into the Bermuda triangle for a final confrontation with the villain; as it moves out of camera range, there's an atomic explosion! Mankind is saved, but our three heroes "were never heard from again." Quite a finale — saddening and yet entirely heroic, and somehow fitting for three masked characters who had caused quite an explosion of their own.

Mil sports what has to be considered the very last word in wrestling masks (*Coloso* photograph).

SEVEN

Glorious Luchadoras of Wrestling
The Lives and Films of the Wrestling Women

Lara Croft, Tomb Raider, and her super-athletic, drop-dead gorgeous cohorts give the impression that Action Heroines are some sort of new invention, when, as with many "new" things, nothing could be farther from the truth. Some of the foremost action stars of early cinema serials were women, the most famous being Pearl White. Perhaps this was too far-thinking for early movie audiences, and so for a number of years women were relegated to more "feminine" roles and types of behavior, and the prime proponent of female "power" came in the form of the seductress, or "vamp."

In the 1940s this began to change. While the men were fighting World War II, women had begun to take on many jobs back home that had always been considered the males' domain. Things had begun to change in the cinema, too, but not in the "mainstream." No, it was in the lowly form of the chapter-play, or cliffhanger (where it had all begun in the first place). The new Pearl Whites had names like Kay Aldridge, Linda Stirling, and Frances Gifford, and they played strong, beautiful action heroines in serials like *The Adventures of Nyoka*, *The Tiger Woman*, and *Jungle Girl*. Another "lowly" art form, the newly-invented comic book, also showcased the new breed of female, of course led by Wonder Woman.

Another extremely popular action heroine was Sheena, Queen of the Jungle, who was still around in comics form until the 1950s, at which point the character transferred to the television screen via the unforgettable Irish McCalla. Tall, blonde, and statuesque, Sheena embodied something that other action heroines had only suggested — a raw and savage sensuality (wondrously accentuated by her leopard-skin bikini). To be sure, Aldridge, Stirling and Gifford were beautiful women, but their costumes appeared quite demure (and in Kay "Nyoka" Aldridge's case, downright manly), and did nothing to emphasize their sexuality. Sheena changed all that, proving that a woman could be both "hot," and kick butt and take names at the same time.

Another quality of action heroines, which had heretofore been largely ignored, was intelligence. Oh, there had been intelligent women in films, but Katharine Hepburn and Bette Davis could hardly be called action stars, not to mention the fact that even intelligent women were not placed in roles or situations that made them the equal of men. Monster movies helped change this. In the 1950s, women in creature features started to become more than just the object of lust for the monsters, or shrinking violets who fainted into the hero's arms at the sight of them. Not that the monster still didn't lust after the heroine (after all, monsters are a notoriously randy bunch), but now they lusted after marine biologists or research scientists who took an active hand in trying to defeat them.

The 1960s was the decade when action heroines really came into their own. The smart, sexy woman who was easily the equal of the male (and sometimes superior) received ample representation in characters like Anne Francis' private eye Honey West, or Diana Rigg as Emma Peel in *The Avengers*, or Tura Satana in Ted V. Mikels' *Doll Squad* (which proved to be the blueprint for *Charlie's Angels* in the '70s). *The Doll Squad* had its Mexican equivalent, *Con Licencia para Matar*, in which Maura Monti led a trio of black leather–clad beauties, each one smart, sassy, and an expert with their chosen weapon. But their path was paved by "the Wrestling Women."

Women's wrestling today is quite different than in its beginnings. With all the pin-up models and porn queens in the ring today, one almost gets the impression that wrestling is a gorgeous lady's primary aspiration. While there may be something to this now, there certainly was not then — women's wrestling, like midget wrestling, has always been viewed as a novelty, and so did not attract women who could use their fame to springboard them into the pages of *Playboy* and beyond. "The Wrestling Women" (Las Luchadoras) changed all that, too. Lorena Velázquez and Elizabeth Campbell were smart, classically beautiful women who not only wrestled, but fought monsters! The films that comprise the Wrestling Women series, especially the first two, are among *the* greatest of a genre that was already over the top in its audacious mixing of disparate elements.

Las Luchadoras contra el Médico Asesino (*The Wrestling Women vs. the Killer Doctor*, a.k.a. *Doctor of Doom*, a.k.a. *Rock and Roll Wrestling Women vs. the Aztec Ape*, 1963)

(Cinematográfica Calderón S.A.) *Prod*: Guillermo Calderón Stell; *Dir*: René Cardona, Sr.; *Story*: Guillermo Calderón Stell, Alfredo Salazar; *Scr*: Alfredo Salazar; *Musical Dir*: Antonio Díaz Conde; *Dir. of Photo*: Ezequiel Carrasco; *Film Ed*: Jorge Bustos; *Cinematography*: Enrique Wallace; *Art Dir*: José Rodríguez; Filmed at Churubusco-Azteca, Mexico.

Cast: Lorena Velázquez (Gloria Venus), Elizabeth Campbell (the Golden Rubi), Armando Silvestre (Miguel), Chucho Salinas (Tomas), Roberto Cañedo (El Médico), Gerardo Zepeda (Gomar), Chabela Romero, María Eugenia San Martín, Ramón Bugarini, Victor Velázquez, Sonia Infante, Jorge Mondragón, Irma Rodríguez, Martha Solis.

Alfredo Salazar's story for *Las Luchadoras contra el Médico Asesino* was an instant hit, and immediately became a standard-bearer for the genre. So much so that it would be recycled several times—twice in the Wrestling Women series itself, and once in the Santo/Blue Demon series—and when not lifted wholesale, at least some of its body parts turned up elsewhere. The original remains the best, however (which is even more amazing considering the fact that it was the first of the series). It had taken Santo and Blue Demon a few flicks to really find their "sea legs," but the Wrestling Women hit the ground running. And the best was yet to come.

There's this nutty doc, see. A Killer Doc, in fact, and he's killing women in order to find a brain for his monster, Gomar (Gerardo Cepeda, Mexico's Eddie Parker). The Doc figures that all his previous test-subject women died because they weren't the right type, and so he needs the hardier breed of female that wrestles. He

The world had never seen anything like the Wrestling Women, nor would it see their like again (pressbook cover).

gets this bright idea after the last woman he subjects to the experiments turns out to be the sister of Gloria Venus (Lorena Velázquez), the tag-team partner of the Golden Rubi (Elizabeth Campbell). The vixens of the ring, ably assisted by their boyfriends, ever-dependable Armando Silvestre and comedy-relief sidekick Chucho Salinas, then engage in a series of pitched battles with the Killer Doc, and bring the film to a rousing climax by dousing the Doc with acid and leaving Gomar in a pile. But wait, it's not down for the full count yet! Just when the wrestling lovelies think it's safe to go back in the ring, the Killer Doctor turns up alive — in a plaid suit and wrestling mask — posing as the manager of (get ready for it...) a masked female wrestler into which he's transferred the brain of a gorilla! The Doc dupes Gloria and Rubi into a match with his new creation, who, surprisingly, does not have her hood torn off to reveal a gorilla! The Doc and his monster wrestler nearly finish off our heroines, but the evil duo escape the ring and ultimately meet their deaths when shot down from a water tower. Damn!

Las Luchadoras contra el Médico Asesino has so many elements going for it, it's hard to know where to start. Having already discussed the audaciously outré plot, how about the two stars? Lorena Velázquez and Elizabeth Campbell were two of the most beautiful and accomplished actresses to appear in Mexican genre films. Lorena, with her regal yet smolderingly sensual bearing, and Elizabeth, an American actress in Mexico, with her Amazonian figure and long blonde hair, made an incredibly alluring and charismatic duo (especially when contrasted against real-life female grapplers like Chabela Pepita, who played the gorilla-brained automaton). Whether wrestling for their lives in the ring or fending off the Killer Doc's thugs (while dressed in negligees), they carry themselves with

guts, style and grace. Of course, the fact that they were actresses and not wrestlers helps.

Roberto Cañedo has a fine turn as the Killer Doc; not only does he appear in a wide array of facial coverings (surgeon's mask, serial-style hood, and wrestling mask), but he also does a *Bowery at Midnight* number posing as ... well, you'll see. As already mentioned, Armando Silvestre and Chucho Salinas offer solid support as the boyfriends, Mike and Tommy, a pair of police detectives. This sends the film off on another weird tangent — as far as couplings go, Lorena and Armando seem like a perfectly natural pair, but the tall, statuesque Golden Rubi's attraction to the short, stocky Salinas is difficult to fathom. At first. She looks like she could eat him for breakfast and spit him back out, and then you realize that's *exactly* what the attraction is! And you thought this was just about women in tights fighting monsters.

In the 1980s Rhino Video released the first two Wrestling Women films on VHS. This normally would have been cause for celebration, but for some reason Rhino felt the need not only to make cuts in the movies, but add amateurishly campy tunes to the soundtrack and re-christen our heroines as the "Rock and Roll" Wrestling Women. Now, Rhino pooh-bah and cult figure Johnny Legend's affection for the Wrestling Women and the Aztec Mummy are well-known, so why he chose to do this with films that were just fine as they were is a mystery. Perhaps he thought the rock and roll songs would help put it over to a larger audience; and maybe if the songs had been better, that would have justified it. But the added music doesn't hurt the films so much (because they're "party movies" anyway); what really galls are the missing chunks of footage and some of the other over-dubs. In the case of *Vs. the Aztec Ape*, it comes at the end when two men enter the arena for the Wrestling

If movies were jewels, these would be 14-karat. *Top*: Roberto Cañedo pretends to comfort Lorena Velázquez. *Bottom*: Gerardo Zepeda menaces María Eugenia San Martín.

Women's latest match, and one remarks on who he thinks will win. The other says (in a line obviously not even in the K. Gordon Murray version), "Yeah, and the loser has to watch this movie again!" This was a very bad decision, and most disrespectful. The Rhino crew managed to keep their attitude in check with their release of *Vs. the Aztec Mummy*, but in this case they made cuts that make no sense. Why, in a movie about an Aztec Mummy, do you gut a key scene of mummy mayhem? What exactly was the point of all this? See these versions if you must, but seek out the dubbed version released to American TV by K. Gordon Murray in the sixties (or, better still, track down the original).

Fortunately, the movies were already so good that they proved almost tamper-proof, and this was even truer with the sequel. *Las Luchadoras contra el Médico Asesino* had already hit a home run, but the next one flew out of the ballpark to become a legend.

Las Luchadoras contra la Momia (*The Wrestling Women vs. the Aztec Mummy*, a.k.a. *Rock and Roll Wrestling Women vs. the Aztec Mummy*, 1964)

(Cinematográfica Calderón S.A.) *Prod*: Guillermo Calderón Stell; *Dir*: René Cardona, Sr.; *Story*: Guillermo Calderón Stell, Alfredo Salazar; *Scr*: Alfredo Salazar; *Musical Dir*: Antonio Díaz Conde; *Dir. of Photo*: Ezequiel Carrasco; *Film Ed*: Jorge Bustos; *Cinematography*: Enrique Carrasco; *Prod. Design*: José Rodríguez Granada; *Sound*: Eduardo Arjona; Filmed at Churubusco-Azteca, Mexico.

Cast: Lorena Velázquez (Loreta Venus*), Elizabeth Campbell (the Golden Rubi), Armando Silvestre (Miguel), Chucho Salinas (Tomas), María Eugenia San Martín (Charlotte), Gerardo Zepeda (the Aztec Mummy), Ramón Bugarini, Victor Velázquez, Chabela Romero, the Malagros Inda Ballet.

In the first film, the character's name was Gloria Venus.

First things first. Though often erroneously reported as such, *The Wrestling Women vs. the Aztec Mummy* is *not* part of the Aztec Mummy series—the ladies fought *an* Aztec Mummy (Tutomec), but not the same creature that appeared in the first Aztec Mummy trilogy (Popoca). For the record, it's not even the same actor; the original Aztec Mummy was portrayed in all three films of that trilogy by Angel de Stefani, while Tutomec was played by Mexico's all-purpose monster portrayer, Gerardo Zepeda. And for many (including myself), Zepeda is *the* Aztec Mummy, for reasons that we shall now explore.

Las Luchadoras contra la Momia may just be the greatest wrestler/monster movie ever made; it remains in an eternal headlock for that title with *Santo vs. las Mujeres Vampiro*. Both are in the running for the title Greatest B-Movie Ever Made. Perhaps the big winner (besides the fans) is Lorena Velázquez, who starred in both, thereby cementing a place in those fans' hearts forever. Like *Las Luchadoras'* version of the Aztec Mummy, Lorena Velázquez is *the* Queen of Mexican genre films; actors and actresses *pray* for a role for which they will always be remembered, and Lorena Velázquez assayed at least two. Her turn as a seductive vampire from outer space in *La Nave de los Monstruos* (see chapter three) is certainly up there as well, but the film itself is not held in quite the same esteem as the other two (which, as discussed previously, is a shame). Lorena's Elizabeth Taylor–like beauty served her well throughout her career, both within and outside of the genre, and unlike many who dismiss genre roles as "just a job," she retains a genuine fondness and affection for hers, and gratitude for the fame they brought her. It's unknown how Elizabeth Campbell feels about it today—after going to Mexico and starring in a number of films, she disappeared from the industry and remains elusive to this day. Together, however, señoras Velázquez and Campbell an unforgettable team.

While it may seem that *Wrestling Women vs. the Killer Doctor* had cornered the market on psychotronica, it only just scratched the surface. Forget about mundane mad doctors and their gangs of everyday thugs intent on transplanting women wrestlers' brains into monsters, this time around our tag-team cuties take on the "Yellow Peril" in the form of Prince Fujiyata of the Black Dragon and his Karate Sisters! It seems that a group of archaeologists have discovered a "codex" (an unfortunate term that when not pronounced distinctly, leads to a whole other set of jokes) which, when deciphered, will lead them to a breastplate that will, in turn, reveal the hiding spot of a long-lost treasure. As it so often happens, the breastplate is worn — and the treasure protected by — the Aztec Mummy! And so begins a series of pitched battles — between wrestling women, karate sisters, prince and mummy. For instance, the film opens with a series of murders (of the archaeologists), and then cuts to a wrestling match! In the quintessential scene, rivaling the Santo's-opponent-turns-out-to-be-a-werewolf sequence from *Santo vs. las Mujeres Vampiro*, the wrestling women are cornered in the mummy's tomb, and the mummy decides it would be a better offensive tactic if he turned into *bat*! Now, the Santo scene is pretty zany, but logical in the sense that vampires can indeed assume the form of a wolf (although not usually in a wrestling ring under a mask); but to have the mummy change into a bat is just insane! And then to have Armando exclaim, in all obviousness, "Look! He's a mummy again!" just ices the cake.

That line of dialogue is basically the same in Spanish or English, but it just *sounds* funnier in the dubbed English version, produced by the infamous K. Gordon Murray. "Infamous" because, to the generally superficial and uninformed "bad movie" cult, he's the guy responsible for dubbing all those wacky Mexican movies. Looking at it another way, he's the guy responsible for providing us the opportunity to see any of those movies at all! Nobody knows why Murray chose the package of Mexican movies that he did (they were probably dirt cheap), but he managed to bring some of the true gems of that genre to an audience that would never have seen them otherwise. At that time there were no 600 cable stations in any language, and so the Mexican films usually played just in Texan or Californian theaters, and then only in their original language. And while it *is* true that the dubbed versions can be side-splittingly funny, it's not so much in the movie itself (which is usually bizarre from the get-go anyway), but in the *way* the lines are read, their very literal translations interpreted in pompous or off-handed ways by the same dubbing actors for every movie in the package. In other words, the voice of Santo in one movie could be the voice of the Evil Scientist in another!

Murray made the fortunate decision to release the films basically uncut — in most cases, they even feature the original title credits, although some of the names are "Americanized" (e.g., "William" Calderón Stell) and all end with the ubiquitous "English version directed by Miguel San Fernando." All told, Murray offered much better representations of the films than the butchered "Rock and Roll..." editions released by Rhino. Putting things in perspective, if K. Gordon Murray hadn't re-dubbed a series of Mexican monster/wrestler classics for television, they never would have been shown on the "Chilly Billy" Cardille-hosted *Chiller Theater* (my childhood *Shock Theater*), I never would have seen them, and this book wouldn't exist, thereby altering the whole time/ space continuum (and, well, you know what happens when you do that).

As indicated earlier, mention the Aztec Mummy, and the made-up visage of Gerardo Zepeda from this movie is the one that immediately springs to mind for most fans. Why? Well, for one thing, this version had a pretty solid launching pad as one of *the* classics of the genre, although the original trilogy (also dubbed by Murray) remains entertaining in a different way. But the main reason is the makeup. The original Aztec Mummy proved sadly lacking in that department, with the mummy looking more like a bedraggled hippie than a monster. But when he met up with the Wrestling Women, he received a mummy makeover, with not only new bandages to replace his raggedy poncho, but a face straight out of a nightmare! Instead of a black mane of hair atop a rather undefined mud-pack face, Zepeda's visage was fashioned into a hideous, grinning, pop-eyed deaths-head with only a few strands of ancient hair covering his skull-like pate. Mexican monster make-ups were never really one of the genre's strong points, but the Aztec Mummy in *Las Luchadoras contra la Momia* proved to be a memorable exception.

In 1989, Lorena Velázquez returned to the scene of her greatest triumph, courtesy of Jonathan Ross, Johnny Legend, and the *Son of Incredibly Strange Films Show.* The TV series, hosted by Ross, spent each of its hour-long segments dealing with a particular psychotronic personality or genre, and one memorable episode treated viewers to what became a primer for wrestler/monster movies for generations to come. Señora Velázquez, still radiant, was all too happy to reminisce — and when taken to Churubusco-Azteca Studios for a trip down memory lane, she got more than she bargained for: as she spoke to the camera, sneaking up behind her, courtesy of

Johnny Legend, was the Aztec Mummy himself! Not Gerardo Zepeda, unfortunately, but a solid approximation. And she wasn't acting — the startled reaction she gives when confronted by her "nemesis" is quite real, according to Johnny ("No, she had no idea," he told me in an interview). But it didn't take her long to adjust; after her initial surprise, she embraced the mummy while saying delightedly, "Oh, my friend, my old friend…" — which pretty much sums up the way we feel about all our monsters.

Las Lobas del Ring (*She-Wolves of the Ring,* 1965)

(Cinematográfica Calderón S.A.) *Prod*: Guillermo Calderón Stell; *Dir*: René Cardona; *Scr*: Jesús "Murciélago" Velázquez; *Music*: Antonio Díaz Conde; *Cinematography*: Raúl Martínez Solares, Enrique Wallace; *Film Ed*: Jorge Bustos; *Prod. Design*: José Rodríguez Granada; *Sound Ed*: José Li-Ho; *Asst. Ed*: Joaquín Ceballos.

Cast: Lorena Velázquez, Elizabeth Campbell, María Eugenia San Martín, Sonia Infante, Rosa María Gallardo, Celia Viveros, Héctor Godoy, Eric del Castillo, Pompin Iglesias, Nacho Contla, Roxana Bellini, Jorge Russek, Perla Walter, Emma Arvizu, Emma Roldan, Jorge Mondragón, Benjamin Ceja, Armando Gutierrez, Manuel Gary, Victor Blanco, Manuel Alvaredo, Nothanael "Frankenstein" León, Gerardo Zepeda, Manuel Donde, Armando Acosta, "Picorro," Juan Garza; Wrestlers: Chabela Romero, Martha Solic, Marina Rey, Refugio González, Cavernario Galindo, Black Shadow, Ray Mendoza, Dorrell Dixon, El Hombre Montaña, Gerardo El Romano, Reyes Oliva.

Not much is known about this film (as well as the following one), as if is considered "lost," — that is, it hasn't been seen on TV, nor is it available on videotape or DVD, either legitimately or "bootlegs," (and if something hasn't turned up bootlegged, you *know* it can't be found). What is known is that it was Lorena Velázquez' last appearance in the series, and that (according to available plot synopses) *She-*

Wolves is more or less a straight wrestling drama, like the ones made featuring the screen incarnation of Huracán Ramírez. Ms. Velázquez has related that she had to quit the series because her boyfriend at the time didn't want her to continue with it. Thanks, jerk!

The movie featured Gerardo Zepeda, whom I previously referred to as Mexico's Eddie Parker, the ubiquitous Universal stuntman who played virtually every famous monster. So it was with Zepeda, who, in addition to his many monsters, played countless henchmen and comedy roles as well. He was a fixture of the Wrestling Women series, appearing in all of them except *The Panther Women*.

Las Mujeres Panteras (*The Panther Women*, 1967)

(Cinematográfica Calderón S.A.) *Prod*: Guillermo Calderón Stell; *Dir*: René Cardona; *Scr*: Alfredo Salazar; *Music*: Antonio Díaz Conde; *Cinematography*: Augustín Jimenez; *Film Ed*: Jorge Bustos; *Prod. Design*: Javier Torres Torija.

Cast: Elizabeth Campbell, Ariadne Welter, Yolanda "Tongolele" Montes, Eric del Castillo, Manuel "Loco" Valdés, Eda Lorna, Genaro Moreno, María Douglas, Jorge Mondragón, Nothanael "Frankenstein" León, Angel Di Stefani, María Guadalupe Delgado.

Like the Republic serial *King of the Rocket Men*, which featured only one Rocket Man, the title of this one promised a whole kaboodle of kitty-women, only to provide a single feline female (played by the beautiful, exotic Tongolele, who cuts quite a figure in her cat-suit). It was Elizabeth Campbell's last time in the ring, but at least she received top billing. Eric del Castillo, normally a heavy, donned a wrestling mask and cape to play "the Angel" (not the same character, nor outfit, seen in the "Demons of the Ring" series), the producers perhaps feeling that another masked hero would help offset the loss of

Lorena Velázquez (how could it?). Replacing Ms. Velázquez was Ariadne Welter, who, in later years, dismissed her role — and the movie — with the comment that she wished all the prints of it would be shot off into space in a rocket-ship! Apparently, she got her wish. Which is unfortunate, because *Las Mujeres Panteras* returned the Wrestling Women series to familiar fantastic grounds, and the available graphic materials show a picture with a lot of potential.

Las Luchadoras contra el Robot Asesino (*The Wrestling Women vs. the Killer Robot,* 1968)

(Cinematográfica Calderón S.A.) *Prod*: Guillermo Calderón Stell; *Dir*: René Cardona, Sr.; *Story/Scr*: Alfredo Salazar; *Music*: Antonio Díaz Conde; *Cinematography*: Raúl Martínez Solares; *Film Ed*: Jorge Bustos; *Prod. Design*: José Rodríguez Granada; *Set Dec*: Carlos Arjona; Filmed at Estudios Churubusco-Azteca, S.A.

Cast: Regina Torne (Gaby Reina), Malu Reyes (Gema), Joaquín Cordero (Dr. Orlac), Gerardo Zepeda (the Killer Robot), Héctor Lechuga (Héctor Lettuce?), Carlos Agosti, Genardo Moreno, José Elias Moreno, Isela Vega, Pedro Armandariz, Jr., Andrés Soler, Augustín Martínez Solares, Pascual García Pena, Eduardo MacGregor, René Barrera, Gloria Chaves.

This was the first Wrestling Women film in color, which meant it was among the first releases on videotape in Mexico. *Las Luchadoras contra el Robot Asesino* was also the first W.W. film to have a "Sexo" version, entitled *El Asesino Loco y el Sexo (Sex and the Mad Killer)*. It was the last Wrestling Women film to feature a tag-team partnership, and the first appearance for a new team. Apparently, they did not catch on, as there would only be one more W.W. film after this one (and that featured a single heroine). Which is too bad, because Regina Torne, at least, proved both beautiful and enthusiastic, and brought a great deal of energy to her role (Malu Reyes was certainly beautiful as well, but brought a little less to the table). Despite great efforts, however, both ultimately fell short of the standards set by Lorena and Elizabeth (although, admittedly, that's a pretty high bar).

The story itself is solid — it should be, as it was a re-write of the first Wrestling Women movie, *Las Luchadoras contra el Médico Asesino*. Since both were written by Alfredo Salazar, at least the producers weren't ripping off someone else's good idea. At least, not obviously ... remember the old Bugs Bunny cartoon in which Elmer Fudd orders the robot to hunt Bugs Bunny, and he inserts into the automaton a card with a picture of the robot's prey? Well, that's exactly how it happens here, robot and all. And to pile it on further, they disguise the obvious eight-foot tall metal man with a trench coat, hat, and sunglasses! Moments like these keep fans (including yours truly) coming back for more. Even the original pressbook is a masterpiece of incoherent lunacy in words and pictures. To wit (sentence construction and emphases exactly as originally printed):

"ORLAC, a brilliant scientist, has invented a MECHANICAL ROBOT, and with the assistance of his helper WALDO, tries to take over a group of scientists to help him convert human beings into humanoid robots.

"AMONG THE MEN captured by the mechanical robot, operated by complicated electronic apparatus, is PROFESSOR REINA, who on learning the object of his kidnapping, refuses to collaborate. Orlac, faced with this situation, directs his robot against the Professor and has him killed.

"GABY REINA, famous wrestler, learning of the death of her uncle, swears not to rest until she finds the assassin. She is assisted by her friend GEMA, and two detectives: ARTURO and CHAVA who finally discover the clue that leads them to the house of ORLAC.

"On being discovered, ORLAC makes them captive and tries to eliminate them by subjecting them to a bracelet of rare metal: Acridium, which was invented by the kidnapped scientist. Acridium in contact with the body upsets the brain and demolishes the will and the entire nervous system, converting them into puppets or Human Robots.

"GABY REINA manages to place the bracelet on the Mechanical Robot, thus attacking his sensitive electronic cells, which makes him insane and uncontrollable. He kills the scientists and Waldo, while Orlac manages to escape through a hidden door. Operating a mechanism which controls the Robot, Gaby finally destroys the monster Robot.

"ORLAC, intent on revenge, kidnaps one of the Female Wrestlers and subjects her to a metallic corset along with the acridium bracelet, which converts her into a terrifying, invincible wrestler, with unnatural strength, in order to confront Gaby in a wrestling match to the death.

"OUR HEROES become wise to Orlac's plan. He escapes with his Robot Wrestler who now carries the name of ELEKTRA. They climb up the metal structure of the wrestling arena, and after an emotional chase, both Orlac and his diabolic creation plunge to a spectacular death."

It's said that a famous director once dreamed up the idea for a movie while under the influence of anesthesia at his dentist's office. I shudder to think of the inspiration for *Wrestling Women vs. the Killer Robot*. Even without Lorena and Elizabeth, it's still wildly entertaining (especially compared to Salazar's *other* variation on his own theme, *Santo and Blue Demon vs. Dr. Frankenstein*).

La Horripilante Bestia Humana (*The Horrible Human Beast*, a.k.a. *Night of the Bloody Apes*, 1968) (Title translation from the pressbook)

(Cinematográfica Calderón, S.A.) *Exec. Prod*: Guillermo Calderón Stell; *Prod*: Alfredo Salazar; *Dir*: René Cardona; *Story/Scr*: Alfredo Salazar; *Cinematography*: Raúl Martínez Solares; *Music*: Antonio Díaz Conde; *Film Ed*: Jorge Bustos; *Prod. Design*: Javier Torres Torija; *Makeup*: María del Castillo; *Prod. Mgr*: Fidel Pizzaro; *Asst. Dirs*: Manuel Alcayde, Valerio Olivo; *Studio*: Churubusco-Azteca S.A.

Cast: José Elias Moreno (Dr. Krallman), Armando Silvestre (Dr. Martínez), Carlos López Moctezuma (Goyo), Norma Lazareno (Lucy), Augustín Martínez Solares (Julio), Javier Rizo, Noelia Noel, Gina Morett, Gerardo Zepeda (The Horrible Human Beast), Juan Fava (The Horrible Human Bean).

This is the last of the Wrestling Women series, even though it doesn't seem that way, because there's only one Wrestling Woman. But still, the original director and scripter were behind the wheel (and Salazar again incorporates elements of *Las Luchadoras contra el Médico Asesino*, although not wholesale as he had in the last one), and so it must be considered as such, even though it was apparent to all on both sides of the camera (and in the audience) that this was the Last Match. Although by no means a clunker, it definitely suffers in comparison with its sister films by virtue of casting (Norma Lazareno is certainly a cutie, but lacks the presence and sheer beauty of her predecessors) and execution — although the elements are there, it just isn't as *fun* as it should have been.

Even so, *La Horripilante Bestia Humana* remains a must-see movie for one very important reason: breasts. There's some gore, too, but that's not nearly as important as the breasts. Now, we can all see plenty of movies with both of those things, but not like this one, for *Night of the Bloody Apes* (as it's known to the gringos) is the only existing version of a fabled "Sexo" movie. And it's the dubbed, American print! The gore consists of some gratuitous blood tossed around, and some (really revolting) real-life operations. And the sexo … ah, yes, the sexo: suffice it to say that the film represents quite a few glimpses of naked breasts (even Wrestling Woman Norma Lazareno plays a couple of scenes in the buff!). Actually, the sexiest scene occurs early on, when the Mad Doctor's nurse decides to lift up her skirt and adjust her stockings and garters right in front of the monster (played with his usual gusto by Gerardo Zepeda). Naturally, the sight drives the monster into a frenzy, so he busts out of his cage and kills her. So, unlike all those legendary Japanese versions of Hammer films that supposedly contain extra scenes of nudity and violence — which you'll never see because they don't exist — this is the real deal. And the final irony is … it's the general release Mexican version that is "lost!"

Just to show that I don't make this stuff up, and that Nobody Does It Better, again I quote from the Pressbook:

"DR. KRAUMAN, eminent surgeon, faces the terrifying reality of his fellow doctors who diagnose the illness of his son, JULIO, 23 years old, as fatal: Leukemia.

"Under the imploring looks of JULIO, the Doctor swears he will save his life.

"Meanwhile, LUCY, a female professional wrestler, throws her opponent from the ring, resulting in a cranium fracture. On her trip to the hospital, the other wrestler is kidnapped by the mad DR. KRAUMAN, who extracts her heart, and makes a transplant for his son, JULIO. In a desperate effort to save his son's life, the doctor injects him with a gorilla's blood to strengthen his resistance.

"The result of the transplant is outstandingly impressive as the gorilla's blood

Pressbook cover for the only existing "sexo" film, known in the States as *Night of the Bloody Apes.*

converts JULIO into a horrifying Human Beast, complete with killer instincts. Escaping from his father's house JULIO terrorizes the entire city, attacking innocent victims and destroying them.

"After a series of impressive adventures [mostly shots of Lucy nude], the POLICE INSPECTOR, LUCY, and her fiancé ARTURO manage to discover the truth. The story ends with the death of the terrifying Human Beast JULIO, dying in the arms of DR. KRAUMAN, who in the throes of overwhelming sorrow, begs forgiveness from his son for having created such a horrible tragedy, driven by his innate father's love and desire to save his life."

At least the doc didn't inject Julio with mongoose blood and turn him into the Golden Age comic book hero The Whizzer (honestly, there really was one!). And speaking of comic book characters, Norma Lazareno, who plays the Wrestling Woman Lucy, takes her falls in a fetching skin-tight suit and mask with ears that conspicuously resemble a certain Caped Crusader ... which provides a perfect lead-in to the final movie discussed in this chapter. Although not officially a part of the Wrestling Women series, it was directed by Cardona and scripted by Salazar, and does indeed feature a wrestling woman — when she's not fighting crime as a masked super-heroine spy! In some ways, it out-outré'd all that had gone before....

La Mujer Murciélago (*Bat Woman*, 1967)

(Cinematográfica Calderón S.A.) *Prod*: Guillermo Calderón Stell; *Dir*: René Cardona; *Scr*: Alfredo Salazar; *Photo*: Augustín Jiménez; *Music*: Antonio Díaz Conde; *Prod. Mgr*: Alfredo Salazar; *Prod. Chief*: Jorge Cardeña; *Sub-Dir*: Julio Cahero; *Film Ed*: Jorge Bustos; *Art Dir*: Javier Torres Torija; *Décor*: Jorge Morales; *Makeup*: Margarita Ortega; *Monster Design*: Alfonso Barcenas; *Underwater Technician*: Alfonso Arnold; *Underwater Photo*: Genaro Hurtado; *Sound Suprvsr*: James L. Fields; *Dialogue Rec*: Eduardo Arjona; *Re-Rec*: Galdino Sampario; Eastmancolor.

Cast: Maura Monti (Claudia/Bat Woman), Roberto Cañedo (Dr. Eric Williams), Héctor Godoy (Mario Robles), David Silva (Don José, a.k.a. No. 1), Crox Alvarado (Inspector), Armando Silvestre (Tony Roca), Jorge Mondragón (Igor), Carlos Suárez (Henchman).

Mexican monster movie makers were nothing if not audacious. From poster art "borrowed" from the covers of American monster magazines, to musical cues for professional productions taken from records that could be ordered from the *back* of those magazines, our south-of-the-border amigos have not been shy about their source material. Only this time, they didn't just lift a werewolf pose or *House of Dracula* riff, they appropriated a whole character! (As Bob Dylan once said, "Good artists borrow; great artists *steal*.") Well, almost; both the American and Mexican characters wore a cape and cowl, and both their names began the same way — but there the resemblance pretty much ends. Batman became Bat *Woman*, and rather than a millionaire playboy who donned gray and black to become a revenge-driven creature of the night, Claudia (played by the beautiful Maura Monti) wore a slinky bikini to match her mask, and became a swingin' super-spy that fought monsters and moonlighted as a masked female wrestler!

Possibly the most strikingly beautiful woman ever to appear in Mexican films, genre or otherwise, Maura Monti was actually from Italy. Like Elizabeth Campbell, Maura came to Mexico, made a lot of movies in a few years (34 in five!), and then retired from film at the request of her husband. They have since divorced, but, unfortunately, she has not graced the screen again. Ms. Monti not only appeared opposite many of Mexico's genre greats, but also many "name" Mexican actors as well, not to mention American horror icons Boris Karloff and John Carradine. Among her many memorable roles was the lead in *Con Licencia para Matar* (*With License to Kill*), a Mexican version of Ted V. Mikels' *The Doll Squad*—and both, by the way, came years before *Charlie's Angels* (the TV show of the '70s, not the recent movies). She was tough, resourceful, and deadly with a crossbow, but still 110 percent woman in her form-hugging leather jumpsuit. Like a comet, her appearance was brief but bright, and she lit up the screen every time she crossed it. But it is for *La Mujer Murciélago* for which she will always be remembered, and rightly so—it's her movie all the way, and she was at her most beautiful, whether clothed in bat-bikini, sleek Parisian fashions, or a sexy green baby-doll nightie (which she wears while fighting the monster!).

Although the monster superficially resembles the Creature from the Black Lagoon, it actually looks more like a cross between that gill man and Enoch, the friendly neighborhood Sleestak from the *Land of the Lost* TV series. But this creature is not some prehistoric throwback, some evolutionary missing link; no, it is a product of science, and its creation scene is one of the most jaw-dropping in all of monster cinema. The creature (named Piscis by his creator) is literally *grown* in an aquarium by—and make sure you're sitting down for this—placing a goldfish and a G.I. Joe with Kung Fu Grip *in* that aquarium, and then boiling the water! In an industry known for audacity, this took the proverbial cake … not to mention the ice cream, plate and knife, too! For all that, though, this creature is actually one of the better-realized visions in the Mexi-monster genre.

Kudos must also go to his (filmic) creator, the ever-reliable Roberto Cañedo (who he had essayed the role of the Killer Doctor in the first Wrestling Women movie). A well-respected actor, Cañedo

appeared in hundreds of Mexican movies and TV shows, and he brings skilled, bravura performances to those genre films in which he starred. Maybe he just enjoyed having acid thrown in his face by shapely females!

The music for *La Mujer Murciélago* also rates special mention. Mexican genre film music is often a hit or miss proposition—when it's good, it can be very good, but when it's bad, it can be completely unsuited to the action on screen (the utterly inappropriate score for *Momias de Guanajuato* immediately springs to mind). But Antonio Díaz Conde's scoring for *Bat Woman* is Right On, in the truest sense of the word. An adept blend of the late '60s "Now Sound," jazz, and "spy" music, it hits the nail on the head in every scene.

Most all of *La Mujer Murciélago's* scenes hit that nail on the head, too. Although considered "B" movies, Mexican genre films were the product of established, respected, hard-working professionals on both sides of the camera, and this expertise shows in every scene of *Bat Woman*. The film and the performances are briskly-paced, breezy, colorful and assured. It takes deft hands all around to pull off a scene like the one in which Bat Woman, *always* knowing how to make an entrance, parachutes (in full bat-cowl and bikini) into the middle of a beach in Acapulco filled with twisting and jiving groovy guys and gals, and not seem as though they're making fun of the subject matter. With a wink and a flip of her bat-bikinied hips, Maura Monti invites us to join in on the fun … and with an invitation like that, it's real easy to suspend your disbelief.

Wrestling women, bat women, panther women, mad doctors, gorillas, monsters, robots, Aztec mummies, fish men, wrestling … the films created by René Cardona and Alfredo Salazar took the already outré concept of the monster/wrestler genre and somehow managed to expand

Panther Women, Bat Women — there was no telling what kind of woman you might meet in the Wrestling Women movies. *Top*: Eric de Castillo on the side of the angels, for once as "the Angel" in *Panther Women*. *Bottom*: The GI Joe–Goldfish creature gives Maura Monti the fish-eye.

Not just another pretty suplex: Wrestling Women outside the ring. *Top:* Maura Monti works her powers of persuasion on Carlos East. *Bottom:* Although they never appeared together as Wrestling Women, Elizabeth Campbell and Regina Torne teamed up for this sex, drugs and rock 'n' roll tale from Albert Zugsmith, the man who produced *High School Confidential* and Orson Welles' *Touch of Evil.*

on it in a way that will be remembered for as long as people enjoy psychotronic cinema. It was the Golden Age of monster/wrestler movies, a short but glorious period When Wrestling Women Ruled the Earth!

Eight

The Undercard

Second-Banana Masked Men

Once the masked-wrestler-as-action-hero-and/or-monster-fighter genre took hold, there was no stopping it. The previous four chapters spotlighted only the most successful purveyors of the form; many more luchadores took up the mask for the screen, some unwillingly, and some who parlayed their screen fame or characters into substantial ring careers. Some found enduring popularity; others lasted for (barely) only one movie. But whether leading the way or bringing up the rear, they all played their part.

Huracán Ramírez

Originally created as a character for the screen in 1952, "Huracán Ramírez" went on to become one of the most famous names in Mexican wrestling. Although the character possessed an on-screen alter-ego (played by either David Silva or Pepe Romay), underneath the mask, except for the first film, was Daniel García (b. 1926), who would wrestle under that mask for decades without ever appearing unmasked on screen. A superlative mat performer, García held as many as four championship belts at once. García had been a boxer in the 1940s, and turned to wrestling in 1952. One of his most famous matches was for the South American Middleweight Championship, when he beat "La Momia"! The wrestler known as "La Momia" did indeed wear a mummy mask, and that trophy hangs today on García's wall. García doffed his mask and retired from the ring in 1988, and the mantle of Huracán Ramírez is carried by his nephew's son, who wrestles as Huracán Ramírez, Jr.

García was a close friend of El Santo he even served as a pallbearer at Santo's funeral, and essayed the role of The Silver-Masked Man in the 1992 semi-biopic *Santo: La Leyenda del Enmascarado de Plata*. Although García wrestled under the Huracán Ramírez name for years, the Rodríguez Brothers, who produced the films, held the rights to the character, thus preventing García from teaming up with other wrestlers on screen (and thus denying film fans some potentially great action).

Huracán Ramírez (1952)

Dir: Joselito Rodríguez; *Scr/Story*: Joselito Rodríguez, Juan Rodríguez Mas, Jesús Saucedo; *Music by*: Sergio Guerrero; *Song*: Antonio Fernández; *Song*: Miguel Ángel Pazos; *Song*: Gabriel Ruiz; *Song*: Consuelo Velázquez; *Cinematography*: Jack Draper; *Film Ed*: Fernando Martínez; *Prod. Design*: José Rodríguez Granada; *Technical Advisors*: Jesús Garza, Enrique Llanes, Jack O' Brien; *Cam. Ops*: Álvaro González, Urbano Vázquez.

The poster that launched a thousand genre-ships. The masked wrestler movie couldn't ask for a better intro.

Cast: Frank Bucher "El Carnicero," Bello Califa, Jorge Casanova, Freddy Fernández, Joaquín Garrido, Jesús Garza "Don Chucho," Leonor Gómez, Carmelita González, Julio Guerrero, Anabelle Gutiérrez, Guillermo "Lobo Negro" Hernández, Tonina Jackson, Yadira Jiménez, Pedro Mago Septien, El Médico Asesino, Jack O'Brien, Camilo Pérez "Bulldog," Salvador Pulido, Joselito Rodríguez, Titina Romay, Ramón Sánchez, David Silva.

Well ... where exactly to place this film? It is one of the seminal pictures of the genre, but it was also part of a series featuring the character of Huracán Ramírez, (although it would be ten years between the first and second installment). It was, in fact, the first Mexican movie to feature a masked wrestler as the hero, and was released before *El Enmascarado de Plata*. But the latter remains better remembered today, because, even though perhaps superior as a movie, *Huracán Ramírez* lacked one crucial ingredient: action. *Huracán* offered plenty of *wrestling* action (and some fine falls at that), but there were no super-villains or death rays or any of the other trappings that made *El Enmascarado de Plata* and *La Sombra Vengadora* sons of the serials in more ways than one.

In all of the character's screen appearances (save the first), Huracán Ramírez was portrayed by the man who wrestled under the mask in real life, Daniel García. In the first film, he was portrayed by Eduardo Bonada, who would go on to make many other (unmasked) appearances in genre films. (The mask, apparently, was the reason he did not continue in the role; he felt he was too good-looking to keep covered up). Bonada, however, did wrestle in the ring for three years under the mask.

The poster art for *Huracán Ramírez* is one of the most striking in the genre (particularly given that it was the first). A model of simplicity, its sole feature, besides the title and credits, is a huge full-face portrait of the title character, resplendent in his ornate mask, glowering, ready to take on all comers. It proved a fitting introductory advertisement for a genre that would do the same.

El Misterio de Huracán Ramírez (*The Mystery of Huracán Ramírez*, 1962)

Prods: Joselito Rodríguez, Juan Rodríguez; *Dir*: Joselito Rodríguez.

Cast: Huracán Ramírez (Daniel García), David Silva, Tonina Jackson, Titina Romay.

Daniel García took over the role of Huracán Ramírez in the ring after Eduardo Bonada went looking for a mirror, and propelled the character's popularity to heights undreamt of, so they decided to do a whole new series of pictures from the original pressbook:

"Fernando Ramírez, who used to be 'Huracán Ramírez,' the fan's idol, is now the owner of a small restaurant he purchased when, with a useless leg, he sold the mask that made him famous to another wrestler. The arrival of Pedrito, his son, causes rejoice in the family. The youngster, besides being a good student, is a real jiu jitsu champion. Pedrito is the only one to notice his grandfather's farce. 'Tonina Jackson' in his wrestling days, he feigns sickness so he is not to tend the restaurant, but has his meals secretly as a starved shipwreck.

"The ex-wrestler becomes enthusiastic when the youngster talks to him about his affection for wrestling and carries him on his small back. The grandfather purchases Pedrito a 'Pancho Pantera' costume, he designs a mask and does a thousand tricks so the youngster can have his first wrestling match at the arena. Pedrito has an overwhelming success and Fernando, who sells sandwiches at the arena, thinks the masked youngster can become a fine wrestler.

"A deadly silent fight starts brooding at the arena, deadlier than those lived at the ring. 'El Principe' and his gang try to take the wrestler with the same name as Huracán Ramírez, acting at the same time as manager of the arena, to pass them the exploiting of the business. Huracán Ramírez wins once and again over all the gangster's ambushes, and in this unknown battle, 'El Principe,' Huracán's second and Fernando's sister's Beau are drawn into it. Aside of this, Pedrito makes an astounding discovery! His father is still Huracán Ramírez. That paralyzed leg and the small restaurant have, explains the father upon finding himself exposed, an innocent camouflage to quiet his wife's anguish every time he wrestles. The youngster keeps silent at his father's request and at the same time doesn't reveal his own secret.

"One day the public at the arena are astounded. There had been a match announced for three against three in which Huracán was to be the leader of the 'clean' team. Supposedly, those who should be his companions, 'El Lobo' and 'Frankenstein' turn against him. They are five men wrestling against one, ready to snatch his mask off him. Naturally they are paid by 'El Principe.' But the public's enthusiasm becomes delirious when 'Pancho Pantera' and 'Tonina Jackson' jump into the arena. The match looks like a deadly duel. At last the winners stand erect, the idol of past remembrance, the glory of the present and the promise of the future: father, grandfather and son."

El Hijo de Huracán Ramírez (*The Son of Huracán Ramírez, 1965*)

Prods: Joselito Rodríguez, Juan Rodríguez; *Dir*: Joselito Rodríguez.

Cast: Pepe Romay, Titina Romay, David Silva, Tonina Jackson, Carmelita González, Freddy Fernández.

This entry could very well have been called "El Hijo del Joselito Rodríguez," for the lead role is essayed by his son, Pepe Romay. Pepe, along with sis Titina, was a fixture in the Huracán series; he appeared in every picture from the previous entry until the last (which he also directed), replacing David Silva as Huracán's civilian identity. Pepe has directed and acted in other films, but his involvement with the genre was limited to the Huracán Ramírez series. David Silva had begun playing Huracán's alter ego in the first film in 1952, and by now was out of shape; it didn't look too convincing when Daniel García took over in the action scenes, and so the mantle passed to the younger Romay. Silva (1917–1976) featured in many classic genre films, including *El Barón del Terror, La Mujer Murciélago* and *Los Campeones Justicieros*, as well as the classic "cult" film *El Topo*.

La Venganza de Huracán Ramírez (*The Vengeance of Huracán Ramírez, 1967*)

Prods: Joselito Rodríguez, Juan Rodríguez; *Dir*: Joselito Rodríguez.

Cast: Pepe Romay, Titina Romay, David Silva, Carmelita González, Carolina Barret, Karina Duprez, Queta Carrasco, Tonina Jackson.

Nearly all the famous masked wrestlers to make names for themselves on the silver screen (and vice-versa) did so by fighting monsters or other fantastic menaces. Not so with Huracán Ramírez, whose films featured bad guys, but of the human variety, and more family comedy/drama. The exception was this 1967 outing, which featured the real Huracán in the wrestling scenes, and his usual screen alter-ego, David Silva, along with Tonina Jackson as Dad and the usual members of the Romay clan. Cute, blonde Titina Romay receives the grooviest exposure, with some hep rockin' production numbers, shakin' her mini-skirt and steppin' out in her go-go boots.

The story follows a mad scientist, Landru, who experiments with serums derived from animals in the hopes that their animalistic qualities can be transferred to humans. Of course, to prove his theories, he has to get into a number of wrestling matches with Huracán and Pop! At the climax, Landru disguises himself as the masked wrestler Vampiro Sangriento (possibly an in-joke, although no one from the film of that title worked on this one). He injects himself with a serum, and proceeds to wage a savage battle with Huracán. Just how savage is revealed when, in a replay of *Santo vs. the Vampire Women*, Huracán Ramírez pulls off his opponent's mask to reveal ... yes, a snarling werewolf! But unlike in *Vampire Women*, the monster doesn't change into a bat and escape; instead, he keels over in the ring, killed by his own potion.

Boffo plot elements, perhaps (there's even a pie fight!), but the personalities pull it off. The wrestling scenes are as good as, and in some ways better than, those in any of the other luchadores films of the time. Huracán Ramírez — or rather, Daniel García — was a great wrestler, and the rest of the regulars, particularly Tonina Jackson, play their roles with warmth and sincerity; at times, you believe they really are a family.

Huracán Ramírez y la Monjita Negra (*Huracán Ramírez and the Black Nun*, 1972)

Prods: Joselito Rodríguez, Juan Rodríguez; *Dir*: Joselito Rodríguez.

Cast: Pepe Romay, Titina Romay, Teresa Velázquez.

Here's the Mexican version of the Elvis movie *Change of Habit*, but with a masked wrestler standing in for the King's swingin' doctor (although the two did share similar sideburns, courtesy of swingin' alter-ego Pepe Romay). Masked wrestlers who help out nuns are hip, but even if they're El Santo, they're not Elvis, so I'm afraid the King takes this match. This was the last appearance in the series for another mainstay — Pepe's sister Titina, who had made a career out of acting mostly in her father's films (five alone in the Huracán series).

De Sangre Chicana (*Of Chicana Blood*, 1973)

Prods: Joselito Rodríguez, Juan Rodríguez; *Dir*: Pepe Romay.

Cast: Pepe Romay, José Chávez, Elizabeth Dupeyrón, Aída Araceli, Marcelo Villamil.

Huracán takes on evil dope dealers in this anti-drug saga. Huracán Ramírez, dope has no hope. The film is full of those awful Seventies styles that people wore then (whether doped up or not). Fortunately, some great wrestling sequences (courtesy of Daniel García) help balance out the bad fashion. By this time, Huracán had been reduced to a role not unlike that of "the Spirit" in Will Eisner's later stories, in which the former central character makes infrequent appearances in his own tales. This would be García's last screen appearance as Huracán, although he would continue to wrestle under the mask for another fifteen years.

NEUTRÓN

Not all of the masked heroes in Mexican cinema became sensations, although most certainly gave it the old college try. The character of Neutrón and his celluloid exploits is probably one of the best realized, and in the early going, via television reruns, he may have been as recognizable as Santo. Just as many (four) Neutrón films as Santo movies were dubbed into

English, making those films accessible to north-of-the-border audiences.

Although played by a former-wrestler-turned-actor, Wolf Ruvinskis, the character himself was not a wrestler; Neutrón was more in the mold of La Sombra Vengadora, a freelance superhero (indeed, he was "the Atomic-Powered Superman"). Of course, he wore a wrestling mask, one of the most impressive in Mexican cinema — jet black with silver lightning bolts above the eyes, and a tassel that brought to mind the old Charlton comic book character the Judo Master. No hint was ever dropped as to his origin. And, just to make sure they were in the ballpark, the films included scenes of Neutrón and his friends working on their moves in a gym.

Anyone wondering why a sixth "Neutron" movie, *Neutrón vs. the Invisible Killer*, is not included here should know that *Invisible Killer* wasn't really a Neutrón film. It was the English-dubbed version of *El Asesino Invisible*, which featured the one-shot hero "El Enmascarado del Oro," whose mask didn't resemble Neutrón's, not at all.

Neutrón, el Enmascarado Negro (*Neutrón, the Black Mask*, 1960)

Prod: Emilio Gómez Muriel; *Dir*: Federico Curiel; *Scr*: Alfredo Ruanova; *Cinematography*: Fernando Colín; *Music*: Enrico C. Cabiati; *Film Ed*: Juan José Munguía.

Cast: Wolf Ruvinskis (Neutrón), Armando Silvestre, Rosita Arenas (Nora), Julio Alemán, Claudio Brook, Ernesto Finance, David Lama, Rodolfo Landa, Jack Taylor [as Grek Martín].

Neutrón contra los Automatas de la Muerte (*Neutrón vs. the Death Robots*, 1960)

Prod: Emilio Gómez Muriel; *Dir*: Federico Curiel; *Scr*: Alfredo Ruanova, Federico Curiel;

Cinematography: Fernando Colín; *Music*: Enrico C. Cabiati; *Film Ed*: Juan José Munguía.

Cast: Wolf Ruvinskis (Neutrón), Armando Silvestre, Rosita Arenas (Nora), Julio Alemán, Ernesto Finance, David Lama, Rodolfo Landa, Jack Taylor [as Grek Martín], Roberto Ramírez Garza.

Neutrón vs. el Doctor Caronte (*Neutrón vs. the Amazing Dr. Caronte*, 1960)

Prod: Emilio Gómez Muriel; *Dir*: Federico Curiel; *Story/Adapt*: Alfredo Ruanova; *Cinematography*: Fernando Colín; *Music*: Enrico C. Cabiati; *Film Ed*: Juan José Munguía.

Cast: Wolf Ruvinskis (Neutrón), Armando Silvestre, Rosita Arenas (Nora), Julio Alemán, Ernesto Finance, David Lama, Rodolfo Landa, Jack Taylor [as Grek Martín], Armando Bianchi.

In the beginning, there was the mysterious Doctor Caronte, a super-villain who, in the style of his pulp magazine forbearers, leaves a distinctive coin at the scene of his crimes. The police are also baffled by the appearance of another mystery man, Neutrón, who they can't decide whether to regard as friend or foe. In a reversal of the usual conventions, Neutrón is garbed in black, Caronte in white (including a white wrestling mask!). The mad doctor has a bow-legged midget assistant named Nick, who sounds like Tattoo from *Fantasy Island*, (amusingly, they walk around hand-in-hand a lot, and Caronte tells Nick, "I can't let anything happen to you — you're my ... good luck piece"). Caronte is after a deadly device called the Neutrón Bomb (Anybody else out there wonder why the hero of the movie and the deadly weapon have the same name?). To obtain the bomb, Caronte employs not only Nick, but Dr. Walker (Claudio Brook), a craven type who murders his colleague to get his part of the formula; and the Death Robots, a hulking herd of misshapen brutes in overalls (more on their amazing origin later). Caronte begins to systematically eliminate the rest of the scientists, until at last he has the weapon, but Neutrón turns it against him in the end. All that is left of the fiend are his clothes and wrestling mask. The best scene occurs when a cab picks up a visiting scientist at the airport, and the driver turns out to be Neutrón in a uniform, cap and all! In the epilogue, Neutrón unmasks himself in front of his friends and associates.

All of this makes for some interesting situations—and major contradictions in the next, even wilder, installment, *Neutrón vs. the Death Robots*. For instance, although he unmasked in front of all the principals in the first film, his secret identity remains intact for the second. Caronte is back; he says he escaped the effects of the bomb, but we all saw him right in the thick of it. Unlike with the serials, no extra shot from that other angle shows an escape; we just have to take his word for it. In the first, the Death Robots are mute, bulky, shambling hulks; but in this one, one of them actually impersonates Neutrón, voice and all! The Death Robots are unique creations; fashioned from organic matter, they are actually baked in ovens! This time out, Caronte still wants a working bomb, so he has stolen the corpses of all the scientists he murdered, and keeps their brains in jars so they can tell him the secrets. Yes, "tell" the secrets, because these brains can talk! Not only is Caronte a criminal genius, he's an accomplished wrestler (which he demonstrates by going toe-to-toe with Neutrón in the finale). Tattoo ... er I mean Nick, crawls to one of those all-purpose destructo levers and literally brings down the house. Neutrón escapes, while Caronte is crushed by the debris.

Or so we thought...

In the next and final entry in the original trilogy, *Neutrón vs. the Amazing Dr. Caronte*, Caronte turns up again, with no explanation of how he escaped death in the previous installment (other than that he's above life and death). He still wants that bomb, but this time so do other interested parties (the Commies), and they're not intimidated by Caronte. And this is where it starts to get weird—not "good" weird, just confusing weird. Caronte, suffering from a lack of confidence, bones up on the ancient texts of Merlin to learn sorcery, telepathy, and soul transmutation. It's suggested that he can now inhabit the other characters' bodies, and appears to do so when he is unmasked as one of the three heroes and apparently dies. (But that fails to account for an earlier scene, before he has gained these powers, in which Caronte is unmasked following a brutal bout with the Commie thugs. A fat-headed spy removes the mask and gasps, "Not you!") At the morgue, when the attendant lets Neutrón look at his friend's corpse, Neutrón says, "Yes, he was Caronte." All right, but then at the climax another one of the leading characters (in civvies) alternately claims to be, then denies being the Bad Doctor, depending on how close the Death Robots are getting. Neutrón shows up disguised as Caronte, and another friend arrives disguised as Neutrón! The Death Robots then proceed to tear their master limb from limb (although this really shouldn't worry Caronte, since he's above life and death).

This rather jumbled ending shouldn't detract from one's enjoyment of an otherwise excellent effort. Sometimes overlooked in favor of films that star "real" wrestling heroes, the Neutrón movies remain classics of the genre, and offer up some of its most bizarre and entertaining moments.

Neutrón contra el Criminal Sádico (*Neutrón vs. the Maniac*, 1964)

Prod: Emilio Gómez Muriel; *Dir*: Alfredo B. Crevenna; *Adapt/Scr*: Emilio Gómez Muriel,

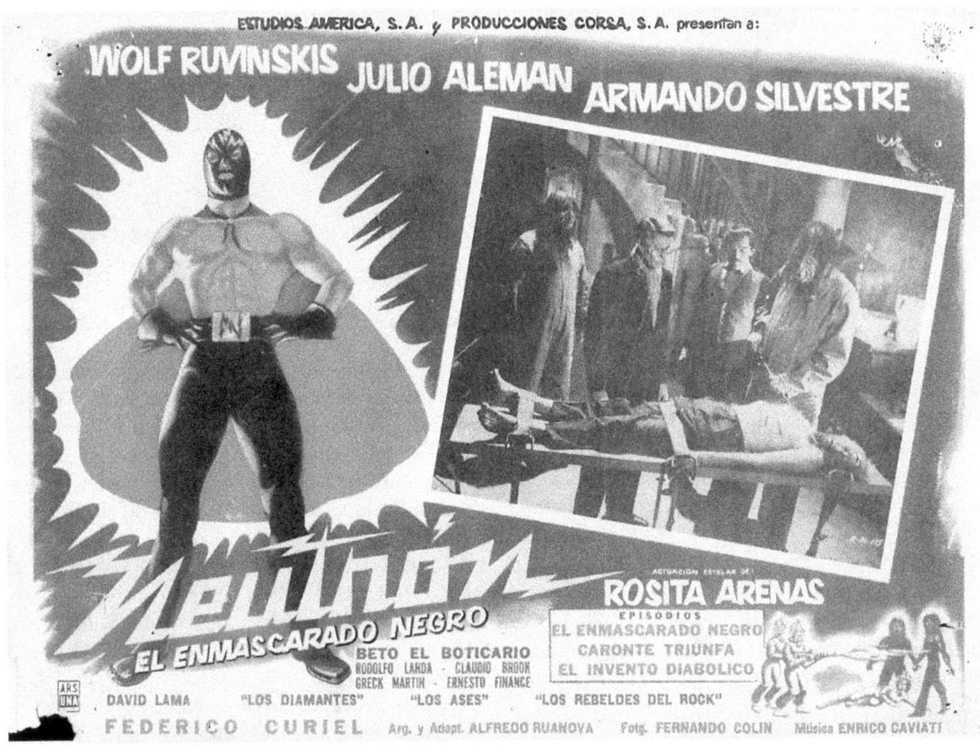

Top: The Death Robots make the scene in the first Neutrón movie. *Bottom*: In the second, they share the billing; here Dr. Caronte checks to see if one of the Robot-dinners is finished basting, while the ever-faithful Nick looks on.

Alfredo Ruanova; *Music*: Antonio Díaz Conde; *Songs*: Pedro Rigual [as Hermanos Rigual]; *Cinematography*: Fernando Colín [as Fernando Alvarez Garcés Colín]; *Film Ed*: Raúl Caso [as Raúl J. Casso]; *Prod. Design*: Arcadi Artis Gener; *Set Decoration*: Fernando Solórzano; *Sound Sync*: Lilia Lupercio; *Cam. Op*: Raúl Domínguez; *Asst. Cam. Op*: Xavier Cruz [as Javier Cruz]; *Orchestra*: Gustavo Pimentel.

Cast: Wolf Ruvinskis (Neutrón), Gina Romand, Rodolfo Landa, Chucho Salinas, José Gálvez, Rita Macedo, Rubén Rojo, Graciela Lara, Guillermo "Lobo Negro" Hernández, Mário Orea, Alberto Mariscal, Nothanael "Frankenstein" León, Antonio Raxel, Julián de Meriche [as Julién de Meriche], Héctor Cabrera, Tito Novaro, José Chávez [as José Chávez "Trowe"].

This fourth Neutrón movie was the last to be dubbed into English — again, not by the K. Gordon Murray crew (which means that it probably won't be so unintentionally hilarious, but will probably provide a truer sense of the film's real atmosphere). The startling and disturbing pre-credits sequence virtually mirrors the opening scene from Michael Powell's *Peeping Tom*, wherein a woman is murdered while her killer films the deed. Cut to titles.

The killer then hides out in an asylum, and Neutrón goes undercover to try and smoke him out — which begs the question: exactly how does a masked man go undercover? (And speaking of masks, Neutrón's changes for both this and the next movie — it's still black, but, disappointingly, the lightning bolts have been replaced by a single "racing stripe" down the middle, ending just above the eyes.) Virtually every member of the asylum's staff and clientele fall under suspicion, and, after a few more murders, virtually all of them claim to be the murderer. The climactic Agatha Christie–like finale reveals that they all done it!

Despite some zany performances from the actors portraying the inmates (and, as usual, a vigorous performance by Wolf Ruvinskis as the hero), *Neutrón con-*

tra el Criminal Sádico, like Neutrón's altered mask, is not quite as distinctive as its progenitors.

Neutrón contra los Asesinos del Karate (*Neutrón vs. the Karate Killers*, 1964)

Prod: Emilio Gómez Muriel; *Dir*: Alfredo B. Crevenna; *Scr*: Emilio Gómez Muriel; *Adapt*: Alfredo Ruanova; *Story*: Alfredo Ruanova; *Music*: Antonio Díaz Conde; *Song*: Armando Manzanero; *Song*: Gustavo Pimentel; *Song*: Lolita de la Colina (as Dolores de la Colina); *Cinematography*: Fernando Colín (as Fernando Alvarez Garcés Colín); *Film Ed*: Raúl Caso (as Raúl J. Casso); *Prod. Design*: Arcadi Artis Gener; *Set Decoration*: Fernando Solórzano; *Cam. Op*: Raúl Domínguez; *Orchestra*: Gustavo Pimentel.

Cast: Wolf Ruvinskis (Neutrón), Ariadna Welter, Chucho Salinas, Germán Robles, Rodolfo Landa, Carlos López Moctezuma, Fernando Luján, Gerardo Zepeda, Fernando Osés, Miguel Arenas, Federico Falcón, Mario Cid, Guillermo Álvarez Bianchi, Xavier Masse, John Kelly, Juan Garza, Imelda Miller.

The final Neutrón film features a cast that reads like a who's who of genre fixtures, including Chucho Salinas, Carlos López Moctezuma, Gerardo Zepeda and Fernando Osés. Also present are the stars of *El Vampiro*, Germán Robles and Ariadne Welter. Ariadne Welter was the sister of famous Hollywood siren Linda Darnell (Blanca Rosa Welter), who later married Tyrone Power. Señora Welter had the bad habit of marrying men who didn't want her to act, so her screen appearances proved sporadic; but in between husbands she managed to make such genre classics as the *El Vampiro* films and *El Barón del Terror*, as well as the (in her opinion) less-than-classic *Las Mujeres Panteras*, in which she replaced Lorena Velázquez as one of the legendary Wrestling Women.

Wolf Ruvinskis (b. 1921) was a former pro wrestler, and had even headed the Mexican wrestlers' union. Besides playing

Another Neutrón series, another mask.

Neutrón, and the unfortunate wrestler who turns into a monster in the seminal *Ladrón de Cadáveres*, he also made two pictures with El Santo: *Santo vs. los Villanos del Ring* (playing a good guy in a bad movie) and *Santo vs. la Invasión de las Marcianos* (playing a bad guy in a good movie).

SUPERZÁN

The character of Superzán (an amalgam of Superman and Tarzan) was created for the screen by Rogelio Agrasánchez, and played by Alfonse Mora, a bodybuilder. Like La Sombra Vengadora and Neutrón, Superzán was conceived as a superhero, and he could even fly! (Later, this ability was dropped.) However, unlike others who developed substantial wrestling careers from a screen persona, Mora never translated his celluloid exposure into ringside success ("He was too afraid of being injured," says Mil Máscaras). The same goes for his film appearances— he certainly had the physical stature for the part, but his personality was rather flat; and in a world filled with outlandish costumes, somehow his appeared a little too glittery, making him seem like the Vegas Elvis of Mexican wrestlers. As such, he was best-suited (no pun intended) to a second-banana role, which he capably played for Mil Máscaras (once) and Blue Demon (twice).

Superzán el Invencible (*Superzán the Invincible*, 1971)

(Producciones Fílmicas Agrasánchez) *Exec. Prod*: Rafael Rosales Durán; *Prod/Story*: Rogelio

The title and the wrestler pictured in the border art say Superzán, but the enmascarado featured in this inset to Superzán's first solo flick is none other than El Santo himself!

Agrasánchez; *Dir*: Frederico Curiel; *Adapt*: Federico Curiel, Angel Rodríguez; *Co-Dir*: Angel Rodríguez; *Photo*: Antonio Ruiz; *SPFX*: Raúl Camarena; *Makeup*: Victoria Celis.

Cast: Superzán, the Champions of Justice (Tinieblas, El Rayo de Jalisco, El Fantasma Blanco, Anibal, El Rostro), Raúl Martínez, Fredrico Curiel, Johnny Laboriel, Julio César Agrasánchez, Jorge Pinguino, Alex Agrasánchez, Rolando Valentino, Chino Chow, El Greco, "El Charro del Misterio," "Arcelia de los Reyes," "Mariachi el Nuevo Azteca."

In his initial solo foray, Superzán encounters that Agrasánchez staple, alien midgets (this time wearing *Phantom from Space*–style helmets!). It's not at all solo action, however; he gets a little help from his friends—an amended Champions of Justice lineup sans the "big guns," (Blue Demon and Mil Máscaras, not to mention Elsa Cárdenas). Superzán needed all the help he could get, really, and perhaps the producers suspected this—on at least one of the colorful Azteca lobby cards advertising the film, the inset photo shows El Santo! Though offering the usual festival of arena wrestling scenes, musical numbers, and campy action sequences, *Superzán el Invencible* really needed a more charismatic lead.

Superzán y el Nino de Espacio (*Superzán and the Space Boy*, 1972)

(Producciones Fílmicas Agrasánchez) *Prod/Story*: Rogelio Agrasánchez; *Dir/Scr*: Rafael Lanuza; *Cinematography*: Antonio Ruiz; *SPFX*: Raúl Camarena; *Makeup*: Victoria Celis.

Cast: Superzán, Caro Laniesti (Carmen), Claudio Lanuza (Silio), Freddy Pecherelly (Beto).

Superzán's first run proved profitable enough to merit a second solo venture, in which he again meets a short alien—only it's not a midget this time, but a golden-skinned boy from the planet Arimina (who wants to impart his vast knowledge of the universe to mankind). As befalls so many benevolent aliens, his initial earth contact turns out to be one of those craven scientific types who thinks he's stumbled onto an extraterrestrial gold mine, and tries to sell the space-lad down the canal to further his own schemes. (The kid had an easy time learning his lines—he merely maintains a somber look while the soundtrack does all the talking "telepathically.")

El Castillo de las Momias de Guanajuato (*The Castle of the Mummies of Guanajuato*, 1972)

(Producciones Fílmicas Agrasánchez) *Dir*: Tito Navarro; *Adapt*: Laura Marchetti; *Story*: Rogelio Agrasánchez; *Photo*: Antonio Ruiz; *Music*: Bernardo Serrano; *Asst. Dir*: José Luis Urqueita; *Makeup*: Antonio Castaneda.

Cast: Superzán, Blue Angel, Tinieblas, Zulma Faiad (Nora), María Salome (Rita), Luis Quintanilla, Tito Navarro, Jorge Pinguino.

Despite the absence of "the Big Three," (Santo, Blue Demon, and Mil Máscaras), this third and final entry in the official "Mummies of Guanajuato" series is still a pretty effective little picture. Blue Angel returns from the previous installment, joined by Superzán and Tinieblas.

The trio of wrestlers, traveling by van to their next match, spot Zulma Faiad and María Salome having car trouble. Being noble heroes (and since the two girls are gorgeous and wearing mini-skirts), they naturally offer their assistance. The sight of three masked wrestlers working on a car along the roadside offers much hilarity. Zulma invites them to the club where she sings, and subsequently performs a torrid number in an outfit designed to display her ample charms. At the same time, the prerequisite gang of evil midgets, under the command of the dying Dr. Tanner, kidnap a Dr. Simmons, who gives Tanner an artificial heart. This enables Tanner to perform a black mass that raises up the Mummies of Guanajuato, and then send them to

The overcrowded *Castle of the Mummies of Guanajuato* (1972).

Tinieblas does the Mummy Stomp in this third, and last, official "Guanajuato" movie.

town on a kidnapping spree. Since the hormones Tanner needs to survive can only be obtained from people in pain, the film offers some surprisingly and sadistic intense torture scenes. Superzán, held prisoner (along with several children) is forced to watch the grisly goings-on. He helps the kids escape; the cops and the other wrasslers bust in; Tanner buys the farm; and the whole joint goes up in flames.

The Three Lucha-teers of this particular outing are not the most charismatic, but their costumes make for some splashy fight scenes, and they handle the action competently enough. But, fittingly, it's the mummies' showcase; they receive for more screen time than in the previous entry, and make the most of it. Not only does *El Castillo de las Momias de Gunaojuato* fea-

ture another great resurrection scene, the mummies (and midgets) perform all the torturing duties, and even partake of some slapstick when they raid the village (when one of the Mummies crashes into a beauty salon and tries to make off with the fat hairdresser, he finds he can't lift her, so he makes off with her petite client instead. Even at this late date, the genre was still capable of producing some inspired moments.

El Triunfo de los Campeones Justicieros

(See Blue Demon chapter for credits and synopsis.)

El Investigador Capulina (*Capulina the Detective*, 1973)

Dir: Gilberto Martínez Solares.

    Cast: Capulina, Superzán, Tinieblas, NOthanael "Frankenstein" León, Alicia Encinas, Carlos Agostí, Bettina Haro Oliva.

Superzán and Tinieblas reunite (and it feels so good) from *The Castle of the Mummies of Guanajuato*, and team up with the always-welcome Nothanael "Frankenstein" León, to aid bumbling wanna-be detective Capulina in his fight against a batch of baddies with a Disintegrator Ray. Capulina offers some pretty amusing bits, like the almost Chaplinesque gag in which he heats tortillas with an iron, or when he sings to crippled children. And it's gratifying to see Nothanael "Frankenstein" León land a leading role (and as a good guy, to boot); León was a staple in genre films from the beginning, and, like the players at Universal or in John Ford's "stock companies," could always be counted on to provide both a familiar face and solid support. Sadly, he passed away in late 2003.

Los Vampiros de Coyoacán

(See Mil Máscaras chapter for credits and synopsis.)

La Mansión de las Siete Momias

(See Blue Demon chapter for credits and synopsis.)

TINIEBLAS

Always a bridesmaid, Tinieblas—which translates as "The Darkness," although his official nickname was "El Gigante" (translation obvious; he is exceptionally tall for a Mexican male)—never had a solo starring role in his own film, but he parlayed his few screen appearances into a wildly successful ring career. His flashy, futuristic costume was a natural for the four-color page, and, like Santo and Blue Demon before him, Tinieblas became a comic book star as well.

Although still active in the ring as of 2004, and still sporting his sidekick (a midget named Alushe who dresses like an Ewok from *Star Wars*), Tinieblas, like many other Mexican ring legends, has a son who wrestles under a near-identical mask and appends "Jr." to the family heritage. Tinieblas, whose real name is Manuel Leal, was a former stuntman. As such, he not only played the Frankenstein Monster in *Santo y Blue Demon contra los Monstruos*, but the head mummy, Satán, in *Las Momias de Guanajuato*, thus making him the only masked wrestler to play a monster in one film, and fight the same type of monster as a hero in another.

El Investigador Capulina

(See Superzán section for credits and other information.)

Las Momias de San Angel

(See Mil Máscaras chapter for credits and other information.)

El Puño de la Muerte
La Furia de las Karatecas

(See Santo chapter for credits and other information on these two films.)

LA SOMBRA BLANCA

Not an actual wrestler, La Sombra Blanca was a character, played by Crox Alvaredo, created for the screen for one film.

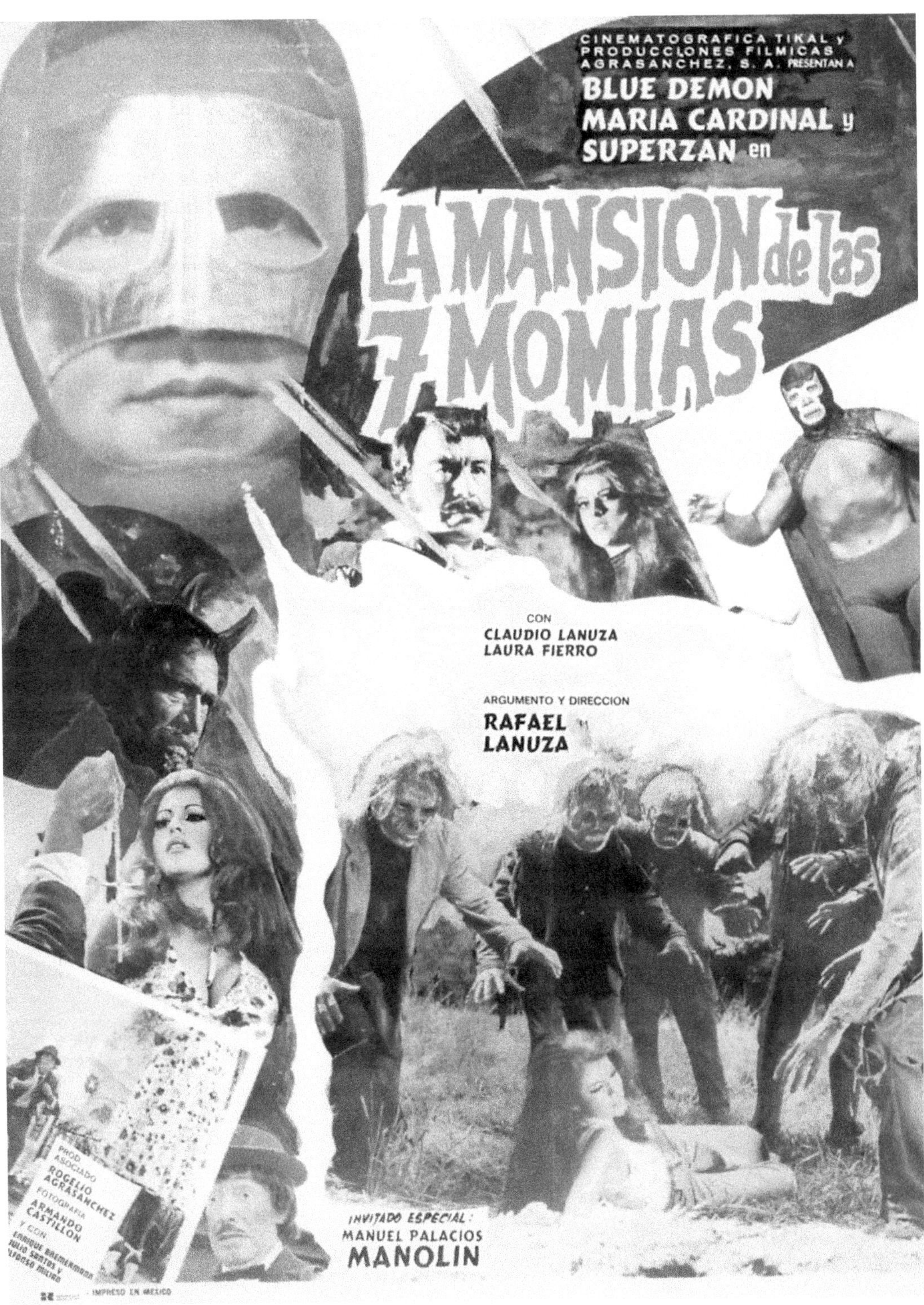

The last (unofficial) movie featuring the Mummies from down Guanajuato way, and they went out the way they came in — with Blue Demon kicking their butts!

La Sombra Blanca (*The White Shadow*, 1963)

Dir: Fernando Fernández; *Scr/Story*: Fernando Fernández, Antonio Orellana.

Cast: Crox Alvarado (La Sombra Blanca), Miguel Arenas, Ramón Bugarini, Rosa Carmina, Lola Casanova, Yolanda Ciani, Julián de Meriche, Jaime Fernández, Consuelo Frank, Mário García, Eulalio González, Félix González, Pepe Hernández, Arturo Martínez, Bruno Rey, Arturo Soto Rangel.

La Sombra Blanca (no relation to either La Sombra Vengadora or El Fantasma Blanco) was the nondescript star of a single nondescript feature in 1963. The distributors' faith in his ability to become a new sensation was apparently pretty lim-ited from the get-go: the wrestler pictured in the border artwork of the Azteca lobby cards for the film is none other than El Santo himself! "The White Shadow" was played by Crox Alvarado, who previously essayed a similar role as "the Angel" in *Curse of the Aztec Mummy* (1957). Alvarado was a key genre actor, appearing in the seminal films *El Enmascarado de Plata* and *Ladrón de Cadáveres*, as well as *La Loba*, *Atacan las Brujas* and *La Mujer Murciélago*, among others. Apparently he had a pretty robust sense of humor regarding his roles, too—Daniel García (Huracán Ramírez) said that Alvaredo would carry a Santo mask around in the trunk of his car; after donning the mask and gathering a

Another one-shot pseudo-mascarado; once again, the distributors seem to doubt the appeal of the star, so who do they feature on the lobby card? Why, El Santo, of course!

crowd, Alvaredo would proceed to unmask, telling the stunned onlookers not to reveal his identity!

LOS ENDEMONADIOS DEL RING

Los Endemonadios del Ring (The Demons of the Ring, 1964)

(Estudios América) *Prod*: Emelio Gómez Manuel; *Dir*: Alfredo B. Crevenna; *Scr*: Manuel Alfredo Ruanova; *Story*: Ruanova; *Photo*: Fernando Colin; *Music*: Antonio Díaz Conde; *Co-Dir*: Tito Novarro; *Makeup*: Graciela Muñoz.

   Cast: Karloff Lagarde (Satán), René "Copete" Guajardo (Angel), Armando Silvestre (Gonzalo), Chucho Salinas (Nando), Jorge Rivero (Tarzan Beto), Fernando Osés, Dorrell Dixon, Johnny Dinamo, Antonio Montoro, Jorge Allende, Humberto Garza, Benny Galan, Jean Safont.

La Mano Que Aprieta (The Clutching Hand, 1964)

(Technical credits same as above)

   Cast: Karloff Lagarde (Satán), René "Copete" Guajardo (Angel), Chucho Salinas (Nando), Gina Romand (Ana), Claudio Brook (Prof. Davenpor), Andrés Soler, María Eugenia San Martín, Fernando Osés, Guillermo "Lobo Negro" Hernández, Tito Novarro, "Picorro."

This was another two-picture series, directed by old hand Alfredo B. Crevenna, that featured characters created for the screen that were played by professional

Too bad these snazzy outfits never made it into the ring.

wrestlers. "The Angel" and "Satán" were portrayed by Karloff Lagarde (a great wrestling name in itself) and Copete (a not-so-great moniker), a tag team with snazzy masks and outfits that (both visually and conceptually) anticipated the coming Santo–Blue Demon pairings. The same technical crew responsible for this dynamic duo also made the 1964 Neutrón films. And backing up the two leads was a solid supporting cast: reliable Armando Sivestre, one of the busier leading men in genre films; Chucho Salinas and his usual goofy comic relief; Jorge Rivero (already starting to hit the big time, he would soon hit even bigger); mainstay Fernando Osés; and Emily Kranz, who, in a few years, would become one of the Dangerous Doll Squad of *Con Licencia para Matar*.

Neither picture set the world on fire, but the second, *The Clutching Hand*, proved better than the first, which was a rather routine ring drama. It wasn't a remake of the 1936 serial of the same name, nor was it a real monster flick, but at least it had Claudio Brook (the 1st Neutrón movie, *Santo in the Wax Museum*) on (clutching) hand to lend an air of Michael Rennie-ness to the proceedings. The hand in question is indeed monstrous, but, alas, it's only a prop used to intimidate potential victims and the hired help. It's never revealed exactly why Brook utilizes the appendage (perhaps he just liked to order stuff from the Captain Company in the back pages of *Famous Monsters* magazine, or maybe he's a serial fan!).

Cinematography: Raúl Martínez Solares; *Film Ed*: Jorge Bustos (as José W. Bustos).

Cast: Jorge Rivero (El Enmascarado de Oro), Carlos Agostí, Miguel Arenas, Karloff Lagarde, Ana Bertha Lepe, Guillermo Murray, Jorge Pons, Adriana Roel.

Another one-shot character created for the screen, El Enmascarado del Oro ("The Gold-Masked Man") tried to go El Santo one precious metal better, but, like La Sombra Blanca, didn't catch on. The man who played him, though, *did* catch on: this was the film debut for Jorge Rivero ("the Half-Naked Man"), who would go on to a successful international career as an action star, and, three years later, would co-star with the Silver-Masked Man himself in a pair of "secret agent" additions to the Santo canon, *Operación '67* and *El Tesoro de Moctezuma*. Rivero's other best-known unmasked role was as one of John Wayne's compadres in Howard Hawks' *Rio Lobo*. Not forgetting his roots, Rivero returned to the (screen) ring ten years after *The Invisible Killer* for *The Lions of the Ring* and its sequel (see below).

Co-star Guillermo Murray (b. 1929) would go on to other genre triumphs as well, including the early "space operas" *Gigantes Planetarios* and *La Planeta de las Mujeres Invasoras*, and his best-known role as Count Subatoi in *The World of the Vampires*.

LOS LEONES DEL RING

ENMASCARADO DEL ORO

El Asesino Invisible (*The Invisible Killer*, 1964)

Prod: Alberto López; *Dir*: René Cardona; *Scr/Story*: René Cardona, René Cardona, Jr.;

Los Leones del Ring (*Lions of the Ring*, 1974)

Dir: Chano Urueta; *Scr*: Rafael García Travesi; *Music*: Sergio Guerrero; *Cinematography*: Fernando Colín [as Fernando Alvarez Garcés Colín]; *Film Ed*: Maximino Sánchez Molina; *Cam. Op*: Agustín Lara Alvarado.

Cast: Jorge Rivero, Rogelio Guerra, Sara García (Doña Refugio), Macaria, Yolanda

Liévana, Guillermo "Lobo Negro" Hernández, Félix González, Eduardo Bonada, Antonio Raxel, Jorge Fegán, Ray Mendoza, Alejandro Cruz "Black Shadow," Cavernario Galindo, Roberto Cañedo, Armando Acosta, Antonio Padilla, Coloso Colosetti.

Los Leones del Ring contra la Cosa Nostra (1974)

Dir: Chano Urueta; *Scr*: Rafael García Travesi; *Music*: Sergio Guerrero; *Cinematography*: Fernando Colín [as Fernando Alvarez Garcés Colín]; *Film Ed*: Maximino Sánchez Molina; *Cam. Op*: Agustín Lara Alvarado.

Cast: Jorge Rivero, Rogelio Guerra, Sara García (Doña Refugio), Macaria, Yolanda Liévana, Guillermo "Lobo Negro" Hernández, Félix González, Eduardo Bonada, Antonio Raxel, Jorge Fegán, Ray Mendoza, Alejandro Cruz "Black Shadow," Cavernario Galindo, Roberto Cañedo, Armando Acosta, Antonio Padilla, Coloso Colosetti, Antonio Padilla "Pícorro," Manuel Dondé, Marcelo Villamil.

By the mid-seventies, wrestling action heroes had just about seen it all — monsters, aliens, mad doctors, spies, midgets, blaxploitation. So, in 1974, inspired by *The Godfather*, they finally met up with the Mafia. Sure, wrestlers had battled plenty of gangsters, but not organized crime, and certainly not in the grim and gritty style portrayed in *The Godfather*. At heart, the story is simple — the Mob is moving in on pro wrestling (No!), and the wrestlers try to stop them.

Yet the simplicity of the story didn't stop the producers from taking three hours to tell it. Then, instead of feeling confident that their epic saga would keep the theater patrons glued to their seats for those three hours, they decided to release it as two films, which was a slight error in judgment. Remember the song that goes "You can't have one without the other?" Well, that's exactly the way it is for *Los Leones*: Neither makes sense unless you see the other. While that might seem to make it the '70s Mexican equivalent of Quentin Tarantino's *Kill Bill* duo, it's not; in the *Kill Bill* flicks there are enough flashbacks (and flashforwards and flashsideways) to keep the audience abreast of the plot. In the *Los Leones* pair, there's no such luck. They just picked a point and literally chopped the film in half. This problem is easily solved in the age of videotape and DVDs, but think of how confused audiences must have been when they first came out!

In this film (or films), Jorge Rivero, who began his career as a distaff Santo in *The Invisible Killer*, returns to the mat, and, befitting his now-star status, plays a dual role, that of twin brothers. And, as befitting his now-polished acting skills, he manages to give each twin a distinctive personality, much like Kane Richmond accomplished in a similar dual role in Republic's classic serial *Spy Smasher* (1942). One twin becomes a pro wrestler, and earns the wrath of the Cosa Nostra by winning a match he's supposed to throw — and winds up dead for his integrity. His twin takes his identity and wrestles under a gold mask (much like the one Rivero wore as Enmascarado del Oro); his wrestling buddies join him to become "the Lions of the Ring" (as opposed to "the Jaguars"). Memorable moments include a granny popping some wise guys with a piece hidden under her shawl; and, when pursued by another buncha mooks on motorcycles, "the Lions" stringing some wire between trees and lopping the bad guys' heads clean off! The film presents some nice twists and turns, and a sting in the tale provides a downbeat ending not often seen in Lucha Libre movies.

Los Leones del Ring contra la Cosa Nostra is surprisingly well-done and violent; though there's nary a monster in sight, but hey, aren't real people always the worst monsters anyway?

RAYO DE PLATA

Campeones del Ring
(*Champions of the Ring*, 1972)

Prod: Juan Manuel Herrera; *Dir*: José A. Venegas; *Music*: Albert Lévy; *Cinematography*: Juan Manuel Herrera; *Set Decoration*: Jorge Mazopier; *Makeup*: Maruja Orozco; *Prop. Master*: Fabio Guzmán; *SPFX*: Sergio Jara; *Electrician*: Gustavo Becerra; *Musician* (piano): Olivia Del Valle; *Musician* (guitar): Antonio Giraldo.

Cast: Rayo de Plata (Frank Braña), Rosa de Castilla, Fernando Soto [as Fernando Soto "Mantequilla"], Amadee Chabot, César del Campo [as Casar del Campo], Fernando Osés, Ángel Menéndez, Guillermo Gálvez.

Yet another single entry into the log, *Campeones del Ring* contains everything a good masked wrestler movie should — except one: a charismatic lead. Rayo de Plata (funnily enough, the name of Gaston Santos' horse in *Swamp of the Lost Monsters*) not only has a name resembling Santo's, but a silver mask as well (distinguishable from the original by the addition of two red lightning bolts, one on either side of the eyes). Ostensibly, the plot concerns gun smuggling, but the film is such a crazy quilt of scenes that it becomes hard to tell. It's almost as if the producers made a list, and checked it twice (or, in some cases, three or four times), just to make sure they shoehorned everything in: let's see, masked wrestling hero, check; male and female wrestling matches, with some boxing thrown in for good measure, check; musical numbers, check; girl in a bikini (lovely Amadee Chabot from *Agente 00-Sexy* and *El Tesoro de Moctezuma*), check; comedy relief, check; and so on and so forth. Rather than this being a liability, however, the packed-to-the-cheesy-gills *Campeones del Ring* is actually a lot more entertaining and fun in its low-budget, comic-book way than some of the latter-day Santos and Blue Demons. It's almost as if Ed Wood had decided to make a masked wrestler movie.

LOS JAGUARES

Including "the Jaguars" may be cheating a wee bit, since their films were made in Colombia rather than Mexico, but substitute Santo or Blue Demon or Superzán for the unfamiliar faces (or masks, if you will), and you've got a production that would be right at home among, say, the many Agrasánchez pictures from the same period. Masked heroes, beautiful women, bizarre villains and situations... They even remembered to include a midget! "Los Jaguares" are cut from the same cloth as Neutrón and La Sombra Vengadora; that is, they are more superheroes than wrestlers (although, like the others, they still liked to dress the part). They also shared their compadres' predilection for "borrowing" images to utilize in their ad art; in this instance, Jim Steranko's "Nick Fury of S.H.I.E.L.D." is transformed into a feline-attired masked wrestler!

Karla contra los Jaguares
(1973)

Dir: Juan Manuel Herrera.
Cast: Los Jaguares, Marcela López Rey (Karla), María Eugenia Dávila (Verónica), King Bryner, Wayne Geroloman.

Los Jaguares contra el Invasores Misteriosos (*The Jaguars vs. the Mysterious Invaders*, 1973)

Dir: Juan Manuel Herrera.
Cast: Los Jaguares, King Bryner, Fedra, Julio César Luna, Gilberto Puentes.

Karla (Marcela López Rey), like "Gatusy" in *Return of the Champions of Justice*, is a super-sexy supervillain with any number of miscreants at her command — a zombie army, a mad doctor, a band of buxom nurses, and a midget. Her latest criminal endeavor is stealing gold from a bank next door to a work-in-progress high-rise. Enter Los Jaguares, dauntless defenders of justice, who wear matching jaguar-print masks, capes, and tights, ride motorcycles, and dismantle whatever opposition stands in their way with a lethal combination of wrestling holds and judo!

The second entry, *Los Jaguares contra el Invasores Misteriosos*, pits the Jaguars against malevolent aliens led by two midgets and a Big Cheese who keeps his back to the camera. The aliens recruit an army of karate men to aid in their conquest, and, for some reason, make them wear masks (not wrestling masks, not monster masks, but a human — more or less—face with black rubber hair that features not only Bettie Page bangs, but huge Elvis-like sideburns and a yellow goatee). The head honcho turns out to be a gorilla from space, and the Jags actually fail to defeat him; he simply grabs the midgets and disappears, and Our Heroes ride off on their trusty cycles to go skydiving.

NINE

Vampires Not Named Drácula, and Other Assorted Creatures
The Wide, Wide World of Mexican Monsters

They are a weird, wild, and wooly bunch, these Mexican monsters. In the '60s, the Monster Boom was in full swing, and Mexico produced some of the most singular variations on the theme that human eyes have ever beheld. Much has been said about the "inadequacies" of Mexican Monster design and makeup, and while it's true that in most cases finances left a lot to be desired, the imagination did not, and that's the most important component in any case. More than anything else, the best of the Mexican monsters brings to mind the work of Paul Blaisdell, creator of *The She Creature,*" the aliens from *It! The Terror from Beyond Space* and *It Conquered the World,* and numerous other memorable monsters. Also forced to work with next-to-no-budget, Blaisdell did not let that hamper his imagination, and his creations linger in the memory long after many slicker hi-tech marvels have faded.

Take Frankenstein. Fans have been raised to appreciate Boris Karloff's sensitive yet powerful performance, or Jack Pierce's unsurpassed make-up, or James Whale's stylish direction, or the presence of Glenn Strange or Peter Cushing. What do fans find when they encounter their Mexican cousins? In various films, Frankenstein's (or, more likely, Frankenstein or Franqestain[!]) monster sports a goatee, or wears a groovy turtleneck, or drives a sports car!

Or how about mummies? Rather than simply limping along while pining for their lost princesses (as was usual for mummies in Hollywood features), Mexican mummies could turn into werewolves or bats, or ride horses. Creatures from lagoons could sprint about freely for hours on dry land. Vampires didn't just hail from Transylvania and overdress, they could be alien midgets.

And those are just the "classic"-type monsters. Besides giving fans a whole new slant on their favorites, Mexican horror created creatures hitherto undreamed of—except, perhaps, in delirium: space cyclops, space gorillas, space midgets, talking space spiders, singing space robots, robots who wear matching uniforms, robots that wear sunglasses and trenchcoats, zombies that fly helicopters. And they all wrestled.

El Mundo de los Vampiros
(*The World of the Vampires,* 1960)

(ABSA) *Prod*: Abel Salazar; *Dir*: Alfonso Corona Blake; *Story*: Raúl Zenteno; *Film Ed*:

Rare example of a vintage ad sheet that was sent to media outlets to promote a particular film.

Juan José Marino; *Sound*: Manuel Topete; *Cinematography*: Jack Draper; *Prod. Design*: Javier Torres Torija.

Cast: Guillermo Murray (Count Sergio Subotai), Mauricio Garcés (Rudolph Summers), Erna Martha Baumann (Leonore Coleman), Silvia Fournier (Martha Coleman), José Baviera (Mr. Coleman), Alfredo Wally Barrón, Alicia Moreno, Carlos Nieto, Mary Carmen Vela.

Directed by the helmsman of *Santo contra las Mujeres Vampiro*, Alfonso Corona Blake, the well-mounted and atmospheric *World of the Vampires* doesn't quite hit the imaginative peak *Mujeres Vampiro* did, but offers some grand, bizarre touches for the connoisseur. Made two years before the Santo opus, *World* stars Guillermo Murray as Count Subotai, another member of the well-dressed vampires club, who seeks revenge on the descendants of the Coleman family for destroying his undead clan centuries ago. One of the film's best (and best-remembered) set pieces features the Count calling his vampiric followers to arms by means of a pipe organ made of human bones. Meanwhile, at a party at the Colemans, family friend Rudolph entertains the guests by performing at the piano. For his next swingin' number, he plays an old Transylvanian tune that's rumored to raise the dead. But it proves to be more than a mere rumor; three guesses as to who it attracts... Subotai hypnotizes Leonore (Erna Martha Baumann) for some subsequent snacking, and makes his excuses. After the guests have left, she heeds the call, and heads over to the Count's castle. The dirty old Count then vampirizes her right in front of her kidnapped dad; the image of the beautiful Baumann's face, befanged and with eyebrows that would put Mr. Spock to shame, is one of the most recognizable in Mexi-films. Even more unforgettable is the image of that face superimposed on a wing-flapping bat! (Undoubtedly Señora Baumann never envisioned this when she was Miss Mexico!) Leonore bites Rudolph, but he only turns into a werewolf. Not right away, though — it has to happen gradually, so that Rudy can perform one last song and dance, a tune that, instead of attracting vampires, kills them (the story earns points here for the novel way that music is used in connection with the undead, especially as a way to dispatch them). Subotai, however, who apparently doesn't have quite the pointed ear for music, withstands the melodic massacre, and so they just push him into a pitfull of stakes. This frees Rudy from his five o'clock shadow problem, but Leonore jumps after her master into the stake-pit and goes down for the Count. This resolves everything, while raising one burning question: Why do so many screen vampires insist on keeping huge open pits of stakes in their lairs? (Isn't that sort of like the Wicked Witch of the West having a sprinkler system installed in every room?)

Orlak, el Infierno de Frankenstein (*Orlak, the Hell of Frankenstein*, 1960)

Prod/Dir: Rafael Baledón; *Scr/Story*: Alfredo Ruanova, Carlos Enrique Taboada; *Cinematography*: Fernando Colín; *Film Ed*: Juan José Munguía; *Prod. Design*: Arcadi Artis Gener; *Prod. Mgr*: Antonio Sandoval; *Conductor*: Rubén Fuentes; *Wardrobe*: Lupita Moreno.

Cast: Joaquín Cordero (Jaime Rojas/Orlak), Armando Calvo (Inspector Santos), Rosa de Castilla (Estela), Irma Dorantes (Elvira Davalos), Andrés Soler (Prof. Frankenstein), Pedro d'Aquillon (Vidal), David Reynoso (Gaston), Carlos Ancira (Eric), Antonio Raxel (Juez Davalos), Carlos Nieto (Gabino), Julián de Meriche, José Pardavé (Velador de Teatro), Carlos Suárez (Hombre con carruaje), José Loza Martínez, Armando Gutierrez (Custodio de prision), Humberto Rodríguez, Roger López (Hermano de Gaston), Chel López (Ayudante de gaston).

This variation on the Frankenstein theme at once recalls *El Monstruo Resuci-*

tado, with its theme of a handsome monster, and anticipates later efforts such as *Frankenstein: The True Story* (1973) and *Frankenstein and the Monster from Hell* (1972). Like in that later Hammer film, Orlak's Dr. Frankenstein is locked up, and acquires an accomplice, Jaime, while so confined. The accomplice not only helps him escape, but assists with his experiments. Frankenstein has already created a monster, and named it Orlak, but it needs a facial overhaul. The doc gives it the face of Jaime — without the original owner having to forfeit his. Jaime, like Ygor in *Son of Frankenstein,* then uses the monster to eliminate his enemies, without Dr. Frankenstein's knowledge. Orlak is only vulnerable to flame (but, then again, aren't most monsters?), and this proves his undoing — when he starts to romance the heroine by candlelight, he gets a little too close to the flame, and his mug starts to melt like Vincent Price in *Tales of Terror!* Orlak then hightails it back to the lab, where he throws his face-sake off the building. Some angry villagers with torches (this is 1960, right?) start a fire to destroy the monster, but trap a little girl instead; Orlak proves himself the true hero by rescuing the child, then walking like a man into the all-consuming flames.

This exceptional early effort featured a particularly strong performance by Joaquín Cordero as Jaime/Orlak. Perhaps best-known for an equally impressive turn as the evil mastermind Dr. Satán in the movie of the same name (and its sequel), Cordero also appeared in the initial pair of Santo films (again playing a mad scientist).

El Barón del Terror (*The Barón of Terror,* a.k.a. *The Brainiac,* 1961)

(ABSA) *Prod:* Abel Salazar; *Dir:* Chano Urueta; *Scr/Story:* Federico Curiel, Antonio Orellana, Alfredo Torres Portillo; *Music:* Gustavo César Carrión; *Cinematography:* José Ortiz Ramos; *Film Ed:* Alfredo Rosas Priego; *Prod. Design:* Javier Torres Torija; *Sound:* Jesús González Gancy; *SPFX:* Juan Muñoz Ravelo; *Cam. Op:* Ignacio Romero; *Prod:* K. Gordon Murray (English language version).

Cast: Abel Salazar (Barón Vitelius/the Brainiac), Rubén Rojo (Ronald Miranda/Marcos Miranda), Rosa María Gallardo (Victoria Contreras), Luis Aragón (Prof. Milan), Ariadna Welter (Bar girl — victim #2), Ofelia Guilmáin (Señora Luis Meneses), René Cardona, Susana Cora, David Silva (Detective Inspector), Germán Robles (Indelacio Pantoya/Sebastian de Pantoya), Roxana Bellini, Mauricio Garcés (Medical Examiner), Magda Urvizu, Miguel Brillas, Federico Curiel, Magda Donato, Carlos Nieto, Francisco Reiguera, Carlota Solares, Víctor Velázquez.

This may be the most famous Mexican monster movie that doesn't offer even a whiff of wrestling. It was produced by and starred Abel Salazar, the man responsible for beginning the Mexican horror boom with *El Vampiro* (1957). Salazar started as an actor in 1941, and was soon producing his own movies, as well as loaning himself out to other outfits. In 1957 he formed his own company, ABSA, and in the next few years produced several memorable genre entries, including *El Vampiro, El Ataúd del Vampiro, El Mundo de los Vampiros,* and, of course, *El Barón del Terror.* Salazar was only in it for the money ("I asked myself why Universal had the profits they had; it was because of the monster films and Deanna Durbin"), but that didn't stop him from making efforts that really hit the coffin nail on the head. (Presumably, he wasn't able to get Deanna Durbin.)

Being that it was his movie, Salazar takes the plum role of Vitelius D'Estera, sorcerer and "seducer of married women and young maidens." A tribunal sentences him to death by fire, but not before he slaps a curse on them, proclaiming he'll be back to collect in 300 years. The picture has offered straightforward Inquisition in-

Azteca lobby card.

trigue until now ... it's when he comes back that the lunacy starts. Vitelius returns via comet (which somehow remains whole after plunging through Earth's atmosphere!). But it's not Vitelius who steps out of the unconvincing hunk of rock onto an obvious studio set, it's one of the most famous monsters of Mexico—the Brainiac!

The Brainiac's weird appearance, both creepy and campy, defies description. The closest Hollywood equivalent would be the monsters created by Paul Blaisdell, in particular the creature from *The Day the World Ended*. But Blaisdell, in all his improvisational genius or wildest nightmares, never imagined anything like this. The huge head (which throbs with an inflating-deflating action) conjures up images of Pinocchio as a werewolf—shaggy hair, arched eyebrows, pointy ears ... and a huge shnozz! Add to this a long forked tongue used to suck brains out of his victims, and tentacles for hands, and voila!—we have on Classic Creep. The fact that he wears a business suit only enhances the effect.

The rest of the film continues at a delirious pace. The hunt is on for the descendants of the tribunal that burned him at the stake, and Vitelius commences the search by letting himself be picked up by a beauty in a bar. When she takes him to a cheap motel, he doesn't even bother seducing her (perhaps because it's obvious she's not a maiden); as soon as she turns her back to disrobe, Vitelius turns into the monster and has lunch! The Brainiac then begins polishing off the unfortunate progeny of the tribunal, one couple at a time, in rather kinky fashion: he wines and dines the couple, then he "freezes" his victims and makes the male half of the couple watch while he seduces, then sucks the brains out of the female, before killing the male. Vitelius often can't wait to get it on, though, and so keeps a bowlful of brains in a cabinet, which he spoons out and gulps down like frozen yogurt!

Films like this make life worth living, and director Chano Urueta (1895–1979) was a specialist in the bizarre. Undaunted by low budgets, he favored weird props and camera effects. For this film alone, he would be assured a place Cinema's Valhalla, but he also made his mark on the monster/wrestler genre by directing a host of Blue Demon's most outré movies (including the first) and helming the late-in-the-game *Leones del Ring* series.

La Cabeza Viviente (*The Living Head*, 1961)

(ABSA) *Prod*: Abel Salazar; *Dir*: Chano Urueta; *Scr/Story*: Federico Curiel, Adolfo López Portillo [as A. López Portillo]; *Cinematography*: José Ortiz Ramos; *Film Ed*: Alfredo Rosas Priego; *Prod. Design*: Roberto Silva; *Sound*: Jesús González Gancy; *SPFX*: Juan Muñoz Ravelo; *Music Sprvsr/Conductor*: Gustavo César Carrión; *Prod*: K. Gordon Murray (English-dubbed version); *Dir*: Miguel San Fernando (English-dubbed version).

Cast: Mauricio Garcés (Roberto/Acatl, "la cabeza viviente"), Ana Luisa Peluffo (Marta/Princess Zochiquatl), Germán Robles (Prof. Mueller), Guillermo Cramer (Xihu the high priest), Abel Salazar (Police detective), Antonio Raxel (Antonio, the archaeologist).

Like *The Brainiac, La Cabeza Viviente* was made by Abel Salazar's ABSA production company, and was directed by Chano Urueta. Unfortunately, little of the wonderful weirdness of *The Brainiac* rubbed off on *The Living Head*, even though it's a combination of Hammer's *Blood from the Mummy's Tomb*, (which starred the volup-

tuous Valerie León in a filmic version of Bram Stoker's *Jewel of the Seven Stars*, and *The Brain That Wouldn't Die*. Like the Hammer film, *The Living Head* presents all the circumstance and rituals usually associated with the creation of a mummy, but it stops short; instead of a marauding mummy killing the desecrators of his tomb under the direction of a high priest (like in the Universals), it's the high priest who comes back to kill (only he's no mummy) desecrators— under the direction of a disembodied head! Though possessing a tantalizing concept, in execution *La Cabeza Viviente* turned out to be the weak link in the ABSA chain of features. Given the personnel involved, one would expect something along these lines to offer a true psychotronic experience, but *The Living Head* is just too slow. This is not to say that it doesn't have its moments (you'd be hard pressed to find a golden-age Mexican genre film that doesn't have at least one or two redeeming scenes), they're just too few and far between.

The Living Head was played by the head of Mauricio Garcés (1926–1989), who appeared in a score of films in the late 1950s and '60s, but concentrated on stage work after that, making only three more movies between 1971 and the time of his death. His co-star, gorgeous Ana Luisa Peluffo, caused quite a stir six years prior to *The Living Head* by appearing nude in three films. Señora Peluffo has worked constantly throughout her career, earning more screen credits than any other actress featured in this book.

Frankenstein, el Vampiro y Compañia (*Frankenstein, the Vampire and Company*, 1961)

(Cinematográfica Calderón S.A.) *Prod*: Guillermo Calderón Stell; *Dir*: Benito Alazraki; *Scr*: Alfredo Salazar; *Music*: Gustavo César Carrión; *Cinematography*: Enrique Wallace; *Film*

Ed: Jorge Bustos; *Prod. Design*: José Rodríguez Granada.

Cast: Manuel "Loco" Valdés, Marta Elena Cervántes [as Martha Elena Cervántes], Nora Veryán, Roberto G. Rivera, José Jasso, Joaquín García Vargas [as Joaquín García Vargas "Borolas"], Quintín Bulnes, Antonio Bravo, Jorge Mondragón, Julián de Meriche [as Julién de Meriche], Jorge Zamora, Alberto Villanueva [as Alberto "Chiquilín" Villanueva], Vicente Lara [as Vicente Lara "Cacama"], José Pardavé, Leonor Gómez.

When remaking the classic Universal monsters and films, Mexican producers could either select the elements that appealed to them most and fashion their own take on the matter, or they could pretty much just remake the source material (as they had done with their version of *The Invisible Man Returns*). South-of-the-border filmmakers had dabbled in monster rallies before, such as *El Castillo de los Monstruos*, which is often cited as the Mexican version of *Abbott and Costello meet Frankenstein*, but *Frankenstein, el Vampiro y Compañía* is the actual remake (if you've seen *A & C Meet Frank*, then you've seen this one).

Manuel "Loco" Valdés was the youngest brother of Germán "Tin Tan" Valdés.

La Invasión de los Vampiros (*The Invasion of the Vampires*, 1961)

Prod: Rafael Pérez Grovas; *Dir/Scr*: Miguel Morayta; *Music*: Luis Hernández Bretón; *Cinematography*: Raúl Martínez Solares; *Film Ed*: Gloria Schoemann; *Prod. Design*: Manuel Fontanals; *Sound*: Jesús González Gancy; *Prod*: K. Gordon Murray (English-dubbed version); *Dubbing Director*: Manuel San Fernando (English-dubbed version).

Cast: Carlos Agostí (Count Frankenhausen), Rafael del Río (Dr. Alvaran), Erna Martha Baumann (Brunhilde Frankenhausen); Bertha Moss (Frau Hildegarde), Rafael Etienne, Enrique García Álvarez, Tito Junco, Antonio Raxel (Count Cagliostro), David Reynoso (The Constable), Fernando Soto.

Invasion of the Vampires and its sequel, *The Bloody Vampire*, were produced by Rafael Pérez Grovas; they are remarkably atmospheric and well-done films, in marked contrast to his efforts twenty years later (such as El Hijo del Santo's first movies, which were cheap, listless affairs). Both vampire movies feature Carlos Agosti as the undead nobleman Count Frankenhausen, and the striking Erna Martha Baumann (from the earlier bloodsucking classic *World of the Vampires*) as his bride, and pit the vampiric duo against the followers of Count Cagliostro, who battle back with an extract from the Black Mandragora plant, which can cure vampirism in much the same manner as the flower that cures lycanthropy in *Werewolf of London* (1935). Some evidence within the films themselves suggest that the sequel was intended to be the first installment, but it was released a year after *Invasión*.

Invasión actor Tito Junco was the brother of *El Enmascarado de Plata* star Victor Junco, and although his reputation was built on villainous roles, his involvement with the genre was limited. His only appearance in a wrestling film came in *The Fury of the Ring* (also 1961), which featured Blue Demon in a wrestling scene.

Carlos Agosti was another fine actor who excelled in villainous roles, and his genre C.V. is impeccable. He appeared in seven films with El Santo, as well as bedevilling wrestlers in *El Misterio de Huracán Ramírez*, *El Asesino Invisible*, *Las Luchadoras contra el Robot Asesino*, and *Investigador Capulina*.

La Maldición de la Llorona (*The Curse of the Crying Woman*, 1961)

(ABSA) *Prod*: Abel Salazar; *Dir*: Rafael Baledón; *Scr*: Baledón, Fernando Galiana; *Cinematography*: José Ortiz Ramos; *Film Ed*: Alfredo Rosas Priego; *Prod. Design*: Roberto Silva;

Sound: Javier Mateos; *Music*: Gustavo César Carrión.

Cast: Rita Macedo (Thelma), Abel Salazar (Herbert), Carlos López Moctezuma (Fred), Domingo Soler (Wild man in bell tower), Rosita Arenas (Emily), Victorio Blanco, Beatriz Bustamante, Arturo Corona, Roy Fletcher, Daniel Jaramillo, Julissa [as Julissa del Llano] (Female stagecoach passenger), Enrique Lucero, Mario Sevilla.

By 1961, the Mexican horror genre, though still rather young, had already shown a predilection for bizarre juxtapositions of characters and situations; they were never content to tell more or less a straight story, but mixed influences at will, creating unique takes not only on classic monsters, but old legends as well. Here, the legend of "the Crying Woman" receives a makeover. This Llorona is more of a vampire, and observes many of the vampiric conventions (such as casting no reflection in a mirror). There is no story of murdered children or betrayal; she's just very evil. She waits for her niece, Rosita Arenas (heroine of the Aztec Mummy and Neutrón series), to inherit the curse, which she must activate by forcing the girl to remove the lance that pins the corpse of the original Crying Woman to a wheel in the cellar(!). Abel Salazar plays the niece's bumbling husband (since Salazar was the head of the company, he took perverse delight in casting himself as a boob). In the end, although La Llorona's influence is strong, the girl refuses to remove the lance, the curse is broken, and the whole enterprise literally crumbles.

Rosita Arenas was Abel Salazar's wife in real life, and settled fully into the role after this picture, her last film in the genre.

El Vampiro Sangriento
(*The Bloody Vampire*, 1962)

Prod: Rafael Pérez Grovas; *Dir/Scr*: Miguel Morayta; *Music*: Luis Hernández Bretón; *Cinematography*: Raúl Martínez Solares; *Film Ed*: Gloria Schoemann; *Prod. Design*: Manuel Fontanals; *Sound*: Jesús González Gancy; *Prod*: K. Gordon Murray (English-dubbed version); *Dubbing Director*: Manuel San Fernando (English-dubbed version).

Cast: Carlos Agostí (Count Siegfried von Frankenhausen), Erna Martha Bauman (Countess Eugenia Frankenhausen), Raúl Farell (Dr. Riccardo Peisser), Antonio Raxel (Count Valsamo de Cagliostro), Begoña Palacios (Anna Cagliostro), Bertha Moss (Frau Hildegarde), Lupe Carriles (Lupe, the innkeeper), Pancho Córdova [as Francisco Córdova], Rafael Etienne (Torture chamber master), Enrique Lucero.

From the original pressbook:

"Count Cagliostro is explaining to a few select students, together with his daughter Ines and her fiancé Ricardo, the discoveries that his ancestors made regarding vampires and how to exterminate them and rid humanity of this plague. The Count is planning a dangerous trip and he explains that he wants his daughter to receive the documents written and compiled by all the Cagilostros who have dedicated their lives and knowledge to the liquidation of vampires. They are interrupted and Gestas, the loyal servant, answers the door … it is a friend of Gestas who has come to beg the Count to see his mistress inasmuch as she is unconscious. The Count can't go, but asks Ricardo to go, inasmuch as he, too, is a doctor. Ricardo finds the Countess in a state of shock … due to a terrible scare. However, when he offers to take care of her, Count Frankenhausen (Carlos Agosti) appears, with his faithful housekeeper, Frau Hildegarda, and in no uncertain terms tells him it is none of his business. After Ricardo leaves, the Count Frankenhausen in a rage beats Lazaro, the servant, for taking it upon himself to bring a stranger into the house.

"Very strange things take place at the home of the Frankenhausens. Every full moon, the Countess's servants disappear, therefore it is getting difficult to find anyone who will serve the Countess. However, when Ines finds out they are looking for a servant — she has Gestas take her to the lady who gets help for the Frankenhausens — inasmuch as nobody knows that she is the Count of Cagliostro's daughter, inasmuch as she has always been away at school. She is introduced into the home of the Frankenhausens and she is convinced that the Count is the vampire her family has tried for centuries to exterminate. Little does she know that the intention of the Count is to sustain himself with her blood. However, he finds himself falling in love with Ines — of course — not knowing who she really is. Frau Hildegarda is very upset inasmuch as she, herself, is in love with the Count.

"The Countess finds a way to get Ricardo to come see her and she gets him to agree to be her ally. However, the Count confides in Ricardo that the Countess is insane and she has an obsession about the Count wanting to kill her. Ricardo finds himself believing the Count and discounting the Countess's belief that she is in danger.

"After the Count declares his love to Ines — and after Ines finds out the Count is really the vampire — the Frau informs the Count who Ines really is. The Count is furious. Everybody is taken to the home of his father-in-law, the Marques. Luckily, Ricardo and Gestas also find out the truth and follow the Count and his party — arriving in time to save Ines from the Clutches of the Count. However, Gestas is killed in the skirmish ... and the Count then, in order to survive, must take his own wife, the Countess' life and although Ines has been saved for the time being — the vampire still lives, and is a threat to humanity."

El Monstruo de los Volcanes (The Monster of the Volcanoes, 1962)

Prod: Rafael Pérez Grovas/Jesús Grovas; *Dir*: Jaime Salvador; *Scr/Story*: Federico Curiel, Al-fredo Ruanova; *Music*: Sergio Guerrero; *Cinematography*: Ezequiel Carrasco; *Film Ed*: Jorge Bustos [as José W. Bustos]; *Prod. Design*: Salvador Lozano Mena; *Art Dir*: Salvador Lozano Mena [as S.L. Mena]; *Set Decoration*: Raymundo Ortiz; *Asst. Ed*: Felipe Islas; *Cam. Op*: Manuel Santaella; *Asst. Cam. Op*: Manuel Luna; *Sound*: Ernesto Caballero.

Cast: Armando Acosta, Víctor Alcocer, Magdaleno Barba, José Chávez, Joaquín Cordero, José Dupeyrón, Jesús Gómez, David Hayat, Ana Bertha Lepe, Salvador Lozano, Margarito Luna, Antonio Raxel, Jorge Russek, Aurelio Salinas, Andrés Soler, Carlos Suárez, Amado Zumaya.

El Terrible Gigante de las Nieves (The Terrible Giant of the Snows, 1962)

(Technical credits same for both films)
Cast: Joaquín Cordero, Ana Bertha Lepe, José Chávez, Elizabeth Dupeyrón, David Hayat, José Eduardo Pérez, Antonio Raxel, Andrés Soler, Amado Zumaya.

In the history of Mexican cinema, there are as many films about the Yeti (two) as there are "serious" dinosaur films, so it's pretty obvious how much clout either subject carries at the box office. Come to think of it, considering the number of Yeti films produced worldwide, they're not that boffo anywhere. This did not stop Mexican moviemakers, however, who, like Hammer, were filming every kind of monster that they could find or dream up; and in particular did not deter director Jaime Salvador from forcing his hand with this pair of jokers from '62. Not that they're comedies, but monster (the same creature appears in both films) inspires plenty of laughter. With a name like "the Lord of the Volcano," or "Terrible Giant of the Snows" (the tropical climate must have proven too much for him, or perhaps he just maintained a summer home), one expects a pretty damned fearsome beast, but this traveling yeti looks for all the world like a big, fuzzy Michelin Man! Of course, a standard savage Yeti would have seemed too mundane in Mexico, so they not only make him intelligent, but perverse: like Boris Karloff in *The Black Cat* (Universal '34), he keeps his dead ex-"wives" all neatly lined up in a row of glass cases!

When two members of a construction crew are mysteriously murdered, chief engineer Jorge (Joaquín Cordero) and the project's financier, Morris, consult Dr. Moctezuma, who believes "the Lord of the Volcano" is responsible. He sure is, and the "Lord" telepathically lures the doc's sexy daughter, Lupe (Ana Bertha Lepe), to his lair, where, even after seeing how he treats his women, she agrees to become his next conquest — but not while her father still lives. Naturally, the horny yeti can't wait, and so he tries to hasten Doc Moctezuma's demise. Jorge won't stand for any of it, though, and disposes of the monster by pratfall — he trips him, and the beast falls off a cliff. The End.

In the sequel, made the same year but taking place "six years later," Jorge and Lupe are hitched, with a little girl, and her dad is convinced that the monster is at work again. He sure seems to be, and Morris, revealed as a baddie at the end of the first feature, is back for another go. But after several more rounds of yeti-fu, the beast is revealed to be merely one of Morris' thugs in a snowman suit.

Museo del Horror (*Museum of Horror*, 1963)

(Cinematograficos Sotomayor) *Prod*: Miguel Sotomayor Martínez; *Dir*: Rafael Baledón; *Scr/Adapt*: José María Fernández Unsain.

Cast: Julio Alemán, Patricia Conde, Joaquín Cordero, Olivia Michel, David Reynoso, Carlos López Moctezuma, Emma Roldán, Sonia Infante, Armando Soto La Marina, Julián de Meriche, Carlos Bravo y Fernández, Guillermo Bravo Sosa, Jesús Gómez, José Pardavé.

The wax museum was quite the busy place in '63; not only did Santo have one of his better adventures in one, but this (as the title suggests) proved to be Mexico's take on both *Mystery of the Wax Museum* (starring Lionel Atwill, 1933) and *House of Wax* (Vincent Price, 1953). The latter's influence is most obvious in the *Museo del Horror* villain's choice of wardrobe — a black slouch hat and cloak — and his chasing the heroine through the streets in said wardrobe (*à la* Vinnie's pursuit of Phyllis Kirk). Julio Aleman, soon to play a big part in the Neutrón series, here portrays another bitter recluse — in this case an ex-actor who kidnaps women and turns them into exhibits in his wax museum. In a sadistic twist on the horrible scenario, the women turned into wax sculptures by the madman are alive when the process begins and regain consciousness just before the wax hits them! *Museo del Horror* also features a nightmarish dream sequence in which rotting corpses rise from their tombs, and a creepy "buried alive" scene. At the climax, the thespian asesino takes a swan dive into an orchestra pit.

Derivative? Certainly. But it's not a question of the influences, it's how creatively they're recycled, and on that level, *Museo del Horror* makes for one great matinee.

Aventura al Centro de la Tierra (*Adventure in the Center of the Earth*, 1964)

(Cinematograficos Sotomayor) *Prod*: Jaime Sotomayor; *Dir*: Alfredo B. Crevenna; *Scr*: José María Fernández Unsáin; *Cinematography*: Raúl Martínez Solares; *Film Ed*: Carlos Savage; *Sound*: Javier Mateos; *Music Suprvsr*: Sergio Guerrero.

Cast: Kitty de Hoyos (Hilda Ramírez), Javier Solís (Dr. Manuel Rios), Columba Domínguez (Laura Ponce), José Elías Moreno (Profesor Díaz), Carlos Cortés (Dr. Pena), Carmen Molina (Julia), David Reynoso (Jaime Rocha), Ramón Bugarini (Apolinar), Carlos Nieto (Novio de Julia), Marco Antonio Arzate, Roberto Meyer (Padre de Julia), Armando

Acosta (Gerente de gruta), Inés Murillo (Turista), Miguel Suárez (Psiquiatra).

Despite the similarity of the titles, this is not really the Mexican version of Twentieth Century–Fox's *Journey to the Center of the Earth* (1959); well, it is, in the sense that the action takes place in "the center of the Earth" (the real-life caverns of Cacahuamilpa), but it plays more like a standard 1950s B programmer. Rather than mere scientific exploration, the purpose of the expedition in *Adventure* is to discover what sort of beast has mauled a teen. Of course, when the Mexican expedition closes in on that center, they meet up with creatures undreamed of even in the fertile imagination of Jules Verne...

On a guided tour of some outlying caverns, a pair of teens sneak off for a little hoochie-koochie, and the boy gets in in the gut from an unseen attacker. His date is pulled gibbering from the scene. A standard 1950s movie expedition (earnest scientists, brash opportunists, and monster food ... er, loyal assistants) hitches up its boots and goes underground to find out exactly what caused the mayhem. Among the group is La Loba herslf, Kitty De Hoyos, who becomes the focus of attention for a member of the local fauna — a furry, winged, bipedal "bat man" who kidnaps her and takes her back to his lair, Blacky Lagoon. He even offers her some of his choicest rats for sustenance, but gets about as far in his advances as the Gill Man ever did. Also encountered are a cyclopian lizard man (not the one from *Ship of Monsters*) and a big spider.

Much has been made of the changeable appearance of the "bat man," which differs greatly from close-up to long shot. In fact, the close-ups have been lifted from another film — they clearly take place inside a room, with windows, doors and shutters painly visible (and certainly not a cavern). But the differences appear no more jarring nor haphazard (and actually a little less so) than the discrepancies found in the 1932 classic *Murders in the Rue Morgue* (wherein Bela Lugosi's simian henchman switches back and forth from a gorilla to a chimpanzee to an orangutan with impunity!).

The leader of the expedition, Professor Díaz, is played by José Elias Moreno, who is probably best known to U.S. audiences as Santa Claus in the 1959 Mexican production of the same name. Dubbed by K. Gordon Murray for U.S. release, *Santa Claus* is nearly as bizarre as the wrestler/monster films (and rivaled as a psychotronic holiday treat only by *Santa Claus Conquers the Martians*. Moreno was last seen by U.S. audiences in his role as the mad scientist in *Night of the Bloody Apes*, made shortly before his death in 1969.

La Loba (*The She-Wolf*, 1964)

(Cinematográficos Sotomayor) *Exec. Prod*: Heberto Dávila Guajardo; *Prod*: Jesús Sotomayor Martínez; *Dir*: Rafael Baledón; *Story/Scr*: Ramón Obón; *Music*: Raúl Lavista; *Cinematography*: Raúl Martínez Solares; *Prod. Design*: Salvador Lozano; *Prod. Chief*: Antonio Guajardo; *Asst. Dir*: Americo Fernández; *Ed*: Pedro López; *Makeup*: María del Castillo; *SPFX*: Antonio Muñoz; *Sound Sprvsr*: James L. Fields; *Sound Dir*: Galdino Samperio; *Dialogue*: Javier Mateos; *Sync. Ed*: Reynaldo Portillo; *Suprvsr*: Miguel Sotomayor Martínez; *Cam. Op*: Cirillo Rodríguez; *Technical Union*: "Insurgentes"; Orquesta de Filarmónicos del S.T.P.C. de la R.N.; *Studios and Laboratories*: Churubusco-Azteca.

Cast: Kitty de Hoyos (Clarisa Fernández, La Loba), Joaquín Cordero (Dr. Alejandro Bernstein), Columba Domínguez (Marcela de Fernández), José Elías Moreno (Professor Fernández), Noé Murayama (Cazador de Lobos "Wolf Hunter"), Adriana Roel (Alicia Fernández), Crox Alvarado, Ramón Bugarini (Inspector), Judith Dupeyrón (Adelita), Jorge Russek (Comisario), José Dupeyrón, Hortensia Santovena, Margarita Delgado.

In this author's opinion, *La Loba* may be the most underrated Mexican horror of them all. And it's a damned shame it has never been dubbed into English, because this one would warm the cockles of the cult-movie lovers' hearts. Not because of any innate weirdness, but because *La Loba* is a taut, atmospheric, and downright scary monster movie. Star Kitty de Hoyos was, in turn, beautiful, haunted, savage and tragic, and her werewolf makeup was perhaps the best ever in a Mexican horror movie. *La Loba* is everything *She-Wolf of London* (1946) wasn't, in spades. The heroine really does turn into a were-creature (it's not just some psycho-babble, with a garden weeder as the real culprit). Señora de Hoyos undergoes the full transformation, and proves to be a most athletic were-woman, performing a number of spectacular leaps as she springs into murderous action (and providing some surprisingly bloody scenes for 1964). An added surprise (and, in the end, bonus) is that, unlike Larry Talbot and his regulation uniform of dark shirt and pants (*The Wolf Man*), or Henry Hull and his tweed cap (*Werewolf of London*), Kitty de Hoyos' werewolf is completely naked, thereby creating some interesting (though discretely handled) situations when she changes back.

Speaking of *Werewolf of London*, Kitty De Hoyos' makeup resembles that of Henry Hull's they go light on the fur in order to emphasize the facial features. And emphasize it the filmmakers do, in a number of wonderfully-lit close-ups that manage to be both sensual and scary at the same time. As if to compensate, her entire body is covered in fur (remember, she's naked), and her hair transforms from a carefully-coiffed 'do into a long, straight mane twice its normal length. This earns my vote for the most effective Mexican monster makeup ever.

In a film that is equal parts creepy atmosphere and full-tilt shock, one gripping sequence combines those elements (and much more) to stand out in a standout film. Kitty's little sister has been snooping around Kitty's bedroom, when Kitty enters. The little girl hides under the bed ... and then Kitty begins to change. For moments of unbearable tension the little girl's eyes grow ever wider, and she can barely suppress a scream as Kitty sheds her garments and transforms. The were-woman even falls to the floor as she changes, not three feet from the child, but fails to notice. As the she-beast explores an opening in the fireplace, the sister makes her way down the trellis, and looks to be home free ... but La Loba has heard the window shut, and in a flash she is upon the child, who escapes into the woods and is saved by Noé Murayama (portraying a werewolf-hunter). Murayama, who usually assayed villains, played against type in this one and excelled, as does every other member (and aspect) of this superior horror.

Ten years later, El Santo would face a whole colony of werewolves, both male and female, in *Santo contra Las Lobas* (which, despite the similarity of titles and makeups, was not a sequel).

Gigantes Planetarios (Giant Planets, 1965)

Prod: Emilio Gómez Muriel; *Dir*: Alfredo B. Crevenna; *Music*: Raúl Lavista; *Scr*: Alfredo Ruanova; *Cinematography*: Alfredo Uribe.

Cast: Guillermo Murray (Daniel Wolf), Adriana Roel (Silvia), Rogelio Guerra (Marcos Godoy), José Ángel Espinosa "Ferrusquilla" (Rey Taquito), José Gálvez (El Protector), Jacqueline Fellay (Mara), Carlos Nieto (Tasilo), Daniel Villaran (Lupecio), Irma Lozano (Anis), Mário Orea (Profesor Walter), Nothanael "Frankenstein" León (Spy), Evita Muñoz "Chachita" (Frijol), Ethel Carrillo, Mario Sevilla (Doctor), Ricardo Adalid, Jorge Zamora ("Nativo de Africa").

El Planeta de las Mujeres Invasoras (*The Planet of the Women Invaders*, 1965)

Prod: Emilio Gómez Muriel; *Dir*: Alfredo B. Crevenna; *Music*: Raúl Lavista; *Scr*: Alfredo

GUILLERMO
MURRAY
ADRIANA
ROEL
ROGELIO
GUERRA
FERRUSQUILLA
JOSE
GALVEZ
EVITA
MUÑOZ
GIGANTES PLANETARIOS
DISTRIBUIDA POR CLASA-MOHME, Inc.
CATCHLINES
RADIO SPOTS
¡DESCUBRA USTED LA VERDAD ACERCA DE LOS
PLATILLOS VOLADORES!
¡MISTERIOSOS VEHICULOS DEL ESPACIO SURCAN EL
CIELO DE NUESTRA CIUDAD.
¡PREPARESE A RECIBIRLOS!
¡Seres de otro mundo han llegado a nuestra ciudad
"GIGANTES PLANETARIOS" ¡Una diabólica misión los ha
hecho atravesar el cosmos en sus fantásticos platillos!
"GIGANTES PLANETARIOS" con GUILLERMO MURRAY,
ADRIANA ROEL, ROGELIO GUERRA y "FERRUSQUILLA".
Hoy, estreno, cine

GUILLERMO MURRAY
ADRIANA ROEL
ROGELIO GUERRA
FERRUSQUILLA
JOSE GALVEZ
EVITA MUÑOZ
GIGANTES PLANETARIOS
CLASA-MOHME, Inc.
GUILLERMO MURRAY
ADRIANA ROEL
ROGELIO GUERRA
FERRUSQUILLA
JOSE GALVEZ
EVITA MUÑOZ
GIGANTES Planetarios
CLASA-MOHME, Inc.
GUILLERMO MURRAY
ADRIANA ROEL
GIGANTES PLANETARIOS
GUILLERMO MURRAY
ADRIANA ROEL
GIGANTES PLANETARIOS
CLASA-MOHME, Inc.
ADVERTISING ACCESSORIES
AVAILABLE TO EXHIBITORS
1-sheet posters
8x10 stills
11x14 colored
lobby cards
Mats:
3-col. ad
One 2-col. scene
One 1-col. scene
One 2-col. ad
One 1-col. ad
One 2-col. slug
One 1-col. slug
C-M inc.
No. C1368
DISTRIBUIDA POR CLASA-MOHME, Inc.
LOS ANGELES - SAN ANTONIO - DENVER
CHICAGO - NEW YORK

Opposite: This ad sheet for *Planetarios* looks like it came straight out of an EC *Weird Science* comic book. *Above*: Lorena Velázquez rallies the troops so that her planet of women can invade us. Please hurry!

Ruanova, Emilio Gómez Muriel; *Cinematography*: Alfredo Uribe.

Cast: Lorena Velázquez (Adastrea; Alburnia), Elizabeth Campbell (Martesia), Maura Monti (Eritrea), Guillermo Murray (Daniel Wolf), Adriana Roel (Silvia), Rogelio Guerra (Marcos Godoy), José Ángel Espinosa "Ferrusquilla" [as José A. Espinosa] (Rey Taquito), Raúl Ramírez (Tono), Ethel Carrillo (Desinea), Graciela Doring (Mujer secuestrada), Guillermo Álvarez Bianchi (Hombre gordo secuestrado), José Chávez (Beto), Enrique Ramírez (Ramón), Aarón Hernán (Hombre secuestrado), Monica Miguel (Fitia), Felipe de Flores (Maestro).

In this pair from Alfredo B. Crevenna, the sequel is by far the superior entry. Although it can't really be called a "serious" science-fiction film in the *2001* sense, the first, *Gigantes Planetarios*, is serious in the sense that it's a fairly straightforward adventure about a group of astronauts (led by Count Subatoi himself, Guillermo Murray) who travel to another planet and save Earth from being blown up. It's reminiscent of one of the really forgettable episodes of *Star Trek*.

Perhaps realizing this, Crevenna pulled out all the interstellar stops on the sequel, *La Planeta de las Mujeres Invasoras*. The second and final phase of Captain Guillermo's two-film mission was, well, where quite a few crews had gone before (but no less fun for it: a planet populated entirely by women! Criswell predicted there would be colonies on the moon; I'll go one step beyond and predict that, based on extensive scientifilm research, there will be entire planets occupied by nothing but gorgeous women, and they will all wear either sheer gowns (the leaders) or really short skirts (every woman who isn't a leader). Films like *El Planeta* and *Cat-Women of the Moon* support this theory.

El Plantea de las Mujeres Invasoras remains memorable for its "all-star" lineup of favorite fantasy femmes; in fact, it could just as easily have been called "The Wrestling Women and Bat Woman on Mars," for it features the trio of Lorena Velázquez, Elizabeth Campbell and Maura Monti, all in their prime. Or, perhaps "quartet" would be more accurate, since the film presents a double dose of Lorena, who plays her own evil twin! (Captain Kirk never had it so good!) The costuming is equally memorable — since Lorena is a queen, she gets to wear a gorgeous gown, while the rest of the women invaders sport the aforementioned short skirts, with funny little helmets that make the whole ensemble resemble a cross between Flash Gordon and the Pope. Captain Guillermo and crew save the earth once again — but in this case, more's the pity!

El Imperio de Drácula (*The Empire of Dracula, 1966*)

(Fílmica Vergara–Cinecomisiones) *Prod*: Luis Enrique Vergara; *Dir*: Federico Curiel; *Story*: Ramón Obón; *Cinematography*: Alfredo Uribe.

Cast: Eric del Castillo (Drácula), Víctor Alcocer, César del Campo, Rebeca Iturbide, Altia Michel, Fernando Osés.

Mexico had influenced Hammer and the modern vampire film by introducing the outsized fangs, and now it was Mexico's turn to *be* influenced by Hammer. This first Mexican vampire film in color borrowed heavily from its counterparts across the sea, particularly Hammer's *Drácula, Prince of Darkness*. This becomes most obvious in the scene wherein the vampire's manservant (Fernando Osés) re-

vives the bloodsucker by killing a young woman and letting her blood drip onto his master's ashes. The vampire, curiously named "Draculstein," is played in a stately-surly manner (*à la* Christopher Lee) by Eric del Castillo. Del Castillo does a fine job (like Lee in *Prince of Darkness*, he has practically no dialogue), and looks both imposing and frightening (although, once again, this apparently was not good enough for Mexican distributors — the poster art, besides featuring many scantily-clad women, adds a large image of Germán Robles, though he has absolutely nothing to do with the film!). Del Castillo would again perform service as a monster (albeit a fake one) four years later in the Santo thriller *Santo en la Venganza de la Momia. El Empiro de Drácula* tries hard to emulate the look and feel of the Hammers, and succeeds admirably.

This was the most important genre appearance for Eric del Castillo (b. 1934), whose other credits include *The Living Head*, two films apiece with the Wrestling Women and Mil Máscaras, and a vigorous performance as the title mummy in *Santo en la Venganza de la Momia*. At the time of this writing, he continues to ply his chosen trade.

La Isla de los Dinosaurios (*The Island of the Dinosaurs, 1966*)

(Cinematográfica Calderón S.A.) *Prod*: Guillermo Calderón Stell; *Dir*: Rafael Portillo [as Rafael López Portillo]; *Scr*: Alfredo Salazar; *Music*: Gustavo César Carrión; *Cinematography*: Agustín Jiménez; *Film Ed*: Jorge Bustos; *Prod. Design*: Javier Torres Torija; *Set Decoration*: Raúl Serrano; *Sound*: José Li-ho; *SPFX*: Roy Seawright.

Cast: Armando Silvestre (Molo), Alma Delia Fuentes (Laura), Manuel Fábregas (Profesor), Elsa Cárdenas (Esther), Genaro Moreno (Pablo), Crox Alvarado (Caveman), Cavernario Galindo (Caveman); Jesús Velázquez (Caveman), Cecilia Leger (Misha), Xochitl

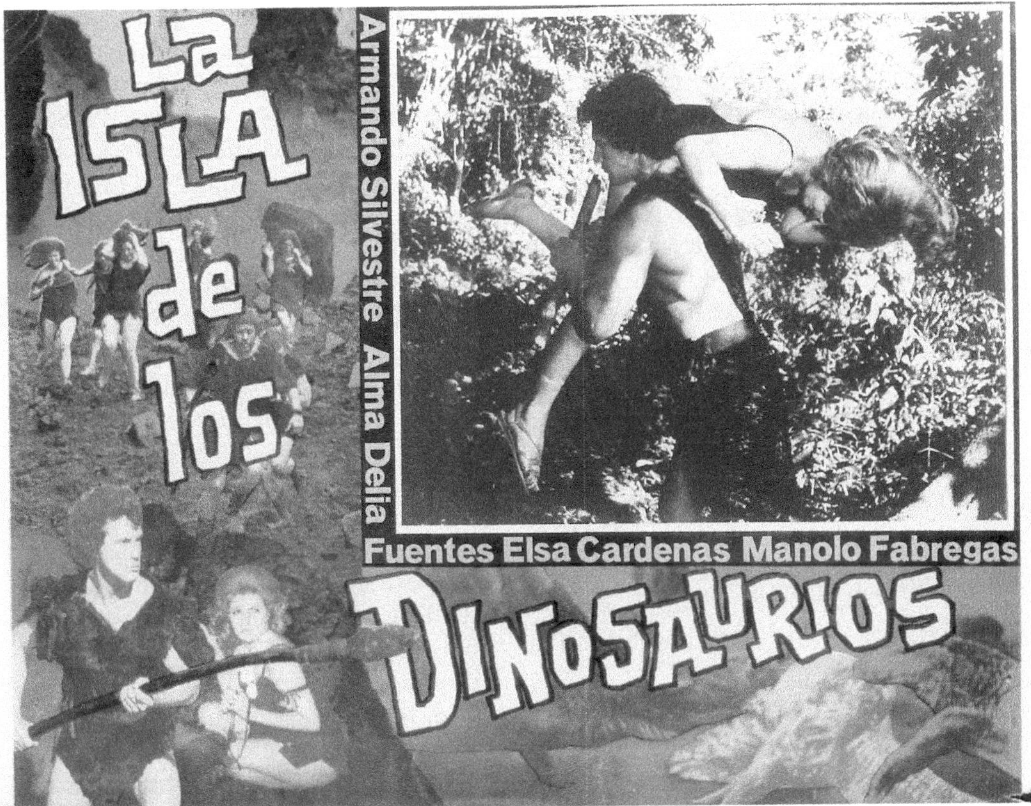

Azteca lobby card.

Flores, Reyes Oliva, Julie Janssen (Cavewoman), Victorio Blanco (Old caveman).

In 1940 Hal Roach produced *One Million B.C.*, starring, among others, Lon Chaney, Jr., as your basic feuding cavemen, who occasionally took time out to battle dinosaurs. Eschewing the time-consuming and costlier services of a Willis O'Brien, Roach decided to dress up real animals (i.e. an alligator with a rubber sail attached to its back) and try to pass them off on the rubes as dinosaurs. The legacy of that film lies in the saurian scenes becoming a staple in the stock footage library, and therefore an indelible part of dino-lore (by its being re-used over and over and over again during the ensuing years).

In 1966, the year that Hammer released its spectacular color remake of that Hal Roach film (but done right this time—in color and featuring the special effects of Ray Harryhausen), Mexico countered by releasing a black-and-white, low-budget dino epic of their own, or mostly their own—*La Isla de los Dinosaurios*. I say mostly their own because *Isla* was the latest (and the last) in a proud line of films that employed stock footage from the original. Yes, when everyone else was turning to color, director Rafael Portillo took it on the cheap in order to match the b & w stock footage.

The story stakes out standard dino-film territory, as a scientist and his companions crash-land on a mysterious island that time forgot, where they encounter many cavemen and dinosaurs. One expedition member falls in love with a local cavegirl, and must make the ultimate choice of whether to stay or go.

La Isla de los Dinosaurios earns points for having "Caveman Wellington" (Cavernario Galindo) finally play a namesake. Roy Seawright receives credit for the film's special effects, although heaven knows why, because they're all lifted from *One Million B.C.* Perhaps he helped pick out the stock footage used? So you've seen the dinosaurs (literally) a hundred times, but this *Isla* is still worth visiting just to see Armando Silvestre in a fright wig.

Dr. Satán (1966)

Dr. Satán y la Magia Negra (*Doctor Satan and the Black Magic*, 1967)

(Technical credits and cast are the same for both films.)

Prod: Sidney T. Bruckner; *Dir*: Rogelio A. González; *Adapt*: José María Fernández Unsáin; *Music*: Luis Hernández Bretón; *Cinematography*: José Ortiz Ramos; *Film Ed*: Carlos Savage; *Prod. Design*: Jorge Fernández; *Set Decoration*: Carlos Arjona; *Sound Ed*: José Li-Ho; *SPFX*: Enrique Gordillo; *Asst. Ed*: Jesús Paredes.

Cast: Joaquín Cordero (Dr. Satán), Sonia Furió, Noé Murayama, Aurora Clavel, Luz María Aguilar, Carlos Agostí, Armando Acosta, Carlos Cardán, Guillermo Hernández, Lila Kiwa, Nothanael "Frankenstein" León, José Luis Llamas, Carlos López Figueroa, Fernando Saucedo, Michel Strauss.

This duo bears no relation to the Republic serial *The Mysterious Dr. Satan*. That classic cliffhanger of the 1940s featured primo character actor Eduardo Cianelli as an evil mastermind who uses water heater–like robots in an attempt to defeat masked hero (but not wrestler) "the Copperhead." Mexico's Dr. Satan was a devil-worshipping crime boss who uses business suit–wearing zombies to carry out his nefarious schemes. Dr. Satan's undead henchmen are the standard chalk-faced, dark-circles-under-the-eye (i.e. easily made-up) zombies, who, although freshly risen from their graves, are still nattily-attired in dark matching suits. They have to be, as the stylish Dr. Satan (Joaquín Cordero, excellent in the part, and clearly having a wonderful time being evil — his eyes literally light up!) is quite the rake himself, preferring a Dracula-like cloak. And his namesake makes appearances in the flesh, in creepily lit, fog-bound scenes that emphasize the Devil's horns and huge bat-like wings, recalling similar shots from *Curse of the Demon* (1958).

The first of the series was an adept mix of sci-fi and Satanism, but the sequel, *Dr. Satan and the Black Magic*, pulled out all the stops. Joaquín Cordero returns as the Doc, and he again brings zombies — only this time they're pretty female zombies in mini-skirts! The original hero is back too, pitting his medical lieutenant against an evil Asian mastermind who just happens to be a vampire. With op-art colors, spy gadgets, and sports cars galore, one wishes they would have mined this formula further; but apparently the filmmakers decided to quit while ahead, as this was the last appearance of Dr. Satan.

The evil Asian mastermind (rugs are Oriental; people are Asian) was played by Noé Murayama, one of Mexico's best-known screen heavies. He made over 200 films, as well as appearing on television and in theater, and is fondly remembered by genre fans for his superb efforts in, among others, *La Loba*, *Operación 67* (with El Santo), and *Blue Demon vs. the Infernal Brains*. He died on August 25, 1997.

Star Joaquín Cordero (b. 1926) was a popular leading man known for his good-guy roles, but his turns in genre pictures often proved villainous, including the first two El Santo films, and *Orlak, el Infierno de Frankenstein*. Cordero's other genre credits include *Museo del Horror*, *La Loba*, and *Las Luchadoras contra el Robot Asesino*. He remains active in the profession as of this writing.

Autopsia de un Phantasma
(*Autopsy of a Ghost*, 1967)

Prod/Dir/Scr: Ismael Rodríguez; *Dialogue*: Pedro De Urdimalas; *Story*: Mário Hernández, Carlos Piñar; *Music*: Raúl Lavista; *Cinematography*: J. Carlos Carbajal; *Film Ed*: Fernando Martínez; *Art Direction*: Roberto Silva; *Makeup*: Margarita Ortega; *Asst. Dir*: Mario Llorca; *Sound Ed*; Raúl Portillo.

Cast: Basil Rathbone (Canuto Pérez), John Carradine (Satán), Amadee Chabot (Galena Pulido), Cameron Mitchell (Prof. Moleculo Pulido), Carlos Piñar (Jaime Blondo), Famie Kaufman (Vitola), Javier López (Chabelo), Arturo Castro "Bigotón" (Judge), Susana Cabrera (Susana), Pancho Córdova (Pinedo), Delia Magaña (Beggar), Pompín Iglesias (Pompin), Mário García (Agente 0), Nacho Contla (Nacho), Manuel Palacios (Manolin), Estanislao Schillinsky (Cab driver), Manuel Trejo Morales, Ahui Camacho.

If you thought John Carradine overplayed in *Las Vampiras*, just wait until you see *Autopsy of a Ghost*. He leers, howls and cackles his way through the role of the Devil Himself, playing it with such heated, over-the-top energy that one begins to fear he'll spontaneously combust. He's joined by other old pros Basil Rathbone (his last film) and Cameron Mitchell (as a mad scientist). Rathbone seems to be enjoying himself playing as Don Carlos, the ghost of the title, who is doomed to wander as a spirit forever unless a female mortal falls in love with him. At least, that's the gist of the idea, but the picture moves in so many directions at once that it's hard to tell. Rathbone wears a Beatles wig; Amadee Chabot wears a bikini (although she's nowhere near water); and a talking skeleton wears nothing at all. There's a female robot, and a man in schoolboy clothes who's not Angus Young from AC/DC. There's a judge and jury composed of a private eye and some hippies. There's so much going on, it becomes difficult to keep up with, but you'll sure have a grand time trying. And, as far as last films go, Rathbone receives a much better send-off than either of his *Son of Frankenstein* co-stars, Boris Karloff and Bela Lugosi.

Con Licencia para Matar
(*With License to Kill*, 1967)

Prods: Eduardo Galindo, Jesús Galindo; *Dir*: Rafael Baledón; *Story*: Alfredo Ruanova; *Music*: Gustavo César Carrión; *Cinematography*: Agustín Jiménez; *Film Ed*: Jorge Bustos; *Prod. Design*: Francisco Marco Chillet; *Set Decoration*: Carlos Grandjean; *Costume Design*: Julio Chávez, Francisco Rubio; *Asst. Ed*: Joaquín Ceballos; *Cam. Op*: Manuel Santaella; *Asst. Cam. Op*: Fernando Galicia; *Music*: Los Rockin' Devils.

Cast: Fernando Casanova (Morrison "the Chief"), Maura Monti (Diana/T009), Emily Cranz (Emily/T001), Barbara Angely (Barbara/T002), Leonorilda Ochoa (Leonor), Noé Murayama (Dr. Klux), Claudia Islas (Adrian Horácio Salinas), Carlos Nieto (Roberto), Martha Yolanda Pirez, Ricardo Carrión (Raúl Velez), Carlos Guarneros, Alfonso Pérez Avalo, Ruben Morales García, Héctor Bonilla, Raúl Padilla, Juan Garza, Adolfo Magaldi, Julián de Meriche, Carlos Suárez, Los Rockin' Devils (Their devilishly rockin' selves).

Santo and Blue Demon weren't the only action heroes to play the spy game in Mexico in the 1960s—their beautiful and frequent co-star, Maura Monti, not only essayed the role of the immortal "Bat Woman," but also turned up as the leader of a crack unit of action heroines called "the Tigresses" in this 1967 effort by ace director Rafael Baledón. If it sounds like *Charlie's Angels*, it should, but this was made seven years before the American TV show ever hit the small screen. Maura and the other Tigresses split their time between battling robot-zombie men (although how much man remains after transforming into both zombie and robot is open to debate) led by Noé Murayama, and modeling the latest mod fashions at the local discotheque (where they, and in particular

Miss Monti, shimmy with abandon). Each woman is an expert with her chosen weapon — Diana (Maura Monti) the bow-and-arrow; Barbara (Barbara Angely) with the sword; Emily (Emily Kranz) with the pistol; and Leonor (Leonorilda Ochoa) is a master of disguise. Baledón's handling is breezy and assured, and the movie's cup runneth over with fine action scenes, colorful set-pieces, wacky gadgets and an irrepressible attitude. Maura Monti was almost a genre unto herself; as well as appearing in this film's sequel, *Munecas Peilgrosos*, and *La Mujer Murciélago*, she played a bad-girl spy in *Cazadores de Espías* and another bad girl (in the Tura Satana mold) in *Los Sicodelicos*, leading an all-star female bunch that included Wrestling Woman Elizabeth Campbell and Agent 00-Sexy, Amadee Chabot.

Invasión Siniestra
(*Sinister Invasion*, 1968)

(Fílmica Vergara/Columbia) *Prod*: Luis Enrique Vergara; *Dir*: Juan Ibáñez; *Scr*: Jack Hill, Vergara; *Photo*: Raúl Domínguez; *Music*: Enrico Cabiati; *Prod. Mgr*: José Luis Cerrada; *Makeup*: Tony Ramírez.
    (Note: Technical credits are the same for all four of the following Karloff films.)

Cast: Boris Karloff (Prof. Mayer), Yerye Beirute, Carlos East, Maura Monti, Christa Linder.

Sereneta Macabra (*Macabre Serenade*, a.k.a. *House of Evil*, a.k.a. *Dance of Death*, 1968)

Cast: Boris Karloff (Matias Mortewald), Julissa, Andrés García, Angel "Ferrusquilla" Espinzosa, Beatriz Baz, Quintin Bulnes, Manuel Alvarado, Carmen Velez.

La Cámara del Terror
(*The Fear Chamber*, a.k.a. *The Torture Zone*, 1968)

Cast: Boris Karloff (Dr. Mantell), Julissa, Carlos East, Isela Vega, Yerye Beirute, Sandra Chávez, Eva Muller, Santanon, Pamela Parmeli, Fuensanta.

La Muerte Viviente
(*The Living Dead*, a.k.a. *The Snake People*, a.k.a. *Isle of the Snake People*, 1968)

Cast: Boris Karloff (Carl van Molder), Carlos East, Rafael Bertrand, Santanon, Tongelele, Quintin Bulnes, Martinique, Julia Marichal, Yolanda Duhalt.

Mexican genre films' thespian link to the Universal classics from which they drew so much inspiration began in 1959 with the appearance of Lon Chaney, Jr., in *La Casa del Terror*, and continued with the likes of Basil Rathbone and John Carradine in various productions discussed elsewhere in this book. But the actors' crowning jewel, one supposes, would have to be Boris Karloff; and, indeed, he appeared in four Mexican films, the last four features he would make before his death. Karloff didn't actually travel to Mexico, as his health was rapidly failing; his scenes were shot in Los Angeles by Jack Hill, whose own crowning achievement was *Spider Baby*. The effect is somewhat akin to Bela Lugosi's scenes in *Glen or Glenda?*. The films, produced by the ubiquitous Luis Enrique Vergara, are all somewhat sleazy, and contain none of the sense of fun that Vergara had brought to his previous ventures with John Carradine or the masked wrestlers.

For instance, in the first, *The Sinister Invasion*, Karloff has invented a death ray (although he doesn't like to call it that), which is coveted by some aliens. To kill the professor and steal the device, the aliens utilize the local serial rapist and killer (Beiyrute), and keep him under control by feeding him victims. He even rapes and murders Maura Monti, and this sort of thing is just not done. Much more time than necessary is devoted to this nasty subplot; and Karloff repeats his standard "silver-haired daddy" role from well, pretty much any film after *Son of Frankenstein*.

At least Boris gets to be bad in the next one, *Macabre Serenade*. It's another old chestnut — the relatives-fighting-over-the-inheritance plot — but with an eye-gouging murderer (who may be a ghost) on the loose. And not only are people getting their eyeballs gouged out, some are done in by various and sundry mechanical toys which Karloff's long-dead brother (the original peeper-gouger) built. The estate goes up in a blazing *House of Usher* ending, thankfully taking with it most everybody else who hadn't already met their demise.

The Fear Chamber was not a television "reality show," but Karloff's third movie for Vergara. Back in "siver-haired daddy" mode, this time Karloff discovers a living rock. The rock lives on glandular secretions which can only be obtained from a terrified human, and so the rest of the film is more or less a parade of young women in various states of undress being offered as sustenance to the stone (an advance agent for his fellow rocks, who want to conquer the world). It sounds more entertaining than it really is, and the question of how the rocks survived before this remains unanswered (as is often the case with movies featuring menaces that can only survive on a substance found in an alien world).

In his final film, Karloff does the Murder Legendre bit (from 1932's *White Zombie*) as a plantation owner who employs a zombie workforce, but seems otherwise unconnected to the voodoo rituals, cannibal feasts and human sacrifices that comprise most of the rest of the action … until he's revealed as the one everybody is sacrificin' to, the evil voodoo god Damballah! As usual, a big-bang finale climaxes the proceedings, wiping out everybody but the hero and heroine. Karloff puts on a

brave face, but he's served no better here than in *Voodoo Island* (1957). Karloff was not served well, period, by his last pictures, but at least he went out working, and that's the way he wanted it.

It's unfortunate that Bela Lugosi didn't live longer, as I suspect he surely would have found employment in Mexico. He wouldn't have been in any worse physical shape than Karloff, and plying his trade south of the border couldn't have been any worse than working for Ed Wood. Although, judging from the quality of Karloff's final efforts, maybe it could.

Capulina contra los Vampiros (*Capulina vs. the Vampires*, 1971)

Prod: Gaspar Henaine [Capulina]; *Dir*: René Cardona Jr.
Cast: Capulina, Carlos Agosti, Juan Gallardo, Rossy Mendoza.

Although scattered technical information and/or display art (lobby cards, posters, stills, etc.) are readily available for certain Mexican genre films. The films themselves, unfortunately, are not. At the time of this writing, *Capulina vs. the Vampires* happens to be one of those films.

Juan Gallardo, who played one of the lead vampires here, specialized in villainous roles, although this and his four appearances with Santo are his only real genre work. He continues actively in the profession to this day.

Chanoc vs. el Tigre y el Vampiro (*Chanoc vs. the Tiger and the Vampire*, 1971)

(Cinematográfica RA) *Prod*: Rafael Pérez Grovas; *Dir*: Gilberto Martínez Solares; *Scr/Photo*: Raúl Martínez Solares; *Story*: Grovas; *Music*: Manuel Esperón; *Film Ed*: Gloria Schoemann; *Animal Wranglers*: Humberto and Miguel Gueurza.
Cast: Gregorio Casal (Chanoc), Germán

Top: Amadee Chabot, a co-star of both El Santo's and John Carradine's, headlined the saucy spy spoof *Agente 00-Sexy*. *Bottom*: Chanoc was a Tarzan clone who made a whole slew of solo films, as well as co-starring with El Hijo del Santo.

"Tin Tan" Valdés (Tzekub), Miguel Gurza (Count Frankenhausen), Aurora Clavel, Lina Marin, Ramón Valdés, Humberto Gurza, Raulito.

Chanoc was the name of a popular, long-running comic book character whose adventures began in 1959. Chanoc, a junior-grade Tarzan, was accompanied in his exploits by Tzekub, an old coot, and Chucho Chucho, the series' resident Cheetah stand-in. His success led to a series of motion pictures, produced over the span of many years, the first one being made in 1966. The first Tzekub was played by zany former director Chano Urueta, who was winding down his career on the other side of the camera, playing old coots. *Chanoc* producer Rafael Pérez Grovas was the man not only responsible for some of El Santo's final films (and his son's initial forays), but for the earlier efforts *Invasión de los Vampiros* and *El Vampiro Sangriento*, which also featured a vampire named Count Frankenhausen. The tiger of the title is actually Frankenhausen's pet, and why he receives top billing is a mystery. Nominally the hero, Chanoc takes a back seat to the antics of Tin Tan, and the whole affair is rather shoddily perpetrated, although it remains preferable to *El Hijo del Santo y Chanoc vs. Los Vampiros Asesinos*, produced by Grovas ten years later, by which time the only person who cared was the son of Santo himself.

Gilberto Martínez Solares (1906–1997) was an incredibly prolific director whose resume included some great genre pics. His most well-known feature to American audiences is *La Casa del Terror*, with Lon Chaney, Jr., but by the time it reached this side of the border as *Face of the Screaming Werewolf*, little of Solares' style remained. Other significant features that can still be viewed in their unbutchered form include: *Blue Demon contra las Invasoras*, *El Mundo de los Muertos*, *Misterio en las Bermudas*, and his other most famous

flicker, the all-star *Santo y Blue Demon contra los Monstruos*.

Capulina contra las Momias (*Capulina vs. the Mummies, 1972*)

(Panorama Films/Estudios América) *Prod/Dir/Scr*: Alfredo Zacarias; *Photo*: Raúl Domínguez; *Music*: Carlos Camacho; *Asst. Dir*: Javier Duran; *Art Dir*: Raúl Cárdenas; *Makeup*: Graciela González.

Cast: Gaspar "Capulina" Henaine, Jacqueline Voltaire (Jackie), Freddy Fernández, Enrique Ponton, Manuel Donde (El Muerto), Citlali Breceda, Argentina Candelario, Dinorah Carrejo, Susana Alvarez, Leticia Perdegon, Sessi Castia (the Mummy Girls).

Originally entitled *Capulina contra las Momias de Guanajuato* (before a name change at the eleventh hour), this Capulina vehicle is the first in a line of unofficial sequels to *The Mummies of Guanajuato*—in that they make use of the monsters and makeups associated with those films, but don't use the location. Capulina plays a taxi driver who finds handyman work with yet another off-kilter member of the medical profession, who just happens to be engaged in the scholarly pursuit of bringing mummies back to life. When they're revived, these ancient dead look normal, so actual mummies really don't have that much to do, and mainly serve as backdrops for Capulina's comedy routines (which are executed with his usual vigor). British-born blonde Jaqueline Voltaire fares almost as well as Capulina, and is quite the dish in a variety of revealing outfits. The real Mummies of Guanajuato exhibit is seen briefly; and the Mummy Girls, with their shrouds and skull-faces, should be a rock-and-roll band.

El Hombre y la Bestia (*The Man and the Beast, 1972*)

Dir: Julián Soler; *Adapt*: Alfredo Ruanova; *Music*: Ernesto Cortázar; *Cinematography*:

Xavier Cruz [as Javier Cruz Ruvalcaba], *Film Ed*: Raúl Caso [as Raúl J. Casso]; *Cam. Ops*: Alberto Arellanos Bustamante [as Alberto Arellanos], Agustín Lara Alvarado.

Cast: Enrique Lizalde (Dr. Enrique Duval/Eduardo Rail), Sasha Montenegro (Bettina), Carlos López Moctezuma (Dr. Ramos), Eduardo Noriega (Licenciado Menéndez), Nancy Compare (Nora Ramos), Julián Pastor (Inspector Blanco), Mauricio Ferrari (Abel), Rebeca Silva (Prostitute), Juan José Martínez Casado (Pablo), Jorge Fegán, Pedro Regueiro, José Luis Avendaño, Marcos E. Contreras [as Marco Contreras], Arturo Guzmán, Odila Dupeyron, Susana Alvarez, Jorge Victoria, Guillermo Segura.

Finally, Mexico gets around to adapting *Dr. Jekyll and Mr. Hyde*, and draws a great deal from the Christopher Lee version of the tale produced in 1971 entitled *I, Monster*. *El Hombre y la Bestia* stars Enrique Lizalde as Dr. Duval & Mr. Rail. This same year, Lizalde starred in another film by the same team responsible for this one, *Satanas de Todo los Horrores*, one of the few Mexican excursions into Poe territory.

Dr. Duval's friend, Dr. Ramos, was played by genre stalwart Carlos López Moctezuma, who had originally been tapped for the lead in *El Vampiro*. He made memorable meanies in many a film, including *The Curse of the Crying Woman* and *Night of the Bloody Apes*. Moctezuma also appeared in two actioners devoted to the exploits of the superhero "Rocambole"—*Rocambole contra la Secta del Escorpion* and *Rocambole contra las Mujeres Arpias*.

Capulina contra los Monstruos (1973)

(Panorama Films/Estudios América) *Prod*: Alfredo Zacarias; *Dir*: Miguel Morayta; *Scr*: Alfredo Zacarias; *Music*: Carlos Camacho; *Cinematography*: Raúl Domínguez; *Film Ed*: Francisco Chiu; *Prod. Design*: Raúl Cárdenas; *Cam. Op*: Alberto Arellanos Bustamante [as Alberto Arellanos].

Cast: Gaspar "Capulina" Henaine, Gloriella, Héctor Andremar, Irlanda Mora, Marcos E. Contreras [as Marco Contreras] ("El Lobo" the Wolf), Manuel Bravo, Guillermo Amador (Frankenstein), Salvador Zea (the Vampire), Juan Garza (La Momia/the Mummy), Jorge Victoria, Nothanael "Frankenstein" León, Ernesto Juárez, Gustavo del Castillo, Jorge Casanova, Armando Acosta, Carlos León.

Capulina had already met a host of wrestlers, vampires and the Mummies of Guanajuato, so for his last genre picture he held a "monster rally" of his own and pitted himself against the "big four" of classic monsterdom: Frankenstein's Monster, Drácula, the Wolf Man and the Mummy. It's pretty silly stuff (admittedly, the Capulina pictures were made especially to appeal to kids), but *Capulina vs. the Monsters* comes off no worse than, and is comparable to, the much later American film *The Monster Squad* (1987). But if you're the type of person who balks at their monsters being made light of, then I'd advise against watching this one. Movies like *Abbott and Costello Meet Frankenstein* and *The Ghost Breakers* (starring Bob Hope, 1940) achieve the rare feat of sprinkling genuinely scary moments amongst the comedy, and the monsters in each are placed in situations that underline their inherent creepiness. Not so in *Capulina vs. the Monsters*, which features plenty of silent film–style speeded-up chase scenes; monsters being held off by Cap's onion breath; and a pillow fight! Silly or not, the makeup for all four of the featured fiends is surprisingly good, and actually looks better than that featured in some of the straight monster movies produced around the same time.

Chabelo y Pepito contra los Monstruos (*Chabelo and Pepito vs. the Monsters*, 1973)

(Estudios Churubusco–Alameda Films) *Prod*: Alfredo Ripstein Jr.; *Dir*: José Estrada; *Scr*: Toni

Sbert; *Photo*: Manuel Gómez Urquiza; *Music*: Dergio Guerrero; *Asst. Dir*: Mario Llorca; *Makeup*: Carmen Palomino; *Prod. Chief*: Enrique Morfin; *Film Ed*: Eufemio Rivera y R; *Deco*: Carlos Grandjean; *Dialogue Rec*: Eduardo Arjona; *Re-Rec*: Ramón Moreno; *Sound Ed*: Sigfrido García.

Cast: Xavier "Chabelo" López, Martín "Pepito" Ramos, Silvia Pasquel (Alicia), Pedro Reiguero (Gerardo), Nothanael "Frankenstein" León (Spectrum 2), Eduardo Casab, Ramiro Orci, Emma Grisso, Manuel Zepeda.

Universal produced all of their "monster rally" epics within the span of roughly six years. Mexico's first, *El Castillo de los Monstruos*, arrived in 1957, and they didn't decide to pull the plug until sixteen years later, with the release of *Chabelo and Pepito vs. the Monsters*. The first time the classic monsters had gathered in Mexico, they bedeviled a comedian; in the last, they battle two—although (as one might suspect from the title) not an Abbott and Costello–like team. Chabelo and Pepito, like Brown and Carney in the 1940s, were established solo comics who just happened to make a few pictures together. Chabelo's gimmick was that he was a grown man who talked like a small boy (amazingly, this sustained a four-decade career). The picture itself like *Capulina contra los Monstruos* was aimed at the smaller set, and featured much the same monster lineup (plus a gorilla and some robots). And, like the Capulina picture, when taken on those terms, it is generally successful.

TEN

Men Can Die but Legends Live Forever

The Legacy of the Silver-Masked Man

Before we close the book on Mexican wrestler/monster movies, let's first find cinematic closure with the films of the Son of Santo. Although perhaps ill-equipped at the time to don his father's cinematic mantle, Jorge certainly gave it his best shot; it wasn't his fault that the genre's time had more or less passed.

Chanoc y El Hijo del Santo contra los Vampiros Asesinos (*Chanoc and the Son of Santo vs. the Killer Vampires*, 1981)

(See page 92 for technical and cast credits.)

In this film, El Santo literally and figuratively passes on his mask and mantle to his son. The picture's well done opening has the potential to get a person all choked up. Too bad the rest of the movie just makes one want to choke. Perhaps that's a bit harsh, but it's an opinion shared by the star himself! For one thing, the picture was made near the very beginning of his career, both as a wrestler and film star, and one can safely say that, although enthusiastic enough, he simply was not ready. Today El Hijo del Santo is the greatest wrestler in Mexico, and both his film and public persona have matured, but back then his inexperience showed (though there were glimmers of promise). Also, *Chanoc y El Hijo del Santo contra los Vampiros Asesinos* carried too many musical numbers, and too many uninspired comedy scenes between Carlitos and Tzekub. The movie was shot on-the-cheap by producer-on-the-cheap Rafael Pérez Grovas. But the film's cardinal sin was treating Santo's son like a garden-variety superhero, and having him spend far too much time as his unmasked alter-ego, Marcos Vargas.

Now, the real identity of "Marcos" is a point of contention among Mexi-film scholars — even in his civilian identity, "Marcos" looks as if he's wearing a disguise: a huge pudding-bowl of blow-dried hair and large dark shades, leading many to believe that "Marcos" is indeed Jorge Guzmán. I had the opportunity to ask him this, point-blank, in one of our interviews, and he merely smiled.

Smiling and/or laughing is certainly what Carlos Suárez had in mind when he concocted his idiotic Carlitos sidekick schtick, but he was more annoying than amusing in El Santo's films, and he's even

Santo lives, in the new millennium (July 2000 magazine cover).

worse here. At least the weird musical numbers have camp value.

El Hijo del Santo en Frontera sin Ley (*The Son of Santo in the Lawless Border*, 1983)

Dir: Rafael Pérez Grovas.

    Cast: El Hijo del Santo, Mil Máscaras, Eliazar García, Carmen del Valle.

Recycling much the same formula as two years before, with generally the same results a routine crime drama with too many songs, too much comedy, and too much "Marcos," *El Hijo del Santo en Frontera sin Ley* offered one major difference. Producer-on-the-cheap Grovas was running this show even cheaper than usual, and, shades of Ed Wood, ran out of money roughly halfway through the project. Enter Mil Máscaras, who stepped up to the plate and saved the movie, both by furnishing the completion money, and adding his own inimitable persona as co-star. His veteran cinematic presence takes a lot of weight off Santo Jr.'s shoulders; and as it was Mil's crew that filmed most of the wrestling and action scenes, they come off much better than in the previous effort. However, it was not enough to pump life into a dying genre, and it would be nine years before the Son of Santo would make another film.

Santo: La Leyenda del Enmascarado de Plata (*Santo: The Legend of the Silver-Masked One*, 1992)

(Televicine) *Exec. Prod*: Gabriela Obregon; *Dir/Scr*: Gilberto De Anda; *Photo*: Fransisco Bojorquez; *Music*: Jorge Castro; *Makeup*: Guillermina Oropeza; *Prod. Mgr*: Jaime Alvaro; *Asst. Dir*: José Amezquita; *Film Ed*: Enrique Murillo; *Cam. Op*: Alejandro Martínez; *Sound Engnr*: Miguel Sandoval.

    Cast: El Hijo del Santo, Daniel García (El Santo), Carlos Suárez, El Tirante, Blue Panther, Espanto, Jr., Tornado, Corbade, Ernesto Gómez Cruz (Lucas Pereda López), Tony Bravo (Marcos Arriaga), Daniela Castro (Martha), Eric Sánchez (Benito), José Carlos Ruiz (don Severo), Luis Guevara, Gilberto de Anda, Alfredo Ramírez.

Finally we're presented with a good vehicle for El Hijo, and a fitting tribute to his father. It is not, as the title might suggest, a documentary, and it's not exactly a bio-pic either. It offers dramatizations of some true-life events, such as the sad and somewhat disturbing (especially to those members of the audience who lost their fathers to heart attacks) death of El Santo, but the film is more concerned with what the legend of El Santo means and inspires, both in his son and the general populace. The parallel stories focus on two sons—one obviously of the son of Santo, and the other, Benito, whose father has been framed by an evil banker (are there any other kind?). Benito hops a bus to the big city to seek El Santo's help, but is crushed to learn that El Santo has died. (El Santo is portrayed by Daniel García, better known as Huracán Ramírez, and one of El Santo's closest friends; he was one of the pallbearers at El Santo's funeral.) Benito is then helped by the Son of Santo, who has been slow to assume his father's mantle (as opposed to real life, where he was destined for the position from day one). Another touching scene occurs when Carlos Suárez (El Santo's real-life manager) takes El Hijo to Santo's secret Santo-Cave, which is filled with crime-fighting equipment and souvenirs of past adventures. El Hijo saves Benito's dad, and accepts his role as successor to his own father. By this time, El Hijo had matured, his screen presence was more assured, and his wrestling style had also progressed to the point where, some whisper, he has actually surpassed his father. But you'd never hear him even *suggest* that, out of respect for his father. And that's what this film is all about, too—a

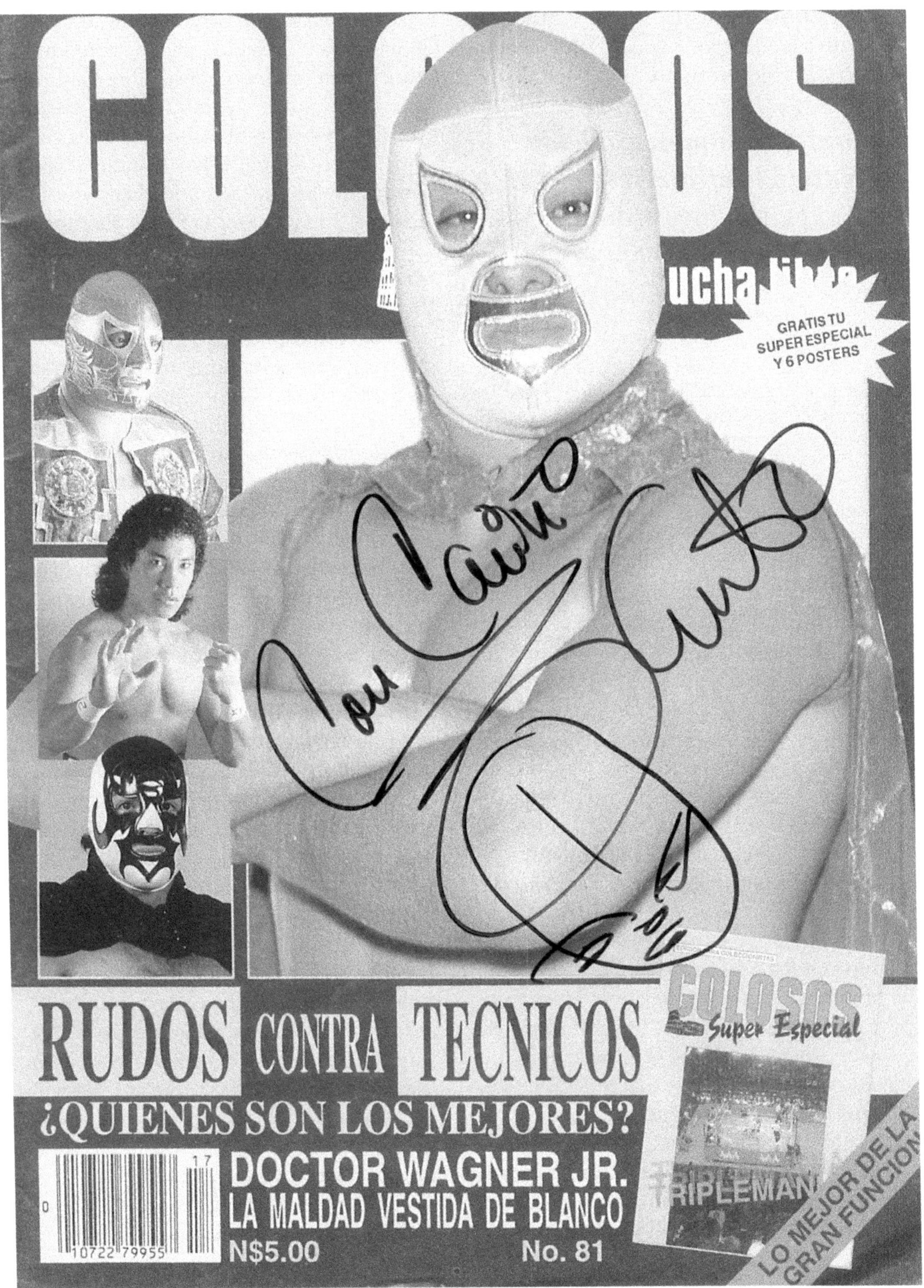

The legacy of the mask lives on, even in El Hijo del Santo's autograph (autographed Santo cover of the March 1982 issue of *Colosos [de la Lucha Libre]*).

son's love for his father. The producer, Gabriela Obregon, would later become Mrs. El Hijo del Santo.

Santo, el Enmascarado de Plata: El Infraterrestre
(Santo, the Silver-Masked Man: Infraterrestrial, 2000)

(Cine Producciones Molinar) *Exec. Prod:* Manuel Medina Martínez; *Prods:* Jesús and Héctor Molinar; *Dir:* Héctor Molinar; *Scr:* Gustavo Rubio; *Photo:* Juan M. Priego; *Music:* Sergio Carmona, Roberto Serrano, Jorge Espino; *Prod. Mgr:* Jesús Molinar; *Film Ed:* Wendy Cervantes, Sandra Salinas; *Sound Ed/SPFX:* Sinergy Studios.

Cast: [El Hijo del] Santo, Blue Panther, Luis Felipe Tovar (Durago Sarmiento), Diana Golden (Dr. Alma Montreal), Manuel Ojeda (Announcer), Héctor Molinar (Capt. del Hierro), Arturo Molinar (Sgt. Ibarra), Turry Molinar (Diego).

The first thing one notices about this movie is that it's simply a "Santo" movie, with no "El Hijo" prefix. On screen, as well as in the ring, Jorge Guzmán has become Santo. Not El Santo, mind you, just "Santo"; and like the superhero who inspired so many other masked men, the Phantom, the mask and the identity remain the same, regardless of whether it is a son or a son's son.

Twenty years after his film debut, the son at last makes a movie in the true Santo tradition, returning the Silver Mask to its rightful position as the bane of monsters everywhere! Tradition is important in this movie; not in the sense that it slavishly follows it, but that it updates the legend without losing sight of what made it a legend, and the quality control and care is apparent throughout the film. Santo still has a secret crime lab (and all kinds of impressive modern gadgets), but he's not so much of a superhero, and the "Marcos" tomfoolery is wisely dispensed with. The production values are impressive, and there is

a stylistic echo of El Santo's team-ups with Blue Demon in Santo's pairing with long-time friend and ring-rival Blue Panther. Even more precisely, *Infraterrestre* recalls the films wherein El Santo had to battle a "bad" Blue Demon, as Blue Panther is controlled by the underground aliens providing the title menace. Echoing Hammer's *Five Million Years to Earth* (1967), we learn that the aliens landed on Earth long ago, but were driven underground by the inclement atmosphere. Too bad they picked the year 2000 to try and make their grab, as Santo, eternal silver-masked champion of justice, is there to thwart their plans for conquest! Now the circle is complete.

Infraterrestre, though intended for a theatrical release, went straight to cable and video. In 2000, Gabriela Obregon told me that Santo's next film venture would be a remake of *The Mummies of Guanajuato*, but as of 2004, no further film projects featuring Santo have surfaced. Will *Infraterrestre* be the last of the Santo films? One certainly hopes not, although if it is, at least we can all be thankful it was a movie worthy of the name of Santo!

So exactly what is the state of the monster/wrestler film genre in 2005? Well, strictly speaking, there isn't one. Oh, wrestling is as popular as ever in Mexico, and Santo is still the name to be reckoned with; Jorge Guzmán's superlative skills and family pride have kept the name in its rightful place in Lucha Libre hierarchy — at the top. And Jorge plans to keep it that way; he has already designated an heir to the mask. He told this author that he will never unmask for money, nor will he give up the identity. In the mid-to-late 1990s a rash of Mexican superstars hitched their wagons to WWF or WCW — to their, and their fans', everlasting regret. Besides being subjected to humiliating, racist promotions, such respected names as Pierroth, Juventud Guererra, and Rey Misterio, Jr., wooed by empty promises of more money

Santo Claus! (Christmas 1987 cover of *Lucha Libra* magazine).

or movie careers, shed their masks. Of course, none of the promised perks materialized, and the aforementioned group of wrestlers, plus others of the same ilk, sold out their legacy and heritage. Naturally, Santo was approached, and, though he never intended to give up the mask, he listened to what they had to say. When it was revealed that not only would unmasking be mandatory, but the mask and the identity would become the sole property of WWF, he told them where to go in no uncertain terms.

He is also determined to keep El Santo's filmic work available for public consumption, and has undertaken a vigorous new campaign to not only re-release El Santo's films in quality prints and editions, but to have them subtitled as well, thereby reaching a whole new audience and attracting a whole new legion of fans. Many films which had previously received little or no exposure north of the border are seeing the light of day, and now cannot only be understood, but appreciated even more (without the detrimental effects of bad dubbing).

And while the masked wrestler movie genre has become stagnant, the mask has busily been making inroads into other areas of pop culture. The late 1990s saw a short lived *Power Rangers*–influenced Saturday morning live action kids' show entitled *Los Luchadores*, and the new millennium brought with it a *Ren and Stimpy*–like cartoon show featuring its own wacky tag-team. Surf band Los Straitjackets wear Mexican wrestling masks when they perform, and so the millions of viewers who tune in to the *Late Night with Conan O'Brien* show get to hear not only the purest surf instrumentals of the modern era, but see them played by guys wearing something that, even if they don't know what it is, appears pretty darn cool. Mega-popular rocker Rob Zombie doesn't wear a mask, but has featured authentic masked wrestler characters in many of his music videos, including what may be his most popular, a tribute to the Munsters' "Dragula" hot-rod. And one of the featured characters in Zombie's comic book, *Creepshow International*, is "El Superbeasto," a masked wrestling hero in the best tradition of ... well, hmm ... actually, there's never been one like him, and Rob is helping to keep the spirit alive!

The Mexican monster/masked wrestler film genre's day has certainly passed, but, like anything that leaves an impression, it will remain alive in the hearts and minds and vaults and creations of fantasy film fans everywhere. It was a world in which, built on a bizarre notion to begin with, anything could and did happen; where men and women in masks and tights fought every manner of supernatural menace conceivable (and many inconceivable) with suplexes and strangleholds; a world in which all a mad scientist needed to create a super-beast was a goldfish and a G.I. Joe doll; where mummies turned into bats, ring opponents turned out to be werewolves, and midgets in rat costumes just turn out.

It was a world created for and by film, a medium for which it can truly be said, "Men can die, but legends live forever."

THE END

Bibliography

Books

Agrasánchez, Rogelio. *Mexican Horror Cinema (Posters from Mexican Fantasy Films)*. Mexico: Agrasanchez Film Archive, 1999.

______, and Charles Ramiro Berg. *Poster Art from the Golden Age of Mexican Cinema*. Mexico: University of Guadalajara/Agrasánchez Film Archive, 1998.

Clarens, Carlos. *An Illustrated History of the Horror Film*. Capricorn Books, 1967.

Gifford, Denis. *Horror Movies: A Pictorial History*. London: Hamlyn, 1973.

Hardy, Phil. *Encyclopedia of Horror Movies*. New York: Harper and Row, 1986.

______. *Encyclopedia of Science Fiction Movies*. London: Aurum Press, 1984.

Harmon, Jim, and Donald F. Glut. *The Great Movie Serials: Their Sound and Fury*. Garden City, N.Y.: Doubleday, 1975.

Hogan, David J. *Who's Who of the Horrors and Other Fantasy Films*. Cranbury, N.J.: A.S. Barnes, 1980.

O'Neill, James. *Terror on Tape*. New York: Billboard Books, 1994.

Peary, Danny. *Cult Movie Stars*. New York: Simon & Schuster, 1991.

Rovin, Jeff. *The Fabulous Fantasy Films*. S. Brunswick, N.J., and New York: A.S. Barnes; London: Thomas Yoseloff, 1977.

Rugoff, Ralph. *Circus Americanus*. London: Haymarket, 1999.

Tombs, Pete. *Mondo Macabro: Weird and Wonderful Cinema Around the World*. New York: St. Martin's/Griffin, 1998.

Vale, Victor, and Andrea Juno. *Incredibly Strange Films*. San Francisco: V/Search, 1986.

Wilt, David E. *The Mexican Filmography: 1916 Through 2001*. Jefferson, N.C.: McFarland, 2003

Periodicals

Blue Demon: Memorias de una Máscara, 1999. Pub. Clio (Mexico).

Cine Confidencial presenta los Idolos del Ring y el Cine Mexicano, May, 1999. Pub. Corporativo Mina S.A. de C.V. (Mexico).

COLOSOS de la Lucha Libre. Pub. Medios Especializados (Mexico).

Cult Movies. Pub. Buddy Barnett.

Famous Monsters of Filmland. Pub. Warren.

Fantastic Monsters of the Films (1962–1963). Pub. Black Shield; eds. Paul Blaisdell and Bob Burns.

Filmfax (The Magazine of Unusual Film and Television), #49, March/April 1995. Pub. Michael Stein.

From Parts Unknown. Ed/pub. Keith J. Rainville.

El Loco. Ed. Miriam Linna; pub. Norton Records.

Lucha Libre. Pub. B.F. Mora y Asociados, S.A. de C.V. (Mexico).

Luchas 2000. Pub. Shibalba Press S.A. de C.V. (Mexico).

Mad Movies, #18, 1978, "Le Cinéma Mexicain." Ed. Jean-Pierre Putters (France).

Mexican Film Bulletin. Ed/pub. David Wilt.

Monsters of the Movies, #4, Dec. 1974, "Superheroes in Distant Lands," by Donald F. Glut. Pub. Marvel/Curtis.

MonsterScene. Pub: GoGo Publications.

Psychotronic Video. Pub/ed. Michael J. Weldon.

Santo Street. Ed/pub. Brian Moran.

SantoScene. Ed/pub. Robert M. Cotter.

Scary Monsters. Ed/pub. Dennis Druktenis.

Screen Thrills Illustrated (1962–1965). Pub. Warren.

Somos Uno, El Santo Special, October, 1999. Pub. Editorial Televisa S.A. de C.V. (Mexico).

Super Lucha. Pub. Reproducciones Curazao S.A. de C.V. (Mexico).

Terror Fantastic, #12, Sept. 1972, "Especial: Santo." Pub. Midesa (Spain).

Websites

La Arena
http://www.highspots.com/arena/prof/elsanto.htm

Atomic Dragon's Lucha Archive
http://www.savethegalaxy.com/stillport.html

Cinema Diabolico
http://www.onr.com/user/doggz/gallery.htm

The Films of El Santo
http://www.wam.umd.edu/~dwilt/santo.html

Horror-wood Webzine
http://www.horror-wood.com/meximon.htm

Internet Movie Database
http://www.imdb.com/

The Official El Santo Website
http://www.elsanto.com.mx/

Professional Wrestling Online Museum
http://www.wrestlingmuseum.com

Santo and Friends
http://www.santoandfriends.com

www.ingramcontent.com/pod-product-compliance
Ingram Content Group UK Ltd.
Pitfield, Milton Keynes, MK11 3LW, UK
UKHW051853150726
7214IPUK00021B/406